Advance praise for *Economic Sanctions in Criminal Justice*

"Dr. Ruback's authoritative volume is a must-read for scholars and policy-makers interested in shaping behavior through economic sanctions. Impressively, Dr. Ruback's book summarizes and integrates 20 years of inter-disciplinary empirical research on economic sanctions by his and others' research teams to develop cogent and practical policy recommendations."

—**Brian Cutler**,
Professor, Ontario Tech University

"Dr. Ruback has been the leading expert on economic sanctions in the US for decades. This book is an essential resource for anyone worried about the financial penalties that are stacked on to people who get caught up in American criminal justice systems. Many are driven more deeply into pov-erty, which cannot be good for their successful reintegration into society."

—**Kevin R. Reitz**,
James Annenberg La Vea Professor of Law,
University of Minnesota

"A wide-ranging study of the ethical, criminological, legal and policy impli-cations of economic sanctions in US criminal justice. By combining this analysis with extensive empirical research into all phases of the imposition of money sanctions, Ruback provides an invaluable addition to the rapidly growing criminological literature on fines, restitution and related penalties in the criminal justice system."

—**Pat O'Malley**, PhD, FASSA,
Distinguished Honorary Professor,
School of Sociology,
Research School of Social Sciences,
Australian National University

Economic Sanctions in Criminal Justice

A Multimethod Examination of Their Imposition,
Payment, Effect, and Fairness

R. Barry Ruback

OXFORD
UNIVERSITY PRESS

Oxford University Press is a department of the University of Oxford. It furthers
the University's objective of excellence in research, scholarship, and education
by publishing worldwide. Oxford is a registered trade mark of Oxford University
Press in the UK and certain other countries.

Published in the United States of America by Oxford University Press
198 Madison Avenue, New York, NY 10016, United States of America.

Library of Congress Cataloging-in-Publication Data
Names: Ruback, R. Barry, 1950– author.
Title: Economic sanctions in criminal justice : a multimethod examination
of their imposition, payment, effect, and fairness / R. Barry Ruback.
Description: New York, NY : Oxford University Press, 2022. |
Includes bibliographical references and index.
Identifiers: LCCN 2021031201 (print) | LCCN 2021031202 (ebook) |
ISBN 9780190682583 (paperback) | ISBN 9780190682606 (epub) |
ISBN 9780190682613
Subjects: LCSH: Corrections—United States—Finance. |
User charges—United States. | Fees, Administrative—United States. |
Justice, Administration of—Economic aspects—United States.
Classification: LCC HV9469 .R74 2021 (print) | LCC HV9469 (ebook) |
DDC 365.068/1—dc23
LC record available at https://lccn.loc.gov/2021031201
LC ebook record available at https://lccn.loc.gov/2021031202

DOI: 10.1093/oso/9780190682583.001.0001

9 8 7 6 5 4 3 2 1

Printed by Marquis, Canada

For Jasmin and for our daughter Miriam

Contents

Acknowledgments

As an undergraduate I took a seminar in Group Dynamics taught by Irving Janis, a social psychologist best known for his book *Victims of Groupthink*, which described the pressures toward consensus and conformity in small groups that led to limited analysis and poor decision-making by presidential cabinets. Professor Janis had worked in the Research Branch of the War Department during World War II, and, at every class, he demonstrated how social science research can be applied to understanding and ameliorating problems in the real world and he insisted that this understanding should be communicated to policymakers and the general public.

Following Professor Janis, this book, representing 23 years of work, is an application of law and social science to a current issue in criminal justice: the imposition and payment of economic sanctions in the criminal justice system. This issue has become more important in recent years for four reasons: (1) the increased costs of the criminal justice system and the concomitant trend to place the costs somewhere other than on taxpayers; (2) the imposition of greater levels of punishment, particularly incarceration, which is very expensive; (3) a desire for intermediate punishment, from both liberals who are concerned about the overuse of incarceration, and conservatives, who are concerned about the unjustified expense of long periods of imprisonment; and (4) a concern that victims receive some form of compensation that restores them to their pre-crime status.

The research described in this book involved multiple research methods, multiple types of research samples, multiple levels of analysis, and multiple statistical analytic procedures. The goal was to look for consistent findings across these various dimensions in order to provide evidence that the findings were robust and the conclusions were warranted. Although the levels of consistency were not always as high as we would want, the work does indicate that most of the findings could be replicated, and it is in connection with these consistent findings that my policy suggestions are based.

This work would not have been conducted without the support of state and federal agencies. In Pennsylvania, both the Pennsylvania Commission on Sentencing and the Pennsylvania Commission on Crime and Delinquency provided grant support for this research as well as interest in learning more about the imposition and payment of economic sanctions in the state. The Restitution in Pennsylvania Task Force provided opportunities for me to discuss the research with practitioners and lawmakers around the state. The Pennsylvania Commission on Sentencing and the Administrative Office of Pennsylvania's Courts provided data on hundreds of thousands of sentencing decisions. At the federal level I received grant support from the National Institute of Justice and from the Law and Social Science Section of the National Science Foundation.

I also want to thank Penn State University, which provided initial support for this research through the Criminal Justice Research Center and which provided me with a sabbatical year during which I was able to complete the manuscript.

This research was conducted with the support and advice of Mark Bergstrom and Cynthia Kempinen, the Executive Director and Associate Director, respectively, of the Pennsylvania Commission on Sentencing. For the studies described in Chapters 3, 4, and 5, I am thankful for the assistance of the judges and the particular help of Tom Young, the Chief Probation Officer, in Centre County, Pennsylvania.

Finally, the research described here was conducted with the help of 14 graduate students, to whom I am especially grateful: Sarah Bowles, Alison Cares, Valerie Clark, Ben Feldmeyer, Andrew Gladfelter, Stacy Hoskins Haynes, Lauren Knoth, Brendan Lantz, Melissa Logue, Kim Ménard, Maureen Outlaw, Gretchen Curtin Ruth, Jennifer Sikorski, and Jordan Zvonkovich.

1

Introduction and Overview

Justice is expensive. So is injustice. These kinds of judgments are usually made in terms of money, and an economic focus makes sense in the context of criminal law and procedure since money has long played a role in how society deals with unlawful behavior. These economic sanctions, the court-imposed financial obligations that follow a criminal conviction, are useful because they apply a metric that is understood by everyone.

The notion of using money as a means of resolving criminal and civil problems goes back almost 4,000 years, to the Code of Hammurabi (Van Ness, 1990), and there are several Biblical injunctions regarding payment after crimes. In the Middle Ages, victims were entitled to compensation for injuries (adjusted for their rank in society), and, by the twelfth century, the king was entitled to a fee for administering the system (Klein, 1997).

America has a long history of making criminals pay for criminal justice. Being accused has sometimes been enough to warrant fees, and being inno-cent has not necessarily been a way to avoid the debt. In the Salem witch-craft trials in 1692, for example, the prisoners were charged for their food and lodging, and nonpayment could mean confiscation of their property or being sold as an indentured servant (Baker, 2006). Prisons in the South were expected to turn a profit (Oshinsky, 1996). In 1846, Michigan became the first state to charge jail inmates for the costs of medical care (Parent, 1990).

Money is also the medium in contemporary America by which the tort system compensates victims for injuries. And, in the case of large numbers of victims caused by terrorism (Feinberg, 2005) and corporate malfeasance (Bennett, 2014), the legal system uses money to cover the harms suffered. Fines for civil violations are also common, including fines for minor building violations that, through penalties for nonpayment, can snowball into hun-dreds of thousands of dollars (Ashford, 2019).

Economic Sanctions in Criminal Justice. R. Barry Ruback, Oxford University Press. © Oxford University Press 2022.
DOI: 10.1093/oso/9780190682583.003.0001

In the past 30 years, economic sanctions following criminal convictions have been more frequently imposed—25% of prisoners received economic sanctions in 1991, but, by 2004, the figure was 66% (Harris et al., 2010). This trend toward increasing the use of economic sanctions is likely to continue because of increased costs, increased retribution, a desire for intermediate punishment, and concern for the losses incurred by victims and their families.

In terms of the costs of administering criminal justice, expenses have risen substantially along with the large number of people under correctional supervision, more than 6.6 million at year-end 2016 (Kaeble & Cowhig, 2018). Corrections alone account for about 7% of state budgets (Scott-Hayward, 2009). Because of these rising costs and the absence of increasing revenues to cover them, jurisdictions are now more likely to make offenders pay for at least part of these costs, including the costs of supervision and incarceration (Olson & Ramker, 2001; Butterfield, 2004). This emphasis on economic sanctions to cover costs generally means that the concern is primarily that the money be paid, not that the offender be disciplined or reformed (O'Malley, 2009a, p. 4).

Regarding retribution, the past 50 years has seen a large increase in the use of criminal justice supervision, particularly in the use of prison. In 1974, there were 216,000 prisoners in a state or federal prison (Bonczar, 2003). There are about 1.3 million prisoners currently under the jurisdiction of state correctional authorities and about 200,000 under federal jurisdiction (Carlson, 2020). Much of the increase has been due to stringent drug laws but also to the use of mandatory minimums and "three-strikes" laws. Minorities have been especially likely to be incarcerated under this regimen (Alexander, 2012).

Related to the high use of incarceration is the increasing need for intermediate sanctions that are more severe than probation alone but less severe—and less expensive—than imprisonment (Tonry & Lynch, 1996). Probation accounts for about 56% of individuals under correctional supervision, roughly 3.7 million individuals (Kaeble & Cowhig, 2018). Thus, changes in probation that increase its effectiveness and that provide opportunities for treatment and deterrence could have a major impact on community corrections.

In addition to these concerns about offenders and the costs to society, there are also concerns about crime victims, particularly about increasing the likelihood that victims will receive restitution for their losses (Office for Victims of Crime, 1998). Every state now has a statute authorizing restitution, and 20 states have elevated restitution to a constitutional right (Tobolowsky et al., 2010; Haynes et al., 2015).

The amounts of money involved in economic sanctions are in the billions of dollars. In the federal system alone, at the end of fiscal year 2018, total criminal debts owed to the United States were $27.29 billion (US Department of Justice, 2019, p. 29, table 8A), the total criminal debts owed to victims or other parties (e.g., insurance companies) was $99.40 billion (p. 32, table 8B). Total payments received for criminal debts to third parties in fiscal year 2018 was $553 million.

Because of the increased role of economic sanctions in contemporary criminal justice, numerous scholars have written about its importance at all stages of the system: policing for profit (Blumenson & Nilsen, 1998), pay-only probation (Georgia Code, §42-8-103 [2015]), pay-to-stay incarceration (Plunkett, 2013), cash-for-freedom diversion (Logan & Wright, 2014), offender-funded probation (Albin-Lackey, 2014), cash register justice (Eisen, 2015; Appleman, 2016), charging for justice (Laisne et al., 2017), mercenary criminal justice (Logan & Wright, 2014), the commodification of criminal justice (Appleman, 2018), poverty capitalism (Edsall, 2014), and poverty-based punishment (Rodriques, 2018). The dozens of articles in the past 10 years on the imposition, enforcement, payment, and effects of economic sanctions all confirm the common recognition that money is the currency of criminal justice (O'Malley, 2009a, p. 24).

In this book, I focus on the major legal and social science questions involved in economic sanctions. Other scholars have used similar terms to describe these court-imposed financial sanctions, including financial obligations (Tobin, 1996), legal financial obligations (Harris, 2016), criminal financial obligations (Clerk of the Superior Court, 2020), criminal justice debt (Bannon et al., 2010; Levingston & Turetsky, 2007), monetary sanctions (Harris, 2016), and monetary penalties (Vander Giessen, 2012). I use the term "economic sanctions" because it has been used by others, particularly the Model Penal Code: Sentencing (American Law Institute, 2020). Although I use it to be inclusive of all economic obligations that follow from a criminal conviction, it does not include financial obligations imposed on defendants before conviction, most prominently bail. Nor does it include such legal obligations as child support, alimony, and bankruptcy payments, all of which are relevant to the debt faced by many criminal defendants but which are broader than my concern here with criminal justice–related sanctions.

The term "economic sanctions" is not perfect, however, because it indicates that these court-ordered obligations are penalties imposed by the legal system. Whether all economic sanctions, including restitution, are penalties deserves some discussion. Moreover, although the term "economic sanctions" focuses on financial considerations, these obligations have precursors and effects that include nonfinancial factors—justice, impartiality, integrity, fairness, equity—at least as important as money. I touch on these issues throughout the book and particularly in the last chapter.

The Meaning of Money

Goetzman (2016) argued that civilization advanced because of the need to develop commerce and finance. According to Goetzman, both writing and mathematics arose in order to promote commerce, as did the concepts of time, probability, and ethics because all resulted from the need to predict and control the changes in human behavior that followed from financial innovations. One of the virtues of money is that, because it is a symbolic medium, it takes the place of commodities and labor in providing value (Ferguson, 2008; Goetzman, 2016). More generally, the world runs on money because it has four useful features (Ariely & Kreisler, 2017, pp. 7–8): (1) generality—it can be used to buy almost anything; (2) divisibility—it can be applied to any size item; (3) fungibility—it is interchangeable with itself, such that a particular piece of money is not needed to pay someone; and (4) storability—it can be used at a later time.

Rather than being solely a neutral technological tool whose only effect was to advance civilization, as Goetzman implies, however, it is important to recognize that finance is also used "to codify and enforce relationships built on power and luck as much as to facilitate voluntary and rational decision-making" (Martin, 2016). This unfairness fits within a larger framework that acknowledges that factors beyond the control of individual persons, like economic recessions, can profoundly affect the nature and extent of exchanges involving money. According to Appelbaum (2019), the focus of our economy on maximum efficiency has resulted in income and wealth inequality and stagnant living standards for all but the wealthiest individuals in society.

One of the results of this greater inequality is that the differences between the rich and the poor become even greater. For example, Ferguson (2008, p. 13) noted that the poor suffer from a lack of reliable places where they can save and efficient credit networks where they can borrow. The fact that the poor often have no bank account and poor credit means that they have to pay to cash checks and take out expensive payday loans, a problem that is especially serious for ex-prisoners (American Civil Liberties Union, 2010; Benoit, 2020). As one senator put it, "It's expensive to be poor in America" (Gillibrand, 2020).

In the criminal justice system, money has both the strengths and weaknesses of money in the larger society. Like contracts and torts law, where money is now the principal remedy for resolving disagreements (O'Malley, 2009a, p. 4), criminal law has come to adopt the general idea that economic sanctions can be used to handle many offenses, most of which are misdemeanors and less serious crimes. Economists have also argued that money is better than imposing time as a penalty (e.g., an offender having to spend time in prison or jail), in that it can be used by governments and victims to buy things (Becker, 1968). Because money is fungible, it can serve multiple purposes: it can be used to punish, deter, rehabilitate, and express moral condemnation. But fungibility also means that the money offenders use to pay their criminal justice–related economic sanctions is not being used to pay for expenses related to housing, food, education, transportation, or family. Thus, economic sanctions can have different effects on offenders depending on whether they are poor, as most offenders are. Furthermore, although economists tend to equate money and time as penalties, it is not the case that judges and legislators agree with this assessment (O'Malley, 2011, p. 58).

Purpose of the Book

This book discusses how economic sanctions are currently being used in the United States, and particularly in Pennsylvania. These sanctions are among the issues that have been at the forefront of criminal justice reform in the past few years, and major legal and policy developments are under way across the country. The book includes a discussion of many of the philosophical, legal, psychological, and criminological issues related to the use of economic sanctions in sentencing and corrections, including punishment, reintegration into the community, and the treatment of crime victims. Research on decision-making by judges and probation officers regarding the imposition and monitoring of economic sanctions is presented, and the effect of paying economic sanctions on offenders' recidivism is also analyzed. Aside from the criminal justice issues involved, the book examines societal issues related to poverty (e.g., ability to pay) and to poverty's intersection with race, since economic sanctions in some states have been disproportionately imposed on minorities.

The focus of the book is on my multimethod, multilevel research into decision-making about the imposition, monitoring, and collection of economic sanctions in one state, Pennsylvania. The research methods used included statistical analyses of existing databases (from the Pennsylvania Sentencing Commission and the Administrative Office of Pennsylvania Courts), the collection of data from multiple sources within counties (court records, probation files, clerk of courts records), surveys of individuals (victims, offenders, judges, district attorneys, probation officers), a field experiment that involved examining the effects of letters to probationers on the payment of restitution, and the addition of archival data (on recidivism) to the data from the field experiment. The book also includes policy issues regarding how the use of economic sanctions contributes to fairness and unfairness regarding society, offenders, and victims.

I have minimized the presentation of statistics to make the book as accessible as possible, and I have focused on effects that were significant across studies and across statistical models, suggesting that the convergent findings are valid. Rather than use statistical significance as the sole indicator of importance, I have tried also to concentrate on results that are substantively important.

The remainder of this first chapter is an overview of the types of economic sanctions currently used in the United States. Discussed are the purposes of sentencing, especially punishment, deterrence, and rehabilitation, and how well, in theory, economic sanctions address these purposes.

Sentencing and Economic Sanctions

Sentencing after a criminal conviction looks both to the past and to the future and involves three parties (the victim, the offender, and society). For the past, sentencing is aimed at punishing the criminal and, if relevant, at restoring the victims for their losses. Looking to the past involves factors about the crime (the type, seriousness, harm caused, and offender's culpability; Blumstein et al., 1983) that are relevant to issues of blame, just deserts, and the restoration of equity. Blame and just deserts relate primarily to the offender, whereas considerations of equity relate to restoring the victim and society to the condition they were in before the crime was committed.

For the future, sentencing is aimed at preventing future crime by deterrence or by rehabilitation. Usually, we think of incarceration as one way to reach these goals. However, even though incarceration rates in the United States are high (higher than virtually every other country in the world), most convicted criminals do not serve time after sentencing often because the time they have already served awaiting trial covers the sentence. Given this time served, the most common sentence is probation.

Future-oriented sentencing is concerned with the likelihood that the offender will offend at some point, and thus judges are concerned with reducing crime through deterrence and rehabilitation. Deterrence-oriented sentences are effective if they involve a high penalty because a rational offender would believe that the benefits of any future crime would be less than the costs he or she would suffer if caught and punished. Rehabilitation-oriented sentences are effective if they induce the offender to believe that crime is wrong.

The relevance of these sanctions depends on the intended target. For the crime victim, restitution is the only relevant economic sanction. It is past-oriented, aimed at restoring the victim, with little or no consideration of punishing the offender. For the offender, fines (monetary penalties) and forfeitures of property used in a crime are past-oriented economic sanctions designed to punish the offender for prior behavior (with little or no consideration of reparation to a victim), and fees are future-oriented in the sense that they pay for ongoing supervision (e.g., probation) and monitoring (e.g., drug tests). For society, past-oriented economic sanctions are aimed at making the offender pay for the costs of prosecuting the offender and future-oriented sanctions are aimed at helping society deal with future problems (e.g., future victims, through payments to the state's victim compensation fund) and helping to pay for continuing supervision (Ruback & Bergstrom, 2006). These issues are discussed more fully in Chapter 8 in terms of policy recommendations regarding economic sanctions.

Beyond these primary goals, economic sanctions also have secondary purposes. Restitution can help with offender rehabilitation. Fines, forfeitures, and fees can serve to deter as well as to punish. Costs can serve to punish as well as to restore equity with society. Restitution, fines, and fees and costs are addressed in greater detail later.

Economic sanctions are legally required transfers of money or other value from an offender to a crime victim or a governmental agency (American Law Institute, 2020; Model Penal Code: Sentencing, § 6.04 A–D). They are typically one of several conditions of a criminal sentence, usually additional penalties rather than sole sanctions (Hillsman, 1990). However, imposition does not mean payment, and, in fact, enormous amounts of the monies that are owed are unpaid. In the federal system, for example, the Justice Department is seeking to recover $97 billion in fines, fees, and restitution (Rothfeld & Reagan, 2014).

The primary criticism of monetary sanctions is that they "are inherently inequitable" (Walsh, 2014, p. 71) in that they are unfair to many offenders who have little or no money but who face charges of hundreds or thousands of dollars, which they are unlikely to ever be able to pay. Many must choose between paying the sanctions and paying necessities (Cook, 2014). The poor already have only limited access to formal borrowing institutions, which means that they face higher interest rates and limited amounts that they can borrow (Haushofer & Fehr, 2014; Pleggenkuhle, 2018). Aside from affecting their time under criminal justice supervision, these economic sanctions may adversely affect their ability to obtain employment, credit, and housing (Harris et al., 2010). These negative effects of economic sanctions are discussed more fully in Chapter 3.

Based on a survey sample of 12,173, the Board of Governors of the Federal Reserve System (2020) reported that 6% of all adults had some type of court costs and legal fees. The percentage was close to 20% for families that had an immediate family member in prison or jail. Families that had current unpaid legal expenses, fines, or court costs were most likely to have family income under $40,000. Of black families, 12% had current unpaid legal expenses, fines, or court costs, compared to 9% of Hispanic families and 5% of white families. Most families that had unpaid legal expenses were likely to have credit card debt (66%), to have medical debt (43%), to have been denied credit in the prior year (52%), and either to not have a bank/credit union account or to have used an alternative financial service in the prior year (52%). Aside from the expense of these high-cost alternatives (check cashing places, pawn shops, and payday lenders), offenders have difficulty raising their low credit scores (Benoit, 2020).

Moreover, in addition to having to deal with criminal charges, the mere fact that most offenders are poor is likely to adversely affect all of their important decisions because scarcity necessitates extra cognitive demands that make rational decision-making more challenging (Mani et al., 2013). Also, poverty is associated with negative affect (unhappiness, anxiety, depression) and physiological stress (Haushofer & Fehr, 2014), both of which seem to lead to changes in economic behavior, including more of a focus on the present and a lower willingness to look at the future (e.g., less willingness to save). Negative affect and stress might have these effects because they increase reliance on habitual rather than mindful goal-directed behavior and because they cause individuals to focus on a few salient cues, which would be especially likely to be present-oriented rather than future-oriented.

The impact of economic problems resulting from an inability to pay living expenses and criminal justice debts are likely especially great with less education. Although their focus was on white non-Hispanics without a college degree, Case and Deaton's (2020) findings linking lower education to drug use, alcohol use, and "deaths of despair" are consistent with their argument that hopelessness and humiliation arise in the face of economic uncertainty and perceived failure. Research on criminal justice economic sanctions specifically has found similar negative effects (Harper et al., 2021).

Types of Economic Sanctions

In contemporary criminal justice, there are a several different types of economic sanctions. Logan and Wright (2014) and Appleman (2016) developed a taxonomy of these different types of sanctions, some of which are charged in only some states.

I. Pre-trial fees:
   A) *Booking fees*: Charges to a defendant at an arrest (although these are probably unconstitutional)
   B) *Bail fees*: Also includes administrative charges in addition to money bail
   C) *Dismissal fees*: Fees paid to the police or courts to dismiss minor criminal charges
   D) *Deferred prosecution fees*: Fees to enter a program (e.g., community service, drug treatment) so as to defer prosecution or divert from trial
   E) *Public defender application fees*: Charges for applying to use a public defender
II. During trial:
   A) *Court fees*: Payment for undergoing the criminal justice process to recoup the costs of investigation, prosecution, public defender, trial, arrest warrants
   B) *Disability and translation fees*: Costs of interpreters
III. Post-conviction fees:
   A) *Jail and prison fees*:
      1) Charges for room and board, which are typically of one of three types:
         a) Per-diem fee: A standard daily fee for incarceration
         b) Itemized charging fees: Fees for individual items (e.g., clothing, meals, doctor visits that the inmates cannot provide for themselves)
         c) Upgrade fees: Fees for better accommodations
      2) Prison phone call fees
      3) Work-release participation fees

    B) *Statutory penalties*:
      1) Fines
      2) Money and property forfeiture
    C) *Post-conviction levies*: Repayment for investigation, prosecution, arrest warrants, seating a jury
    D) *Criminal restitution*: Funds to compensate victims for their losses
    E) *Probation and parole supervision fees*:
      Especially high if the fees are private probation fees
    F) *Community service fees*: Fees to cover the cost of required community service
    G) *Expungement charges*: Fees to remove a conviction record
IV. Additional financial charges:
    A) *Penalties, interest, and collection fees*
    B) *Child support debt*

As can be seen in this typology, most of the different types of sanctions are fees of one kind or another. In this book, and as discussed in more detail in Chapter 2, I focus on three general types of economic sanctions: fees, fines, and restitution. Most of the research discussed in the book relates to the imposition, payment, and effects of paying restitution.

I need to note here that these economic sanctions apply to convictions for felonies and serious misdemeanors. In contrast to the considerable litera-ture on the extent to which courts operate using the funds they collect from fees and costs, there is other work suggesting that most misdemeanors are not handled through court decisions. In her analysis of how misdemeanor cases are handled in New York City, which she calls "Misdemeanorland," Kohler-Hausmann (2018) argued that the lower criminal courts were more concerned with managing and monitoring people over time (what she calls "procedural hassles") than with adjudicating guilt and punishing convicted offenders. Based on her analyses, in 2015, 54% of misdemeanor cases resulted in some kind of dismissal, about 20% resulted in a misdemeanor convic-tion, and the remainder resulted in a conviction for a noncriminal offense (pp. 68–69). From a cost-benefit standpoint, however, using a managerial model rather than an adjudicative model means that police and courts do not have to invest the time and effort to meet legal and constitutional standards for convictions. Not having convictions also means that economic sanctions are not and cannot be imposed.

Advantages and Disadvantages of Economic Sanctions

The strongest arguments for economic sanctions were made by the economist Becker (1968), who discussed economic sanctions as part of a more general consideration of using public resources to enforce legislation so as to prevent crime and apprehend offenders. Becker argued that economic sanctions are advantageous because they conserve resources since society does not have to pay for the cost of punishment. Absent collection costs, "the social cost of fines is about zero" (p. 180). Posner (1986, p. 208) added that society saves money by not having to build or administer prisons, by not having to support the dependents of the incarcerated, and by being compensated by the funds criminals pay. O'Malley (2011, p. 57) further argued that economic sanctions have the advantage of punishing but not stigmatizing offenders.

In addition to these strengths outlined by Becker, Posner, and O'Malley, economic sanctions have several advantages over both traditional probation and incarceration in jail or prison. First, economic sanctions use a measure that is understood by everyone, and especially by the legal system. Second, economic sanctions provide flexibility in that they can be adjusted to an offender's specific circumstances, although they often are not (Hillsman et al., 1987). Paying economic sanctions is a punishment for most offenders, especially the poor (Hillsman et al., 1987). For wealthy offenders, the amounts (theoretically) could be increased so that the adjusted punishment is approximately equivalent to what is experienced by those with fewer assets. Third, economic sanctions can be used to serve different purposes, including helping the victim, restoring justice to society, and punishing the offender (McGillis, 1986).

Fourth, economic sanctions can be used to provide intermediate punishments. At the low end of punishment is traditional probation, which typically includes several conditions, such as reporting regularly to a probation officer, not leaving the county without permission, and not meeting with convicted felons (Petersilia, 1997). These conditions, which can number as many as 25 or more, are often not enforced because probation officers may have caseloads of more than a hundred and may lack the time to adequately supervise offenders. In addition, because probationers often move, probation officers may not supervise the offenders even if they had the time and resources because they may not even know where probationers are (a problem that we faced in our study of restitution; see Chapter 5). Thus, probation alone is generally not very punitive.

At the other, more punitive, extreme is incarceration in prison and, for less serious crimes, incarceration in jail. As of December 2018, there were 6.41 million individuals under correctional supervision, approximately 1.5 million of whom were in prison (Maruschak & Minton, 2020). Incarceration in prison is expensive and has major effects on inmates' social and physical lives, both in prison and after release (Western, 2006). And, although there may be some effect of incarceration on reducing recidivism, the results are clear that, beyond some point, there is no added deterrence benefit of additional time in prison (Pennsylvania Commission on Sentencing, 2009). Prison is disruptive of family life and social networks, makes employment more difficult, and may reduce inmates' long-term health (Schnittker

& John, 2007). Incarceration is highly punitive and, particularly for those serving long sentences, may be counterproductive.

Compared with incarceration, economic sanctions are about as effective in deterring future crime, at least for some lower-level crimes (Gordon & Glaser, 1991), but they are substantially cheaper because the state does not have to pay for housing (Morris & Tonry, 1990). Moreover, economic sanctions can avoid the stigma and secondary effects of incarceration, such as loss of employment and dependents who would otherwise have to rely on public assistance (Gordon & Glaser, 1991).

Because of dissatisfaction with the lack of supervision of probation and the harsh punitiveness of incarceration, there have been numerous calls for intermediate sanctions, which would give judges and probation officers additional tools to help offenders learn skills, gain employment, deal with substance abuse problems, and address social and behavioral problems. A further advantage of economic sanctions is that they can be delivered more consistently than other types of sanctions, an important strength because continuous punishment, in which punishment is delivered after every response, deters behavior better than intermittent punishment, in which punishment is delivered after some, but not every, response (Brennan & Mednick, 1994). In general, it would be easier to impose financial penalties after every crime than to impose incarceration after every crime. There is also evidence that fines following a speeding ticket based on an automatic radar system (i.e., one that, in certain speed camera zones, always detect a violation) lead to fewer subsequent violations (Dušek & Traxler, 2020).

Despite these advantages, it is important to understand that economic sanctions also have disadvantages. Becker (1968, p. 195) recognized that economic sanctions have problems, although he suggested these problems could be answered. First, they allow offenders to purchase their criminal behavior, just as goods are bought in the marketplace. That is, criminals could simply see economic sanctions as the cost of doing business. Becker's response was that a "fine *can* be considered the price of an offense, but so too can any other form of punishment; . . . fines are prices measured in monetary units, imprisonments are prices measured in time units, etc." To stop corporations from seeing fines as licenses to commit crimes, the US Sentencing Guidelines made fines highly punitive by requiring judges to consider both the pecuniary gain obtained and the monetary cost of the harm (O'Malley, 2011, p. 69).

A second problem is that economic sanctions are not useful if "the harm exceeds the resources of offenders . . . victims could not be fully compensated by offenders, and fines would have to be supplemented with prison terms or other punishments in order to discourage offenses optimally" (p. 196). As discussed later in Chapter 3, offenders' inability to pay clearly limits the usefulness of economic sanctions.

A third criticism is that economic sanctions are simply ways to punish "debtors" to society. Although Becker recognized that this "debt" is not one that either victims or society agreed to, as is the case with ordinary commercial transactions, he also recognized that the tradeoff between prison sentences and fines placed an especially low value on the time in prison of people who could not afford to pay.

Beyond these problems, economic sanctions invoke three larger issues. First, as noted earlier, economic sanctions relate directly to issues associated with wealth and poverty, including race, class, education, job skills, and employment. There is also the issue that convicted offenders, especially those who have been incarcerated, face structural impediments and interpersonal biases, beyond the monetary amounts they owe, that make reintegration difficult (Western, 2002).

The second larger issue is that a focus only on economic sanctions is too limiting. Applying economic incentives to the criminal justice system is the same error made by economics more generally: "that financial incentives are the primary driver of human behavior" (Duflo & Banerjee, 2019). Aside from financial incentives, incentives can be moral or social (Levitt & Dubner, 2006, p. 17) in that people care about self-respect, status, and social connections. Human behavior is also affected by people's desire to be seen by others in a positive light and to be treated and treat others fairly (Tyler, 2011, pp. 17, 38–40). Moreover, by focusing only on economic incentives, economic sanctions can undermine social and moral sanctions (Gneezy & Rustichini, 2000); in this study, parents were found to prefer to pay a penalty for the late pickup of their children from daycare rather than follow the rules and not inconvenience the staff.

The third larger issue is that equating the harm from a crime to money is difficult and viewed by many as inappropriate. In this vein, O'Malley (2011) argued that economic sanctions are inappropriate for crimes like murder and rape because the harm cannot be translated into a specific amount of money.

The most complete statement about economic sanctions was published by the American Law Institute (ALI), an organization founded in 1923 to improve the law. It consists of judges, lawyers, and law professors and publishes summaries of common and statutory law, called Restatements of the Law, as well as proposals for model statutory codes. In 2020, the ALI published the Model Penal Code: Sentencing (MPCS; American Law Institute, 2020) which was drafted by Kevin Reitz (Reporter) and Cecelia Klingele (Associate Reporter).

In general terms, the MPCS (§ 6.06) argues that economic sanctions can be part of a criminal sentence, that the total amount of these sanctions should be fixed and realistic, and that the enforcement of these sanctions should not exceed 3 years from the date of sentencing or from release from incarceration, if that date is later. If an economic sanction is not paid within the required time, then the sanction can be converted to a civil judgment. The MPCS limits economic sanctions to those that do not prevent the offender from being able to pay reasonable living expenses and family obligations, what the MPCS calls "reasonable financial subsistence" (RFS). The consideration of RFS at sentencing is, like the law for consumer bankruptcy, to enable ex-offenders to become a productive part of the community and to lower the likelihood that they will need to reoffend (p. 172). The MPCS suggests that economic sanctions can be used as a potential substitute for incarceration but that incarceration cannot be a substitute for economic sanctions. The MPCS prohibits the agencies that collect economic sanctions from receiving the monies collected and also prohibits fees for failing to pay the sanctions. If there are multiple types of economic sanctions imposed, victim restitution takes precedence over the other types of sanctions.

The revised MPCS (2020, § 6.04 A–D) includes provisions for six types of economic sanctions: (1) restitution, (2) fines, (3) costs, (4) fees, (5) assessments, and (6) asset forfeiture. The MPCS is discussed again in the final chapter, which focuses on policy.

Outline of the Book

In the remainder of the book, I provide more context for the research my students and I conducted, systematically present that research, and then suggest some policy implications of the findings from those studies.

Chapter 2 discusses the three purposes of economic sanctions: (1) punishing the offender, (2) funding the government, and (3) compensating the victim. Because state and local governments have in recent years imposed more types of economic sanctions, especially fees, costs, and forfeitures, there is some detailed discussion about these sanctions. The chapter also examines the constitutional status of economic sanctions as outlined in court decisions, particularly the US Supreme Court. There is a brief overview of the laws in the 50 states, the District of Columbia, and the federal government regarding the three major types of economic sanctions: fines, fees, and restitution.

Chapter 3 provides an overview of the research that my students and I have conducted, research that combines perspectives from criminology, psychology, and law. It also discusses the need for and use of multiple research methods and multiple levels of analyses in addressing issues that affect public policy. The research used state-wide data from courts, data from individual counties for both adult and juvenile offenders, surveys of victims, surveys of offenders, and surveys of judges. The chapter also includes some discussion of the advantages and disadvantages of focusing on a single state. The chapter discusses three studies of economic sanctions in general that rely on statewide data or on data from multiple counties.

Chapter 4 looks at the imposition of restitution in Pennsylvania. It summarizes our studies that addressed the question of when, where, and for whom restitution is ordered. The chapter discusses seven multimethod studies that look at the imposition of restitution from the state, multi-county, and single-county perspectives, and which examine both legally relevant factors such as offense type, offense seriousness, and prior record and demographic factors (race, age, gender) in judges' decisions.

Chapter 5 describes studies that look at the payment of restitution. Most court-ordered restitution is not paid. One study describes from victims' perspective the system of how restitution is ordered and paid. A second study looks from the offender's perspective at restitution. In addition to the obvious factor of offenders' inability to pay, this chapter considers other factors that affect the likelihood of payment, including fair treatment (procedural justice) by probation officers. The third study in this chapter is a field experiment which attempted to induce offenders who were delinquent in payment to provide the restitution they owed. The final study in this chapter is a survey of offenders who participated in the field experiment.

Chapter 6 examines the effect of paying restitution on recidivism. Because criminal offenders generally have few assets and limited income, paying financial obligations in addition to living expenses is likely to be difficult and may lead to criminal activity. The chapter examines whether having to pay these sanctions is related to recidivism and particularly to criminal offending aimed at gaining money. The chapter also discusses whether this link between economic sanctions and recidivism is true for all types of economic sanctions. The chapter reviews some of the prior studies mentioned in earlier chapters and presents a recidivism follow-up of the offenders who had participated in the field experiment.

Chapter 7 summarizes the findings and conclusions from the 15 studies presented in the prior four chapters and then describes some specific implications of the research.

The last chapter, Chapter 8, looks at larger issues of economic sanctions. Reitz and Klingele (2019), the reporters of the Model Penal Code raised three concerns about economic sanctions: they are *unprincipled* (they violate legal standards and discriminate against the poor), they are *unsuccessful* (they are generally unpaid and, as presently constituted, do not meet the purposes of sentencing), and they are *unending* (local and state governments are continuing to impose economic sanctions and other legal financial obligations in order to meet budgetary needs). I will be touching on these issues throughout the book, and I return to them in the final chapter. Also, in the final chapter I discuss how the existing research can be used to inform policy, particularly regarding questions of whether there should be different types of economic sanctions, what those types should be, and what amounts of economic sanctions should be imposed. The chapter also includes some discussion of alternatives to monetary sanctions, such as community service.

Summary

This chapter introduced the concept of economic sanctions and provided an overview of the three types of sanctions (fines, fees/costs, and restitution) that were the subject for the research conducted in Pennsylvania. The next chapter examines the legal context of economic sanctions.

2

Fines, Fees/Costs, Forfeitures, and Restitution

In this second chapter, I look more closely at the primary types of economic sanctions by focusing on the three primary goals of imposing debt on criminal offenders: punishing the offender (fines), funding the government (fees and forfeitures), and restoring the victim (restitution). The distinctions among these goals are clear, but in practice there is overlap among them. For example, fines are used to fund government operations, and fees and forfeitures are punitive.

For each of these types of economic sanctions, I give a brief history, discuss how they are currently used, describe the law and court decisions relevant to each type of sanction, and then look more broadly at factors across the states that are related to the kinds of statutes that exist in the states. I also examine how well each particular sanction meets the relevant goal and the implications of focusing only on that goal.

Punishing the Offender

Fines are monetary penalties for crime. Nationally, they are imposed on 33% of convicted felons (Durose, 2007). Fines can be used as the sole sanction or in combination with other sanctions, from treatment to incarceration (Hillsman, 1990). In some jurisdictions, fines are used as prosecution diversion devices, such that charges are dismissed when the fines are paid (Tonry & Lynch, 1996). Fines can also be targeted to support specific purposes. For example, most fines in the federal system are deposited in the Crime Victims Fund, 90% of which is sent to the states for victim compensation and assistance (US Government Accountability Office, 1999). States, like Pennsylvania, often have similar funds (18 PA. CONS. STAT §1.1101(b) (1) 2014).

Economic Sanctions in Criminal Justice. R. Barry Ruback, Oxford University Press. © Oxford University Press 2022.
DOI: 10.1093/oso/9780190682583.003.0002

The assumption of the Model Penal Code: Sentencing (MPCS; 2020) is that fines have no penological value in that they do not address the goals of sentencing. In contrast to that assumption, some scholars believe economic sanctions do have some value because they can meet the goals of deterrence and rehabilitation. First, as noted in connection with less serious crimes, there is some evidence that, compared with incarceration, fines are about as effective at deterring future crime (Gordon & Glaser, 1991) but are substantially cheaper because the state does not have to pay for housing (Morris & Tonry, 1990). Moreover, fines can avoid some of the stigma and secondary effects of incarceration, such as loss of employment and unsupported dependents who would otherwise have to rely on public assistance (Gordon & Glaser, 1991). Second, compared with simple probation, fines are more punitive and thus can serve as intermediate sanctions between probation and prison (Petersilia, 1997). Third, fines can be flexible in that they can be adjusted to the facts of the case and the circumstances of the offender (Hillsman et al., 1987). Moreover, they can be used alone, with incarceration, with probation, or with both incarceration and probation (Hillsman, 1990). Fourth, evaluating the success of fines is relatively easy and straightforward and is usually determined by an offender's level of payment.

Fines have been criticized for not being rehabilitative (Beckett & Harris, 2011), but the most likely alternative—short periods of incarceration—is also non-rehabilitative (O'Malley, 2011). Doing away with fines makes incarceration more likely since there would be fewer intermediate sanctions available (Ruback, 2011). Moreover, judges also generally do not believe that fines alone can be used as an alternative to probation or incarceration (Cole et al., 1987).

In the United States, many people oppose the use of fines because they cannot be enforced against the poor since they are subject to the 8th Amendment Excessive Fines Clause, and they have little impact on the wealthy (Hillsman, 1990). Fines with absolute maximums can become ineffective if legislatures do not regularly update them to adjust for inflation (Gillespie, 1988–1989). Perhaps the most egregious example of this failure to update is the fact that, at least as late as 1952, some fines in Pennsylvania were still stated in British pounds (University of Pennsylvania Law Review, 1953; see O'Malley, 2011, p. 48). Fines that have a statutorily defined and predetermined amount are regressive and do not meet the goals of individualized justice. Thus, fines in the United States tend to be used primarily in courts of limited jurisdiction, particularly traffic courts (Hillsman et al., 1984). In other words, fines tend not to be penal but regulatory (O'Malley, 2011, p. 55), and the focus tends to be on having aggregate conformity to the rules rather than correcting individual behavior (O'Malley, 2011, pp. 85–88).

Fines are also used in lower courts for minor offenses, such as shoplifting, especially for first-time offenders who have enough money to pay the fine (Hillsman et al., 1987). In the United States, fines are used in 42% of courts of general jurisdiction and in 86% of cases in courts of limited jurisdiction (Weisburd et al., 2008).

In each jurisdiction in the United States there is usually a "going rate" for fines, that is, what is typically imposed for a specific offense (Hillsman & Greene, 1992). Because judges tend to use this going rate for fines, they do not adjust the seriousness of the penalty to the specific defendant. Often, this going rate is low, to accommodate the poorest offenders. Rather than make adjustments at initial sentencing, judges tend to make adjustments to fines at the back end, when they often excuse the remaining unpaid portion or simply let the probation period expire without enforcing the fine. Nationally, offenders in state courts are ordered to pay fines in 38% of all conviction offenses: 36% of violent offenses, 37% of property offenses, 41% of drug offenses, 27% of weapons offenses, and 40% of other offenses (Rosenmerkel et al., 2009, tab. 1.5).

In the late 18th century, there was a shift away from fines because imprisonment's effect on liberty was seen as a fairer punishment (Faraldo-Cabana, 2014). A second reason was that imprisonment was the likely result for individuals who defaulted on their fines. Although Bentham argued for fines that took into account the offender's wealth (O'Malley, 2009b), European countries in the 19th century generally opposed the notion because of a reluctance to thoroughly investigate the offender's assets and a concern that punishment should be equal (i.e., exactly the same amount for everyone).

Today, most countries use fines, which, according to Bentham, have several clear advantages: "they were cheap to administer, produced revenues, could be completely undone in the event of a wrongful conviction being established, could be graduated infinitely to match the magnitude of the wrong, could be matched to the means of the offender . . . and could be used to provide victim compensation" (O'Malley, 2011, p. 550).

Fines are the legally presumptive penalty in many European countries and thus are much more common there, primarily because incarceration is believed to have negative effects and fines are seen as effective in preventing recidivism (Tonry & Lynch, 1996). In Germany, for example, 80% of convicted offenders are ordered to pay a fine (Federal Ministry of the Interior & Federal Ministry of Justice, 2001), and fines are imposed in about 80% of criminal cases in England and Wales (Moxon et al., 1990; Ministry of Justice, 2021). Fines in Europe are usually the sole sanction.

Europe uses two types of fines, *prosecution diversion systems* and *day fines*. As a diversion device, the offender agrees to pay a fine (generally the amount that would have been imposed had the offender been convicted), and the prosecutor dismisses the charges. Day fines, the second type of fine, are based on the degree of punishment needed (relating to the severity of the crime) and a specific monetary amount based on the offender's ability to pay (typically, the offender's daily income). Germany adopted day fines in 1969, both to decrease the use of incarceration for low-level cases and to establish standards on the amounts of fines (Nagrecha, 2020). The notion of day fines has been traced to the French Revolution, and early models were adopted in Brazil in the 1830s and in Portugal in 1852 (O'Malley, 2011, p. 54). Brett and

Nagrecha (2019) have suggested that US jurisdictions should adopt the use of day fines (what they call *proportionate financial sentences*) as a way to ensure that fines are proportionate to the seriousness of the offense and that they take into account the offender's ability to pay.

If punishment is the primary goal of an economic sanction, then three things should be true: (1) the amount of the fine should be highly related to the severity of the offense for which it is imposed; (2) over time, as inflation eats into the value of money, the amount of the fine should be increased every few years to ensure the same level of punishment; and (3) the inflicted punishment should be the same for every offender. Day fines do a better job than flat (and unchanging) fines in being consistently related to crime severity.

In contrast to time, which is constant for an offender (i.e., a day is a day is a day), the value of money changes depending on the inflation/deflation rate. For example, a fine of $1,000 at an inflation rate of 2% per year (about what the inflation rate has been over the period 2015–2020), the real value would be only $905.73 5 years later. After 10 years, at a 2% inflation rate, the real value of the fine would be only $820.35. Given that states do not change the amounts of fines very often (e.g., the last time Pennsylvania changed its fine amounts was 1995; 18 PA C.S.A. §1101; https://www.legis.state.pa.us/cfdocs/legis/LI/consCheck.cfm?txtType=HTM&ttl=18&div=0&chpt=11), the punitive value of a fine has been eroded. Thus, because fines do not retain their punishment value over time (i.e., the amounts of fines are not periodically revised upward by state legislatures), Gillespie (1981) argued that they are not realistic alternatives to imprisonment.

Day fines overcome this and other problems with flat fines (Gillespie, 1981). First, with day fines the punitive power of the fine is not eroded by the failure of the legislature to periodically revise them upward because the day fine uses the offender's current daily income. Second, they force judges to deal with both the seriousness of the offense and the financial ability of the offender to pay the fine. Third, day fines overcome the problem of flat fines because they have "expressive value." That is, because day fines are clearly punitive, even for the wealthy, they cannot be seen as ex post licenses. Fines that are not perceived as punishment (e.g., for minor traffic violations) are judged to be a license for inappropriate behavior that is purchased after being caught. However, it should be noted that, at the extreme, day fines may be unfairly high for wealthy offenders (Stecklow, 2001).

Fees/Costs: Compensating the Government

Whereas fines are punishment based on the offender's conduct, fees and costs are based on government expenditures for arrest, prosecution, and corrections (Logan & Wright, 2014). The primary purpose of fees/costs is to make offenders pay for the expenses associated with their prosecution, incarceration in prison or jail, and supervision when released to the community. Here,

I look first at the larger factors that prompted local and state governments to seek reimbursement from offenders.

Trend Toward Less Government and More Individual Payment

The trend toward the development and imposition of more types and greater amounts of fees and costs fits within a larger movement in the country toward making individuals pay for their individual expenses. One of the first bits of evidence of this trend toward decreasing government expenditures and increasing individual responsibility for paying was individual accounts for retirement, healthcare, and education, by which individuals exercised private ownership and control. This push toward shifting these responsibilities to individuals as part of an ownership society meant that government could, theoretically, spend less money in these areas. This trend toward individual responsibility fits with "some of the strongest-held values of American culture, namely personal autonomy, private property and self-support" (Zelinsky, 2007, p. 97). This "politics of responsibility" (Forman, 2017) led to welfare reform limiting federal benefits to the poor, limitations on the use of bankruptcy to resolve debts, and greater use of incarceration (Osnos, 2020).

Another example of the trend toward less government is higher education. One of the most common conditions in higher education today is that state governments are cutting funding to universities, meaning that private sources are needed to fund athletics and that academic projects, like libraries, suffer from underfunding (Jarvis, 2019). Pressure from state legislatures has kept tuition relatively constant but, because of reductions in state spending per student, universities have had to move to other sources of income to cover other student expenses. In the case of student facilities, the burden has moved to higher fees for students, which, for example, in the case of Louisiana State University increased by almost 300% from 2000 to 2018 (Stripling, 2017).

Less government funding is apparent even in public grammar and high schools, where fees are becoming more common (Hobbs, 2019). In one district in Ohio, for example, there is a $10 student activity fee, a $3 fee for the mass calling alert system, and a $25 fee for school-provided laptops. Students in chemistry pay a $34 fee for chemicals and supplies, and students in anatomy and physiology pay a $35 fee for cat cadavers and course materials. In 2017, 71% of school districts had such fees, which together with textbook sales and rentals and activity costs total about $6 billion. In a school district in Utah where the basic registration fee for high school is $105, a school board member argued that "school fees are a user tax that distributes the costs of education to people that would use it, just like a toll road" (Hobbs, 2019).

In the criminal justice system, fees and costs refer to court-imposed orders to reimburse the jurisdiction (local, county, or state) for the administrative cost of operating the criminal justice system. One way that the terms "costs" and "fees" have been differentiated is that costs describe blanket charges for program admission or participation, whereas fees refer to specific, individual charges for services (Ruback & Bergstrom, 2006). In Pennsylvania, for example, there are costs for the court-processing expenses associated with a court diversion program and a fee to pay for DNA analysis. In other jurisdictions, costs are backward-looking charges for the costs of prosecution, whereas fees are forward-looking charges for future expenses (e.g., probation supervision). However, the terms are often used interchangeably, and that is how they are used in the MPCS and in this book.

Costs and fees are important because the criminal justice system runs both on money from the jurisdiction's operating budget and on money from offenders who pay for their prosecution and punishment through fees and costs. One of the implications of relying on offenders to carry the cost burden is that "[a] government that can fob off costs on criminals has an incentive to find criminals everywhere. And defendants threatened with higher fees through extended trials are all the more likely to be intimidated into pleading guilty—whether they really are or not" (Baker, 2006). The amounts owed are large; 10 million people in the United States, about two-thirds of all current and former offenders, owe $50 billion in fines, fees, costs, and other court-ordered impositions (Edelman, 2017, p. xvi).

Supervision fees, which are the most common type of special condition on probation (Bonczar, 1997), help defray the costs of preparing pre-sentence reports and supervising probationers. Such fees are essential in most jurisdictions since correctional budgets do not cover the costs of supervision; about two-thirds of convicted offenders are placed on community supervision, but only one-tenth of corrections budgets go toward supervision (Petersilia, 1997). Special services, such as electronic monitoring, require additional fees. Not surprisingly, probation officers generally believe that collecting fees takes too much time and infringes on their ability to do what they consider to be more important duties (Morgan, 1995). However, probation officers do seem to have higher collection rates if they are evaluated in part on their collection rates (Wheeler et al., 1989), an issue that I touch on in Chapter 4 and Chapter 7. Some probation departments have become self-supporting through supervision fees, whereas other departments are able to cover only a portion of their costs (Olson & Ramker, 2001). Texas is often considered the most successful state in generating fees, with about 40% of the cost of basic probation covered by fees paid by offenders (Finn & Parent, 1992).

Research suggests that probationers in rural counties are more likely than probationers in urban counties to be ordered to pay probation fees (Ellsworth & Weisheit, 1997). In their analysis of probation fees in Illinois, Olson and Ramker (2001) found that fees were ordered in 55% of the cases, and, on average, probationers paid 72% of the ordered amounts. Multivariate analyses indicated that probation fees were significantly more likely to be imposed in rural than urban jurisdictions when treatment or fines were also imposed, and, in terms of individual characteristics, for white offenders, offenders with higher incomes, offenders with prior convictions, and offenders convicted of a misdemeanor rather than a felony. Probationers were likely to pay higher percentages of their probation fees if they were white, had higher incomes, had lower amounts of fees ordered, were sentenced to pay fines, were sentenced in a rural area, and did not have their probations revoked.

Olson and Ramker suggested that the difference in imposition of fees is attributable to the fact that rural judges are likely to be more responsive than urban judges to their communities and more concerned with the imposition of justice in individual cases than with the processing of large numbers of cases (see also Weisheit et al., 1995). It might also be the case that rural areas have lower available tax bases to support government operations, and therefore they have a greater need to rely on revenues from fees (Olson et al., 2001). With regard to their finding that collection rates were higher in rural areas, Olson and Ramker suggested that judges in rural areas were concerned that offenders pay something, whereas judges in urban areas were concerned that fees should be imposed and enforced only if they were set at a level high enough to justify the time and expense of collection.

There are numerous fees and costs imposed, and most economic sanctions in the United States are fees (O'Malley, 2011). In Pennsylvania, for example, of the roughly 2.8 million economic sanctions imposed each year, most are fees and costs (Ruback & Clark, 2011; see Chapter 3). There is significant variation between counties both in the number of different types of economic sanctions imposed and in the average and median amounts of economic sanctions imposed per case. In general, counties with larger populations and higher percentages of citizens in urban areas impose more and a greater variety of economic sanctions.

Aside from county-level differences, there are also significant offender-level differences. Most importantly, there are differences between individual offenders based on conviction offense. In Pennsylvania, offenders convicted of driving under the influence (DUI) have much higher economic sanctions imposed than drug, person, and property offenders because they are likely to pay fees in order both to regain their driver's license and, if they had been admitted to a diversionary program, to avoid the stigma of a criminal record (Ruback & Clark, 2011). But, in general, fees are likely counterproductive—what O'Malley (2011) calls "economically irrational"—because they cost more to implement than the money that is brought in. Moreover, the use of fees can interfere with other economic sanctions. "Fees cannot substitute for imprisonment, but fines can; fees, unlike fines, are a comparatively recent invention; and one reason why so many Americans are imprisoned is because fines are used so infrequently" (O'Malley, 2011, p. 551).

In a National Institute of Justice report on how correctional costs can be recovered through offender fees, Parent (1990, pp. 10, 23–24; see also Hillsman & Mahoney, 1988) listed eight actions that lead to higher levels of revenue: (1) maximize the agency's incentive to collect fees by ensuring that most fees will be additional revenue and that the fees are high enough to justify collection; (2) emphasize program fees (primarily supervision and room and board) rather than service fees (e.g., drug testing); (3) set fees at moderate levels that most offenders can pay, given their other court-ordered obligations; (4) prioritize the collection of fees; (5) impose fees on most offenders, including misdemeanants; (6) drop individuals who are truly unable to pay or when payment problems first appear; (7) develop clear procedures that are consistently followed; and (8) when payments are not made, use credible enforcement efforts that include a series of responses reflecting increased pressure and greater threat of more coercion.

Fees and costs are particularly unfair to the poor since nonpayment is likely to mean that these offenders have to spend more time under criminal justice supervision, and this unpaid criminal justice debt may adversely affect their ability to obtain employment, credit, and housing (Harris et al., 2011). The MPCS objects to fees and costs because "criminal offenders should not be treated as a special class of taxpayers who may be called upon to pay for criminal justice programs and operations that are otherwise underfunded by state legislatures" (Reitz, 2015). In their study of legal financial obligations in Alabama, Meredith and Morse (2017) found fees were 44% of the total amount of legal financial obligations imposed but 57% on average of the amount assessed to each individual, indicating that, for the average offender, fees accounted for most of what was owed. Of these fees, 71% of the fees were accounted by docket fees (27%), public defender fees (24%), and district attorney collection fees (21%). Crime victims' fund fees accounted for another 9%.

Government's Use of Fines, Fees, and Forfeitures

There is clear evidence that governments rely on economic sanctions to operate and that minorities and the poor owe a disproportionate amount of these sanctions (Goldstein et al., 2020; Harris, 2016; Liu et al., 2019). This concern with generating revenue at the expense of those least able to pay raises questions about the legitimacy of the criminal justice system and about citizens' willingness to cooperate with police, prosecutors, and the courts (Holcomb et al., 2018).

There is also evidence that the focus on raising revenue through fines and forfeitures undermines the effectiveness of law enforcement because crime-fighting priorities are sacrificed. Consistent with this idea, Goldstein, Sances, and You (2020) found that cities that collect a higher percentage of their revenue from fees, fines, and asset forfeitures were less likely to make arrests for violent and property crimes. This tradeoff resulting in subordinating the investigation of crime was particularly true for smaller cities with the number of police officers around 20. Other research suggests that fine and forfeiture revenue is greater for drug arrests than for violent crime arrests and that this revenue-driven law enforcement is likely to result in higher arrest rates for blacks and Hispanics for drugs, DUI violations, and prostitution (Makowsky et al., 2019).

Cities' reliance on fines and forfeitures to fund governmental services, what Atuahene (2020) calls "Predatory Cities," became well known after the 2014 shooting of Michael Brown by a police officer in Ferguson, Missouri. Aside from relying on fines and forfeitures to generate revenue, there was evidence that the imposition of these sanctions was racially discriminatory. In the subsequent report by the US Department of Justice (2015) that examined the Ferguson Police Department, the investigators concluded that

Ferguson's law enforcement practices are shaped by the City's focus on revenue rather than by public safety needs. This emphasis on revenue has compromised the institutional character of Ferguson's police department, contributing to a pattern of unconstitutional policing, and has also shaped its municipal court, leading to procedures that raise due process concerns and inflict unnecessary harm on members of the Ferguson community. Further, Ferguson's police and municipal court practices both reflect and exacerbate existing racial bias, including racial stereotypes. Ferguson's own data establish clear racial disparities that adversely impact African Americans.

The City budgets for sizeable increases in municipal fines and fees each year, exhorts police and court staff to deliver those revenue increases, and closely monitors whether those increases are achieved. . . . The importance of focusing on revenue generation is communicated to FPD officers. Ferguson police officers from all ranks told us that revenue generation is stressed heavily within the police department, and that the message comes from City leadership.

An analysis of municipalities in St. Louis County, Missouri, found the same results (Harvey et al., 2014). In those suburbs of St. Louis, court costs and fines were a significant source of income and were the second largest source in Ferguson. Moreover, the amounts of money collected by the courts were inversely related to the wealth of the municipality. That is, more money was collected in poorer municipalities.

A subsequent report by the US Commission on Civil Rights (2017, p. 3) found that "municipalities that rely heavily on revenue from fines and fees have a higher than average percentage of African-American and Latino populations." The report relied on a study by Kopf (2016), who examined the revenues of approximately 20,000 municipalities. Kopf found that "of the nearly 4,600 municipalities with over 5,000 people, the median municipality received just 0.9% of its revenues" from fines (mostly parking infractions, traffic tickets, fines for missed court appearances) and forfeits (mostly forfeited bail and collateral). Kopf found that African Americans composed about 19% of the population in the 50 cities that had the highest proportion of revenues from fines, but they made up less than 4% of population in the median municipality. Kopf concluded that it was race, not a municipality's poverty rate or average income, that explained this reliance on fines and fees.

In a similar study, Singla, Kirschener, and Stone (2019) examined a stratified random sample of 93 California cities to test whether the increasing use of fines and forfeitures revenues from traffic citations was the result primarily (a) of greater budgetary need from fiscal stress and greater demand for public safety services or (b) racially biased policing. About 85% of these fines and forfeitures were for violations of the vehicle code. In their study, Singla et al. used the Census of Governments definition of Fines and Forfeits (CODE U30).[1]

Singla et al. (2019) found that these fines and forfeitures were not like other nontax revenues, such as utility revenues and intergovernmental grants. This revenue to the California cities was primarily affected by the characteristics of the community and the agencies collecting the revenue. Specifically, cities with larger black and Asian communities were more likely to rely on fines and forfeitures. In contrast, cities with police departments that were more representative of or overrepresentative of their white residents were less likely to rely on fines and forfeitures.

Fines and forfeitures are different from user fees in two ways (Singla et al., 2019). First, user fees are voluntary and optional, whereas fines and forfeitures are not. Second, user fees are comparable to a market where consumers make purchases, whereas fines and forfeitures serve as punishments and deterrents in furtherance of public safety. I return to this issue of user fees in Chapter 8.

A third study, by Sances and You (2017), analyzed local revenues for 9,143 cities with at least 2,500 persons. The researchers found that 86% of the cities collected revenues from fines and court fees and that these fines and fees accounted for 2% of the city's revenues, averaging about $8 per person. Consistent with the US Department of Justice report on Ferguson, Missouri, Sances and You found that the use of fines as revenue was positively related to the percentage of the residents of the city who were black. This effect was reduced if the city council had black members. These fines and fees are regressive, and they may be used against poor and minority city residents simply because they are not likely to complain, or it may be that they represent deliberate efforts to control blacks (Sances & You, 2017), questions that future research needs to examine.

Forfeitures as a Revenue Source

Fees are clearly designed to provide revenue for local and state governments. Similarly, forfeitures have become a key source of revenue for many state and local law enforcement agencies, which I discuss here for the sake of completeness about economic sanctions.

Forfeiture, which can be either criminal or civil, refers to the government seizure of property that is illegal contraband, was illegally obtained, was acquired with resources that were illegally obtained, or was used in an illegal activity. The ostensible rationale for asset forfeiture is that offenders should not enjoy the benefits of illegal activity. More recently, forfeitures have served a secondary purpose (and perhaps a primary purpose) of providing assets to the government that can be used or sold.

Civil forfeitures are the most common type of forfeiture (about 80% of all forfeitures; Blumenson & Nilsen, 1998). In civil forfeitures, the lawsuit is against the property that was used in the criminal activity (Williams, 2002), not against the owner of the property. Thus, because the forfeiture is not seen as punitive, the standard of proof is "preponderance of the evidence." In contrast, criminal forfeiture involves the punitive taking of assets involved in a crime and requires that the owner be convicted of the crime "beyond a reasonable doubt." Historically, civil forfeiture in the United States followed the British Navigation Acts, which authorized as "prizes" the seizure of ships used by pirates and smugglers (Pimentel, 2018) and allowed the federal government to seize ships and cargo when their owners did not pay duties (Carpenter et al., 2015, p. 10).

Since 1970, with the passage of the Racketeer Influence and Corrupt Organizations Act, supplemented by laws in 1984 and 1986 (Spaulding, 1989), forfeitures have become an important part of the federal government's law enforcement's efforts against drug crime. The goal is to remove the profit motive from drug dealing and also provide an incentive to law enforcement agencies to pursue drug offenders. In *United States v. Ursery* (1996), the Supreme Court held that the primary goals of forfeiture are remedial and nonpunitive: making sure that criminals do not benefit from their illegal actions and encouraging property owners to prevent their property from being used in criminal activities. Given these primary goals, the Court upheld the government's profiting from the use and sale of seized assets.

In 2014, the Assets Forfeiture Fund of the US Department of Justice brought in $4.5 billion (Carpenter et al., 2016). Because almost all of these forfeitures (87%) were civil forfeitures, the burden of proof was on "property owners to prove their innocence in order to recover property" (Carpenter et al., 2015, p. 43). As a result of this burden on property owners, virtually none of the roughly 40,000 annual asset seizures is contested (Biewen, 2002).

According to Pimentel (2018), a critic of forfeiture policies, forfeitures punish people who did not commit crime and encourage police to focus on gaining revenue rather than on enforcing laws. As evidence of this distortion of law enforcement priorities, Pimentel described a report from Tennessee showing that police were 10 times more likely to stop cars used in drug transactions that were carrying cash (going west toward Mexico) than to stop cars carrying drugs (going east toward the east coast). Seizing cash was apparently more important to the police than seizing drugs, even though the drugs probably were a greater threat to the public. As additional evidence that the police respond to incentives, Holcomb, Williams, Hicks, Kovandzic, and Meitl (2018) found that law enforcement agencies in states with more restrictive laws concerning civil forfeiture were more likely to use the more generous equitable sharing program of the Department of Justice, under which local agencies can receive up to 80% of the seized assets, rather than their own state's civil forfeiture laws.

The ostensible rationale behind asset forfeitures is that offenders should not enjoy the benefits of illegal activity. In recent years, however, critics have argued that, in an era of limited government revenues, asset forfeitures are used to supplement, and perhaps even to finance, law enforcement operations. Given that money may be the primary motive underlying asset forfeitures, scholars have pointed to several dangers of allowing "policing for profit" (Blumenson & Nilsen, 1998), including a lack of notice to those individuals whose property is targeted, the fact that innocent individuals may be the victims of such seizures, the low standard of proof required for such seizures, civil rights violations, police corruption, and an unjustified focus on drug crimes (Baumer, 2008; Skolnick, 2008).

In a test of the "policing for profit" hypothesis, Worrall and Kovandzic (2008) analyzed overall asset forfeiture proceeds and the proceeds from the US Department of Justice Asset Forfeiture Program. They found that in states where police agencies were limited in their ability to keep monies from asset forfeitures, police were more likely to work with federal law enforcement so that they could keep a larger share of the assets under the Department of Justice equitable sharing provisions rather than work alone. Worrall and Kovandzic suggested that this evidence indicates that police agencies are primarily concerned with revenue generation.

Whether asset forfeiture programs have been effective in reducing the supply of drugs and lowering drug-related crime is not known (Baumer, 2008). Moreover, the monetary incentives for police to focus on asset seizures as a way to increase revenues may be undermined by the fact that some jurisdictions lower their budgets for police agencies that are successful in seizing assets (Baicker & Jacobson, 2007).

Despite their obvious advantages, there are some limits to asset forfeitures. In *United States v. Bajakajian* (1998) the US Supreme Court held that, in addition to ensuring that property is not used in criminal activity, civil forfeitures under federal law also have punishment as at least part of the government's goal. Thus, this punishment aspect means that forfeitures are subject to the excessive fines clause of the Eighth Amendment. In the *Bajakajian* case, the defendant's punishment (forfeiting $357,144 in cash that he was planning to take out of the country) was grossly disproportionate to the severity of the crime and to the actual punishment (a $5,000 fine) imposed by the court.

In a more recent case, the US Supreme Court also limited the use of civil forfeiture. In *Timbs v. Indiana* (2019) the Court held that the excessive fines clause of the Eighth Amendment applies to the states. In this case, Timbs used a newly purchased Land Rover to sell drugs to support his habit. He pleaded guilty and was sentenced to 1 year of home detention followed by

5 years of probation and a fine of $1,200. In addition, his $42,000 vehicle was seized because it had been used to transport drugs. The value of the vehicle was more than 4 times the maximum fine that could have been imposed and more than 30 times the fine that was actually imposed. In *Timbs*, the Court noted that protection against excessive fines dates from Magna Carta because such fines undermine other liberties, including free speech, and can be used for non-penal purposes, such as raising revenue.

There have been numerous claims that law enforcement agencies have misused forfeitures as a relatively easy way to replace tax revenue. For instance, there have been reports of police not bringing charges after a vehicle stop if individuals forfeit property and of the government dropping prosecution in exchange for the defendant agreeing not to challenge civil forfeiture (Logan & Wright, 2014). It is too early to know whether the *Timbs* decision will reduce this alleged abuse.

The MPCS (American Law Institute, 2020, p. 227) argues that forfeitures are criminal punishments and, except for stolen goods and contraband, should be preceded by a criminal conviction. The Model Penal Code also recommends that law enforcement agencies should not be able to retain forfeited assets or the proceeds of those assets since doing so creates three conflicts of interest (pp. 232–233). First, law enforcement agencies are likely to give priority to crimes that generate the most revenue (e.g., focusing on drug purchasers who are likely to have large amounts of forfeitable cash rather than on drug dealers whose drugs cannot be used to increase revenues). Second, law enforcement agents might focus their activities (patrol, investigation, search, arrest) on individuals they believe might have money or property that can be seized. Third, forfeitures generally put the interests of law enforcement agencies against the interests of crime victims. To deal with these conflicts, the MPCS suggests that forfeited assets and proceeds from the sales of those assets be directed to the state's victim compensation fund.

Summary of Using Economic Sanctions to Pay for Governmental Services

Logan and Wright (2014) suggested that the widespread use of economic sanctions to pay for the ordinary costs of criminal justice means that decision-makers are not neutral, offenders are not treated as individuals, and the amounts of the sanctions are based more on the needs of the government rather than the seriousness of the crimes committed. Consistent with that argument, when state funding for prosecutors decreased in Oklahoma, the number of offenders in deferred prosecution programs increased, the amount of the fees increased, and the required supervision period increased, all of which together meant that the local prosecutors had more money in their budgets (Logan & Wright, 2014).

Compensating the Victim

Aside from punishing the offender and funding the government, economic sanctions can be used to restore victims through restitution to where they were before the crime occurred. Restitution is a court-ordered payment by the offender to compensate the victim for tangible financial losses directly related to the crime. In contrast to pure punishment, which to be effective as deterrence must be greater than the harm caused (Brickman, 1977), restitution is "exactly proportionate to the harm caused by the offense" (Doyle, 2007). Restitution is concerned both with the welfare of the victim (Moen, 2013) and with issues of just deserts and justice for both the victim and society (Harland, 1981).

Rationale for Restitution

The idea of restitution is at least 4,000 years old (Van Ness, 1990), as several legal codes from the Middle East (e.g., the Code of Hammurabi [c. 1700 BC], the Code of Lipit-Ishtar [c. 1875 BC]) required restitution for property offenses and other codes required restitution for both property and violent offenses (e.g., the Code of Ur-Nammu [c. 2050 BC], the Code of Eshnunna [c. 1700 BC]). In Leviticus, there is an explicit recognition of the need for restitution: "If anyone sins and commits a breach of faith ... through robbery, ... he shall restore what he took by robbery ... he shall restore it in full, and shall add a fifth to it, and give it to him to whom it belongs" (Leviticus 6: 1–5). Roman Law and Germanic tribal laws also included restitutionary sanctions (Van Ness, 1990).

In the Middle Ages, crime victims were compensated for their losses under a system called *composition*, according to which there was a preset rate for the type of harm that was done (Klein, 1997, p. 153). For homicide, the amount (called a *wer*) depended on whether the victim was a noble or a serf. For injuries, the amount (called a *bot*) depended on the type of injury. As long as offenders paid the compensation they owed, they were protected by the king. However, if they did not pay the restitution they owed, they were considered to be outside the law, and victims could punish them without consequences (Klein, 1997).

For administering this system, the king demanded a fee (called a *wit*). By the 12th century, this fee had greatly increased and payments to victims had dramatically decreased (suggesting a tradeoff that is still present; see Chapter 7). The transition was completed in 1256, when King Louis IX of France ended restitution completely. During the next several hundred years, in addition to fines, kings added such sanctions as torture, banishment, and flogging (Klein, 1997, p. 154).

In colonial America, victims were entitled to restitution. In pre-Revolutionary Massachusetts, for instance, thieves had to pay treble damages to victims in addition to being whipped and standing at the gallows with a rope around their necks. If the thieves could not pay the restitution, they worked as an indentured servant for the victim or a third party. After 1785, when Massachusetts established its first prison, thieves were imprisoned and victims' losses were largely ignored. In 1805, Massachusetts completely eliminated treble damages to victims (Klein, 1997, p. 154). For the next 170 years in the United States, prosecutors and judges gave little consideration to the concerns of crime victims in the prosecution and punishment of offenders (Tobolosky et al., 2010).

This evolution from a victim's right to restitution under the Code of Hammurabi to the substitution of the state for the victim in criminal law and the subsequent elimination of restitution as a sentencing option is summarized by Jacob (1975, p. 37), as quoted in Harland (1980, p. 2).

> The ancient historical evolutionary process thus consisted of several stages: (1) private vengeance; (2) collective vengeance; (3) the process of negotiation and composition; (4) the adoption of codes containing pre-set compensation amounts which were to be awarded the victim in the compensation process; (5) the gradual intervention of lords or rulers as mediators, and payment to them of a percentage of the composition-compensation award; and (6) the complete take-over of the criminal justice process and the disappearance of restitution from the criminal law. . . . During this process the interest of the state gradually overshadowed and supplanted those of the victim. The connection between restitution and punishment was severed. Restitution to the victim came to play an insignificant role in the administration of the criminal law. The rights of the victim and the concepts of composition and restitution were separated from the criminal law and instead became incorporated into the civil law of torts.

The use of restitution was revived in the early part of the 20th century, such that restitution was permitted as part of suspended sentences and probation. By the 1930s, 11 states had legislation permitting judges to order restitution as a condition of probation (Frank, 1992). Beginning with the report from the President's Commission on Law Enforcement and the Administration of Justice (1967), there have been consistent calls to require offenders to pay restitution to victims. For example, the President's Task Force on Victims of Crime (1982, p. 72) recommended that "judges should order restitution to the victim in all cases in which the victim has suffered financial loss, unless they state compelling reasons for a contrary ruling on the record." Until the late 1970s, state statutes broadly stated that restitution may be ordered but did not specify the conditions under which restitution would be appropriate (Harland, 1980, p. 3).

Following passage of the federal Victim and Witness Protection Act in 1982, restitution was established at the national level and, in 1996, became mandatory in almost all federal cases as a result of the Mandatory Victims

Restitution Act (Dickman, 2009). All states have statutory provisions that permit restitution (Tobolowsky et al., 2016), the justification for these laws being their restorative effects on victims or their rehabilitative effects on offenders (Klein, 1997).

Without such a statutory provision allowing for restitution, courts of criminal jurisdiction cannot order the offender to pay restitution to the victim (21A Am Jur 2d, Criminal Law §1051, 15 ALR5th 391, 430). According to these statutes, restitution can be a condition of probation, but, in some states, probation cannot be conditioned on restitution unless the court has first considered the defendant's ability to pay the ordered amount. In some states, the amount of restitution must not be in dispute or must be adjudicated, whereas in other states there is no requirement that the amount be determined. In most states, victims are limited to economic losses that are "easily ascertainable," "specific," "actual," or "liquidated" (Klein, 1997, p. 171; McGillis, 1986, p. 36). With regard to the types of losses, some states use the general language of "losses and damages," whereas others list specific types of losses, such as medical expenses and stolen property. In general, these statutes allow restitution for medical expenses and lost wages. As reviewed in the ALR5th, court cases have also considered such costs as funeral expenses, interest, attorney's fees, travel expenses, moving expenses, future medical expenses, repair costs, and lost profits. Most states do not allow restitution for pain and suffering and other general damages since most judges believe these damages should be sought in civil suits.

The burden of proof for the amount of loss for restitution is, in most states, by a preponderance of the evidence, although some commentators have argued that prosecutors must prove the amount of the victim's loss beyond a reasonable doubt (MPCS; American Law Institute, 2020, p. 205). For restitution, most states specify that the amount of restitution recovered through criminal proceedings should not be included in any later civil recovery (p. 215).

Haynes, Cares, and Ruback (2015) systematically analyzed the restitution statutes in the United States. Following the federal statute, most states mandate restitution in all cases unless the judge provides reasons for not doing so. However, even among these "mandatory" statutes, there is little consistency in that some states require restitution only for violent crimes, whereas others require restitution only for property crimes (Office for Victims of Crime, 1998, pp. 356–357). There are also differences among the states in terms of who can receive restitution. In some states only the victim can receive restitution, whereas in other states family members and victims' estates, as well as agencies that provide assistance to victims (e.g., victim service agencies, compensation programs) can receive restitution. There are also differences among states in terms of whether indirect victims (e.g., insurance companies) and local governments are entitled to restitution (Klein, 1997). In some states, incarcerated offenders must pay restitution, whereas in others offenders must be on probation or parole. States also differ in terms of whether juveniles are obligated to pay restitution.

Although restitution is now largely victim-oriented, historically, it was an offender-focused remedy that was intended to promote the offender's rehabilitation rather than to compensate the victim (Dickman, 2009). Imposing, monitoring, and enforcing restitution orders is expensive, sometimes costing more money than is likely to be brought in. In the federal system, the cost of a single restitution order is $2,000 (Dickman, 2009).

As noted earlier, the rationale for restitution in some states is that it helps to rehabilitate offenders, whereas in other states the rationale is that it restores victims to where they were before the crime (Klein, 1997, p. 156). Consistent with these divergent rationales for restitution, in some states restitution is handled through probation/parole supervision and court-based employment programs, which are offender-focused agencies, or through victim and witness assistance programs and victim–offender reconciliation programs, which are primarily victim-focused agencies.

For the most part, restitution programs are perceived as ineffective because judges often do not impose restitution if they believe that the offender does not have the ability to pay it. Moreover, because the payment of restitution often is seen as less important than the payment of costs and fines, any money collected from the offender goes first to these other economic sanctions. Finally, these programs are often unsuccessful because the tasks of monitoring, collecting, disbursing, and enforcing restitution payments is split among agencies with unclear guidelines for who has the primary responsibility (Office for Victims of Crime, 1998, p. 358).

The rates of imposition of restitution has traditionally been low. In a study from 30 years ago, which examined 12,000 probation cases from 32 large metropolitan and suburban jurisdictions which has the virtue of including several different states, restitution was ordered in 29% of cases and the average restitution order imposed on each probationer was $3,369 (Cunniff & Shilton, 1991; see also http://www.ncjrs.gov/App/publications/abstract.aspx?ID=129490). Aside from imposition rates being low, collection rates of restitution are also traditionally low: 45% in one national study (Smith et al., 1989) and 34% in Cook County (Chicago; Lurigio, 1984).

Concern for restitution demonstrates the importance that should be placed on victims. For the most part, the criminal justice system is focused on offenders rather than victims (President's Task Force on Victims of Crime, 1982). By making restitution mandatory, which I advocate in Chapter 8, my emphasis is on victims rather than offenders. Some scholars have gone even further regarding the focus on victims by arguing that the criminal justice system should be privatized so that the emphasis is on victim restitution rather than on offender punishment (Benson, 2012).

The problems usually faced by offenders are also faced by victims: they are disproportionately poor, unemployed, unskilled, and racial/ethnic minorities. Victims suffer both direct costs, such as lost or damaged property, medical expenses, lost wages, mental health counseling, and drug/alcohol treatment, and indirect costs, such as purchasing protection devices, paying increased insurance costs, moving, and avoiding certain neighborhoods (Kilpatrick et al., 1998). Tangible losses can cause direct tangible harms (e.g., a stolen car), indirect tangible harms (e.g., losing a job because of a lack of transportation), and intangible harms (e.g., stress from financial worries). Receiving restitution can address not only issues of tangible harms, but an order of restitution alone can also have some "placebo value" because it gives victims the impression that their concerns are being taken into account (Walsh, 1986). The largest intangible cost is generally pain and suffering, which about 68% of serious violent victims experience (Langton & Truman, 2013), although there are also intangible costs relating to reduced quality of life and fear of crime. Somewhat dated, but still the best available, estimates of victims' tangible and intangible losses are $19,000 for robbery with injury, $24,000 for an assault with injury, and $87,000 for rape (Cohen, 2005).

In addition to the harms of physical injury (and the resulting medical and hospital charges), lost wages, and property damage and loss, victims often suffer from the same sort of credit, employment, and housing problems facing offenders, which is not surprising because many victims are, have been, or will be offenders (Sampson & Lauritsen, 1990; Shaffer & Ruback, 2002). Victims also suffer increased chances of revictimization (Outlaw et al., 2002) through links between drug and alcohol use, depression, and criminal offending (Ruback, Clark, & Warner, 2014).

Restitution in the Federal System

In the federal system, probation officers are responsible for writing a presentence report, which includes the amount of losses to each victim and the economic circumstances of the defendant (18 USC. § 3664). Probation officers are also responsible for the continuing supervision of offenders and for notifying the federal court of an offender's failure to pay and of any changes in the offender's ability to pay. About 15% of federal offenders are ordered to pay restitution (US Government Accountability Office, 2017).

Under federal law, the imposition of restitution is intended to recognize the loss suffered by crime victims and to ensure that they receive the restitution they are entitled. Restitution is also intended to make sure that the offender both recognizes the damages caused by the crime and pays the debt to the victim (US Government Accountability Office, 2017). Federal law requires that the defendant's conduct for which he or she was convicted must be the proximate cause of the victim's injury or loss, which means that the defendant's behavior was both the factual cause of the harm and that it was closely connected to the harm. Under the law, the defendant's financial resources are to be considered only with regard to whether restitution is ordered, not with the amount of restitution. If restitution is ordered, it must be for the full amount of the victim's loss (US Government Accountability

Office, 2017). Federal law does not permit compensation to the victim for pain and suffering, punitive damages, or breach of contract, but compensation for these harms can be sought in state civil litigation in tort law.

The collection of restitution in federal cases is difficult because individuals may be imprisoned or may have only a limited ability to pay their debt. Thus, it should not be surprising that the total amount of unpaid restitution was $110.2 billion at the end of fiscal year 2016 (US Government Accountability Office, 2017). In large-scale financial fraud cases, where the losses can be in the tens of millions of dollars, collection rates are quite low. A 2005 GAO study found that only $40 million (7%) of $568 million dollars lost to financial fraud was paid in restitution (US Government Accountability Office, 2017).

The US General Accountability Office's (2017) report to Congress included a discussion of the benefits and costs of three ways that restitution could be expanded: (1) allowing restitution for conduct beyond what the offender was convicted of and for the results of behavior that was not reasonably foreseeable, (2) expanding restitution to include losses not specified by statute, and (3) permitting restitution for intangible losses, including emotional distress. Under current law, emotional distress is not compensable as restitution. One of the possible problems is that, as with emotional distress under torts suits, it can be difficult to determine whether the emotional distress is real and how serious is the emotional distress.

Restitution, if imposed and paid, addresses the tangible needs of victims by reimbursing them for the tangible costs incurred from the crime. It legitimizes victims' socioemotional needs by indicating, in an official and public manner, that their victimization was wrong and should be repaired (National Center for Victims of Crime, 2011, p. 4). Restitution may also address victims' emotional needs by holding offenders responsible for and forcing them to acknowledge the harms they caused (Okimoto & Tyler, 2007). Restitution cannot be ordered for pain and suffering, but it can cover medical bills, mental health counseling, replacement of lost or stolen property, and funeral expenses (Office for Victims of Crime, 1998). For damages that are difficult to quantify, like pain and suffering, civil court options are available (National Center for Victims of Crime, 2004). Although restitution can possibly address many victims' needs, it is not ordered in every case where it could be imposed and restitution orders generally do not cover the full costs of the harm suffered by victims (Miers, 2014).

Aside from addressing the needs of victims, many scholars and practitioners alike support restitution because it forces offenders to confront the harms they caused victims, makes them responsible for correcting those harms, and gives them a sense of accomplishment when they have paid the restitution (McGillis, 1986). Consistent with that notion, there is some suggestion in research that victims prefer restitution from the offender over compensation from the state because restitution means that the offender must acknowledge the harm that was inflicted (Bolivar, 2010; Doak & O'Mahony,

2006; Miers, 2014). If those goals are met, paying restitution is associated with lower rates of recidivism for both adult offenders and juvenile offenders, as is discussed in Chapter 3 and Chapter 6. Unfortunately, analyses of recidivism generally look only at gross categories of interventions (e.g., probation, intensive probation, jail, prison) rather than at specific types of sanctions, such as economic sanctions. There are only a few studies examining the relationship between the payment of restitution and recidivism, and their value is limited by relatively small sample sizes and potential problems of omitted variable bias (i.e., possible explanatory factors that were not included in the study) and reverse causality (i.e., a failure to consider that possible explanations are actually effects). In this book, I discuss two studies my students and I conducted that address this gap (see Studies 14 and 15; Chapters 5 and 6).

Review of Research on Restitution

Because most of the research that we conducted in Pennsylvania concerned restitution, I spend some space here providing an overview of the research on the imposition and payment of restitution with juveniles and adults.

Juveniles

Several characteristics of the offender may be related to the imposition of restitution orders. In one study, juveniles who were ordered to pay restitution as a sole sanction differed in four ways from those sentenced to restitution plus probation: those with longer prior records, more serious offenses, lower family incomes, and poorer school attendance were more likely than other juveniles to receive a sentence of paying restitution plus probation. Judges apparently used this background information to decide that juveniles who were "worse risks" should receive more supervision (Schneider et al., 1982). Other studies have found that judges are more likely to impose restitution in cases in which the offender appeared likely to pay (e.g., those in which the offender was employed and better educated; Lurigio & Davis, 1990). Such a finding makes sense because the primary reasons for having offenders pay restitution to victims include meeting victims' financial needs and lowering their distress.

Across six counties (in California, Georgia, Idaho, Oklahoma, Wisconsin, and Washington, DC), Ervin and Schneider (1990) found that juveniles randomly assigned to formal restitution programs had lower recidivism than juveniles randomly assigned to other dispositions (e.g., ad hoc restitution). Ervin and Schneider suggested that this positive effect of restitution was not the result of deterrence, a change in self-image, or increased integration into the community. Rather, their analyses indicated that successfully completing the restitution program was the best predictor of recidivism. The authors suggested that restitution programs in which juveniles make regular payments mean that they perform a tangible action that provides positive feedback on a continuing basis, rather than just at the end, as is the case with most programs (see Chapter 6, Study 15).

Many evaluations of restitution programs for juveniles have indicated that most were successful in terms collecting monies owed (86%), recidivism rates (less than 10%), and provision of community service (Bureau of Justice Assistance, 1988). Similarly, evaluations of local programs have suggested that juveniles in restitution programs were less likely to recidivate (Shichor & Binder, 1982).

In an analysis of the court records of juvenile offenders in Utah whose cases involved robbery, assault, burglary, theft, auto theft, and vandalism, Butts and Snyder (1992) found that recidivism was significantly lower when juveniles were ordered to pay restitution either directly or through earnings from community service. Other studies have also found that juveniles who pay a higher proportion of their ordered restitution are less likely to recidivate (Jacobs & Moore, 1994). One possible reason for this effect is that working and paying the restitution teaches the juvenile to take responsibility for the outcomes of his or her crime. Alternatively, it might be that individuals who are ordered to pay high amounts of restitution simply give up and pay no restitution (Jacobs & Moore, 1994).

Adults

Studies with adults suggest that judges are more likely to order restitution when the offender is better educated and employed, characteristics that make it more likely that the offender will pay the imposed restitution (Lurigio & Davis, 1990). In an experimental test of the effects of notification in Cook County, Lurigio and Davis (1990) sent notification letters to the experimental group of offenders and no letters to the control group. The letters, sent by certified mail, contained a reminder that restitution was a condition of probation, a description of the amount and time of the offender's delinquency in payment, a warning that continued nonpayment would result in a violation of probation and possibly incarceration, and a set of guidelines for making payment. Results indicated that offenders in the experimental group were significantly more likely to pay the restitution, particularly if they had a job and had less experience in the criminal justice system.

If offenders do not have any money, they are often unwilling to make any efforts to pay the restitution (Galaway & Hudson, 1975). The likelihood of payment is increased if offenders are told about the importance of restitution, if they are given employment opportunities, if they are closely supervised, and if they are allowed to pay in installments (Klein, 1997; Rubin, 1988; Schneider, 1990; Van Voorhis, 1985). These factors are similar to research on the payment of fines indicating that payment increases with ability to pay and closer supervision (Hillsman et al., 1987).

There is relatively little research on what factors predict the rate at which restitution orders will be paid in full. McGillis (1986), who relied on agencies' self-reported estimates of payment rates, found no systematic predictors of payment. McGillis was also careful to note that the estimates were not validated by independent examination of case records. Factors that may be predictive include whether the agency has a strong emphasis on victim assistance, the types of cases heard, the presence of enough staff to monitor payment, and the support of the judiciary to punish offenders who do not comply.

Because most offenders are not able to pay restitution orders immediately, they frequently pay over time. There is debate about whether delayed and partial payments are worthwhile (McGillis, 1986, pp. 47–48). At the very least, these payments help reduce some of the victims' economic losses and may help them psychologically if they believe that justice has been at least partially done. On the other hand, delayed and partial payments do victims little good if they need to replace stolen or damaged property immediately. Moreover, some have suggested that continuing partial payments serve as constant reminders to victims of their victimization.

Harland (1980) argued that restitution is imposed unsystematically rather than being based on an empirical determination of the conditions that are associated with effective treatment of the offender and meaningful benefit to the victim. To investigate that assertion, Harland (1981) used data from the National Crime Survey to determine the amounts of restitution owed by defendants to victims of six personal and household offenses: larceny from the home, larceny away from home, burglary, vehicle theft, purse snatching/pocket picking, and unarmed robbery. Most of these victimizations (86%) resulted in something being stolen; in 19% of the victimizations, victims suffered damages. Harland found that most losses were small; 48% of the victimizations involved losses of less than $25, and 73% of the victimizations involved losses of less than $100. These relatively small amounts, Harland argued, mean that paying restitution is possible even for offenders who have no financial resources and are unemployed, unemployable, or underage. Harland also argued that if paying restitution to an individual is more rehabilitative than paying restitution to a corporation, restitution is likely to be successful.

However, there are three limitations of Harland's work. First, the surveys on which it was based are more than 40 years old, meaning that the absolute amounts of money he reported are too low even if the general point is true. Second, as Harland noted, because he relied on the National Crime Survey, his data include both crimes reported to the police and those not reported to the police (68% of his sample did not report). Although including both groups of crime provides a good estimate of the losses for which offenders potentially could pay restitution, in practice many of these crimes are not relevant to the criminal justice system since they are unlikely to be reported to the police and thus do not enter the criminal justice system. Even among crimes reported to the police, only if the offender is arrested, prosecuted, and found guilty does restitution come into play. As a result, Harland argued, the property offenses for which restitution is arguably most appropriate are those least likely to come to the attention of and be cleared by the police (p. 23).

Payment of Restitution

The payment of restitution is crucial if the victim, offender, and system are to benefit (McGillis 1986). In particular, if restitution orders help victims only when they are paid and can be harmful when restitution is expected but unpaid, it is important to know (a) whether and how much restitution is paid (Adair, 1989) and (b) what factors affect payment. Research suggests that generally restitution is not completely paid. For example, in the Cook County (Chicago) probation department, the mean (M) collection rate over a 3-year period in the early 1980s was only 34% (Lurigio, 1984). An analysis of the 561 offenders ordered to pay restitution in North Carolina in the first quarter of 1990 found that only 41% paid all of the ordered restitution, 13% paid some of the restitution, and 46% paid no restitution (North Carolina Sentencing and Policy Advisory Commission, 1994, cited in Sims, 2000).

Vermont has a special Restitution Unit that enforces and collects court-ordered restitution (http://www.ccvs.vermont.gov/support-for-victims/restitution-unit). Even so, from 2004 to 2011, the Restitution Unit had an overall collection rate of only 24% (National Center for Victims of Crime, 2011).

Compliance rates seem to be higher when courts take ability to pay into account (Davis et al., 1991). Research suggests that restitution is more likely to be paid when the amount is reasonable in light of the offender's ability to pay, when enforcement efforts are high, and when the offender is given enough time to pay (Davis et al., 1991).

Other reports, however, indicate that most offenders will comply with restitution orders if they are both well-supervised and allowed to pay in installments (Klein, 1997). Understanding what factors affect payment is important because it is at this point of enforcement that policies can be changed to make restitution more effective as a sanction. For example, if research concludes that increased supervision or employment assistance is necessary to ensure payment, such changes could be applied to existing restitution programs.

The rehabilitative potential of restitution hinges both on offenders' ability to pay and their willingness to pay (Galaway & Hudson, 1975). Offenders who do not have adequate resources to pay restitution are generally unwilling to even attempt payment (Galaway & Hudson, 1975). Accordingly, research has shown that emphasizing the benefits of paying restitution, supervising probationers well, and providing employment opportunities to offenders to help with payment increases compliance with the order (Van Voorhis, 1985; Schneider, 1990; Rubin, 1988). Thus, it appears that emphasizing the importance of restitution payment and providing opportunities to fulfill the obligation can increase the likelihood of payment. Research on the payment of fine orders also supports the finding that the payment of financial sanctions relies heavily on the ability to pay and the emphasis placed on payment during supervision (Hillsman et al., 1987). However, as noted in Chapter 6, paying fines does not have the same effects as paying restitution.

Effects of Payment on Recidivism

Aside from addressing the needs of victims, restitution is intended to rehabilitate offenders and thereby benefit the justice system. By accepting responsibility and repairing the damage to the victim in a tangible way, offenders may reap benefits that remain long after the criminal sanction has ended, including taking responsibility in other aspects of their lives and avoiding criminal behavior in the future. Both reintegrative shaming theory (Braithwaite, 1989) and defiance theory (Sherman, 1993) provide insight into the potential of victim restitution to be an effective means of reducing future criminal behavior. These theories are discussed in more detail in Chapter 6, in connection with our research on the effect of paying restitution on subsequent criminal behavior.

Evidence on Restitution and Recidivism

Overall, paying restitution appears to be an effective means of reducing recidivism. In particular, studies have shown that although formal restitution (i.e., as a condition of probation or assigned through court) may be less effective than more informal restitution arrangements (i.e., residential programs or court diversion), it is still more effective than straight probation or incarceration (Schneider, 1990; Rowley, 1990). Similarly, studies have shown that reoffense rates for restitution cases increase monotonically with the degree of court control (Schneider et al. 1980). In contrast, a study of juveniles in Utah (Butts & Snyder, 1992) found positive effects for restitution regardless of whether juveniles were processed formally or informally, although the effect was more dramatic among the informally processed group. In general, studies examining the effectiveness of restitution among juveniles (Schneider, 1986) have shown that juveniles who pay restitution have lower rearrest rates than juveniles who receive other sanctions.

Research on the use of restitution with adults is limited but shows similar trends. In one study, adults in the Minnesota Restitution Center who had to pay restitution had lower recidivism rates than a group of incarcerated offenders (Heinz et al., 1975). Likewise, another study, which performed a 2-year follow-up of adult parolees, found that those randomly assigned to the Minnesota Restitution Center had fewer new court commitments than those on standard parole (Hudson & Chesney, 1977). In Chapter 6, I present empirical evidence from Pennsylvania on the effects of paying restitution on recidivism.

Implications of Constitutional Law for Economic Sanctions

The imposition and enforcement of economic sanctions directly involves three aspects of constitutional law: neutrality, as required by the Due Process Clause; equality, as required by the Equal Protection Clause; and proportionality, as required by Eighth Amendment (Note, 2015). The Due Process Clause requires fair and neutral administration when a criminal defendant's liberty or property are subject to the judgment of a court. That neutrality is threatened when a judge "has a direct, personal, substantial, pecuniary interest in [the] case" (Note, quoting *Tumey v. Ohio*, 1927, p. 523), as may be true if the funds provide a substantial amount of the operating funds of a court or agency or, as in the case of private probation companies, that have a strong financial incentive to threaten incarceration as a mechanism to induce payment. Currently, 13 states allow for private probation (Edelman, 2017).

The Equal Protection Clause, in combination with the Due Process Clause, was the basis for the Supreme Court's decision in *Bearden v. Georgia* (1983) that defendants cannot be incarcerated simply because they are unable to pay a fine. Although wealth is not a "suspect classification" and uniform fees are not unconstitutional simply because they impose a heavier burden on the poor (*San Antonio Independent School District v. Rodriquez*, 1973; Note, 2015), there are cases that suggest indigent defendants cannot be denied access to the courts because they cannot afford the uniform fees (for a transcript and filing). For example, the Supreme Court has held that a state does not have to provide for appeals of court rulings in child custody cases. However, the Court ruled, if a state does provide for such appeals, it cannot make that right to appeal dependent on whether the parent can afford to pay court costs since the right to parent children is a "fundamental right," *M. L. B. v. S. L. J.* (519 US 102 (1996). This decision followed from an earlier decision in which the Supreme Court held that Illinois, once it granted convicted defendants the right to appeal, could not condition that appeal on the procurement of a transcript if the defendant could not afford to pay for the transcript, *Griffin v. Illinois*, 351 US 12 (1956). It has also been suggested that although *Bearden* prohibits incarcerating a defendant who cannot afford to pay a fine, it does not prohibit a defendant from being placed on probation and paying supervision fees, even though that defendant would be paying more overall than a defendant who was able to pay a fine immediately (Note, 2015).

The Excessive Fines Clause of the Eighth Amendment prohibits forfeitures that are "grossly disproportional to the gravity of a defendant's offense" (*US v. Bajakajian*, 1998, p. 334). In *Bajakajian*, the Court was concerned with the defendant's culpability, not with the amount of money he had failed to declare, and it has been suggested that the same rule could be extended to penalties and fees for late payment or nonpayment (Note, 2015).

Overview of Economic Sanctions in the United States

One of the criticisms of many states' use of economic sanctions is that they are used only so that the jurisdiction receives funds to pay for criminal justice expenses. An alternative view is that economic sanctions serve penological functions—to punish, deter, or rehabilitate. One way to test those ideas is to examine state laws to see whether "law on the books" reflects one view over another. To do that, Jordan Zvonkovich and I used an inductive approach to determine whether a state's use of economic sanctions is primarily to pay for criminal justice or to achieve penological goals of punishment, deterrence, and rehabilitation (Zvonkovich & Ruback, 2017).

We analyzed a database created through the National Consumer Law Center (2016), in conjunction with the Criminal Justice Public Policy Program at Harvard Law School, concerning fines and fees independently coded from statutes for all 50 states and Washington DC. To that, we added information about each state's use of restitution and service to crime victims. Finally, we merged those data with information from the census concerning factors related to an economic explanation for the use of economic sanctions (e.g., gross domestic product [GDP], percent living in poverty, average income) and factors related to policy (e.g., indicators of conservatism).

The data contain detailed information on the state-dependent fines, fees, restitution, and forfeitures. State-level variables from the US Census Bureau, Uniform Crime Reports (UCR), Bureau of Justice Statistics (BJS), and measures of the political environment within each state were added as well as controls. State-level measures include unemployment, poverty, economic diversity, residential stability, incarcerated population, and demographics.

To measure the magnitude of sanctions in each state we included the maximum fine for a felony-level offense, the lowest classification of theft, the highest classification of assault/battery, the highest classification of robbery, and the maximum fine for a first DUI offender in the lowest blood-alcohol content category in each state. Data for these maximum fine variables are mostly complete. Finally, we included a variable, also from the Harvard project, that accounts for whether a state considers offenders' ability to pay prior to assessing sanctions.

We included several measures in an attempt to classify states in terms of how punitive they are. First, we included a variable to account for the amount of revenue that a state acquired as part of the Department of Justice's equitable sharing plan (Institute for Justice, 2015). Under this plan, local and state law enforcement agencies are afforded a portion of federal forfeitures taking place in their state for cooperating. From the BJS, we included incarceration statistics for 2010, including any private prison populations. Last, there are variables to account for the state death penalty policy and whether or not the state engages in offender-funded ("for profit") probation.

In order to account for state differences in crime we included both violent and property UCR rates at the state level for 2009–2014. To attempt to isolate which criminal justice system are well-funded and which may be relying on economic sanctions as a means to generate additional revenue, three BJS variables that measure total expenditures in 2010 and 2011 were also included. To control for political conservatism, we coded states based on the political party of the winner in the state of the prior three presidential elections and their last three governors.

In general, there is wide variation in how states impose fines and fees. For statutory fines, the range across states was from 6 to 952, with a mean of 157.0 and a median of 50. For mandatory fines, the range was from 0 to 462, with a mean of 50.4 and a median of 18. For fees, the range was not quite as great. The range for statutory fees was from 8 to 118, with a mean of 36.6 and a median of 33. The range for mandatory fees was from 0 to 89, with a mean of 26.0 and a median of 22.

To determine whether the number of laws states impose regarding fines and fees related to each other and to the amount of money states collect from criminal forfeiture, we correlated these three variables. The only significant correlation across states was the number of statutory fees and the amount of money collected through criminal forfeiture ($r = .41$, $p < .01$). This correlation indicates that states with more statutory fees also collect more money through criminal forfeiture. This association makes sense, in that states relying on offenders to pay the costs of criminal justice through fees also seem to rely on criminal forfeitures to fund the costs of law enforcement. States with more statutory fees also spend more on the justice system ($r = .29$, $p < .05$) and have larger private prison populations ($r = .46$, $p < .01$). Similarly, states that take in more money through criminal forfeitures also spend more on the justice system ($r = .38$, $p < .01$) and have larger private prison populations ($r = .64$, $p < .01$).

Our assumption was that those states that rely on statutory fees and criminal forfeitures to fund their criminal justice operations do so because they need the money. Consistent with that notion, states with higher unemployment rates are also likely to have more statutory fees ($r = .32$, $p < .05$) and collect more money through criminal forfeitures ($r = .31$, $p < .05$).

A multiple linear regression of the total number of statutory fees in a state on economic predictors (state GDP, percent unemployed), political predictor (percent voting for a Republican governor), and criminal justice variables (size of the private prison population, total criminal justice expenditures) was significant ($F(5, 44) = 3.66$, $p < .01$, Adj $R^2 = .214$). The only individual predictor that was significant was the size of the private prison population. The same variables used to predict the amount of money collected through criminal forfeiture was also significant ($F(5, 44) = 8.43$, $p < .001$, Adj $R^2 = .431$). Again, the only individual predictor that was significant was the size of the private prison population.

Given that an economic indicator of poverty is related to economic sanctions related to funding the government, it makes sense that the 17 southern states have more statutory fees (M = 50.0) than the 12 midwestern states (M = 34.8), the 13 western states (M = 29.8), and the 9 northeastern states (M = 25.0), as southern states tend to be poorer than the other regions (F, (3, 44) = 3.24, $p < .05$). The difference between the southern states and the northeastern states is significant. The midwestern and western states do no differ significantly from the other two groups.

Summary

This chapter provided detailed information about the rationale for, imposition of, and effects of economic sanctions designed to punish the offender (fines), compensate the government (fees, costs, forfeitures), and compensate the victim (restitution). It was noted that punishing and compensating are not independent and that poorer states (particularly in the South) tend to have more fees for compensating the government. The next chapter focuses on Pennsylvania, providing a legal context for economic sanctions in the state, giving an overview of the research we conducted, and then examining the imposition of fines, fees, and restitution.

Note

1 Revenue from penalties imposed for violations of law; civil penalties (e.g., for violating court orders); court fees *if* levied upon conviction of a crime or violation; court-ordered restitutions to crime victims where government actually collects the monies; and forfeits of deposits held for performance guarantees or against loss or damage (such as forfeited bail and collateral) (US Bureau of the Census, 2006, pp. 4–40).

3

Overview of the Research

All of the studies presented in this book were conducted in Pennsylvania. This chapter provides an overview of the law in Pennsylvania regarding economic sanctions and an overview of the research studies, including the rationale for focusing on one state. The chapter ends with a summary of the research we conducted that examined multiple economic sanctions across the state.

The Law in Pennsylvania Regarding Economic Sanctions

Unlike some states (e.g., Texas) where courts are controlled at the county level, Pennsylvania has a unified court system, which means that courts are managed at the state level. The Pennsylvania Unified Judicial System (UJS) is overseen by the Administrative Office of Pennsylvania Courts (AOPC). There are about 165,000 criminal cases processed annually by the courts of general jurisdiction (Courts of Common Pleas) in the state (AOPC, 2020). In the state, there are about 117,000 criminal convictions each year (http://www.pacourts.us/news-and-statistics/research-and-statistics/dashboard-table-of-contents/statewide-criminal-dashboard-common-pleas-court). According to the Pennsylvania Commission on Sentencing (PCS), which monitors sentencing after conviction in Pennsylvania's District Courts (the courts of general jurisdiction), there are about 75,000 judicial proceedings each year, with some individuals being sentenced for more than one criminal conviction (Pennsylvania Commission on Sentencing [PCS], 2017).

This summary of Pennsylvania law on economic sanctions is based on a 2014 Superior Court of Pennsylvania case (*Commonwealth of Pennsylvania v. Rivera*, 95 A.3d 913) and a guide to the imposition of fines, costs, and restitution written by the Pennsylvania branch of the American Civil Liberties

Economic Sanctions in Criminal Justice. R. Barry Ruback, Oxford University Press. © Oxford University Press 2022.
DOI: 10.1093/oso/9780190682583.003.0003

Union (ACLU; see https://aclupa.org/sites/default/files/wysiwyg/sentencing_
guide_2020-03-11_1.pdf).

Fines

According to Pennsylvania law, fines are punitive and a direct consequence
of the criminal conviction. "A fine is a monetary amount equal to the severity of the crime . . . used to ensure that a person does not receive a pecuniary gain from the offense" (*Rivera* at 916) and can be imposed only after the
court considers the defendant's ability to pay the fine and the burden that
the fine will place on the defendant (42 Pa.C.S. §9726 (c) and (d)). The court
can impose a fine only if the fine will not prevent the defendant from paying
restitution to the victim (42 Pa.C.S. §9726 (c)). The court must find and state
in the record that the defendant has sufficient financial resources to pay the
fine. However, even if the defendant lacks the present ability to pay the fine,
the court may still impose the fine if the defendant will be able to pay the
fine. The courts have interpreted 42 Pa.C.S. §9726 (c) and (d) as not covering
mandatory fines.

Costs

Costs reimburse "the government for the expenses associated with the criminal prosecution" (*Rivera* at 916). They are intended to make the government
whole and are collateral to the sentence. Costs are not mandatory, and the
court can reduce or waive costs depending on the defendant's ability to pay.
Under Pennsylvania law, costs cannot be considered a condition of probation
because they do not serve a penal or rehabilitative purpose. That is, they are
not considered punishment. And, because they are "not reasonably related
to the rehabilitation of the defendant" (42 Pa.C.S. §9754 (c)), unpaid costs by
themselves cannot be the basis for revoking or extending probation.

   Aside from not being a condition of probation, a cost can be imposed
only if there is a statute that authorizes it. The costs must be related to the
conviction charges and must be for costs that are beyond those that "fall
within the ambit of usual services provided" (*Commonwealth v. Cutillo*, 440
A.2d 607, 609, Pa Super.Ct. 1982). The term "costs of prosecution" is acceptable to cover authorized court costs such as the cost of experts and the money
used to buy drugs. Ordinary salary costs are generally not recoverable.

   A defendant must receive a bill of costs at the sentencing hearing and can
object at that time to individual costs. Costs cannot be imposed retroactively.

Restitution

Restitution "compensates the victim for his loss and rehabilitates the defendant by impressing upon him that his criminal conduct caused the victim's

loss and he is responsible to repair that loss" (*Rivera* at 916). Like costs, restitution is not considered punishment.

Restitution can be imposed in Pennsylvania under one of two rationales. If it is part of the sentence, then the defendant's ability to pay cannot be considered (18 Pa.C.S. §1106(c)(1)(i)). The restitution order does not expire with the end of probation. However, if restitution is imposed as a condition of probation, then the defendant's ability to pay must be considered and the duty to pay the restitution ends with the end of probation, even if all of the ordered restitution has not been paid.

Restitution can be imposed as part of a sentence only in connection with losses that result directly from a crime for which the defendant was convicted. These losses can be for property loss as a result of theft, conversion, or damage decreasing its value or for personal injury to the victim. Restitution must be determined by the court, not some other agency (e.g., the probation department). The amount of the restitution must be supported by facts determined at an adversarial evidentiary hearing and made as findings on the record.

From 1978 to 1995, the controlling statute in Pennsylvania gave courts the power, but did not require them, to order restitution. According to the statute, courts were to consider the extent of the victim's injuries and could also consider any other matters, including the offender's ability to pay. Courts had the power to order restitution according to any payment schedule within the time limit set by the maximum term of imprisonment to which the offender could have been sentenced. Restitution in Pennsylvania is considered a type of restorative sanction, and, in 1994, the state sentencing guidelines recommended restorative sanctions for crimes of relatively low seriousness. Restorative sanctions (a) are least restrictive in restraining the offender's liberties, (b) do not involve confining the offender, and (c) focus on restoring the victim to pre-offense status (PCS, 2012, p. 12).

In 1995, as part of a comprehensive change in criminal statutes, Pennsylvania implemented a statutory change making restitution mandatory (18 Pa. C.S.A. §1106 (1)). Under the statute, victims, either individuals, businesses, or the state, whose property was stolen or damaged or who suffered personal injury as a direct result of a crime were entitled to restitution. Moreover, the statute explicitly stated that restitution awards were not to be reduced by any payments that had been made to the victim from such sources as the Crime Victim's Compensation Fund, other governmental agencies, or insurance companies. That is, if victims had received partial or total compensation, offenders still owed the total restitution amount, although the payments were to be made to the government agency or insurance company that had paid the victim. And, according to the statute, judges were to impose full restitution regardless of the offender's financial resources.

The statute also established priorities for the payment of restitution, with the victim receiving payment first, the Crime Victim's Compensation Board receiving payment second, other government agencies that provided reimbursement to the victim third, and insurance companies providing reimbursement under an insurance contract last. Under the statute, the district attorney must recommend the amount of restitution to be awarded. This information usually comes from the victim and is often collected by the victim and witness advocacy office.

The mandatory nature of the 1995 restitution statute should have resulted in a substantial increase in the number of restitution orders because the legislature was clearly trying to eliminate possible reasons why judges had not previously been ordering restitution. In Chapter 4, I present a study that examined the effect of the 1995 statute.

In 1998, the Pennsylvania General Assembly enacted legislation that made the county probation department the agency responsible for collecting restitution and ordered that 50% of money collected had to go to paying restitution, with the remainder going toward costs, fines, and fees. The law also permitted a wage attachment for the purposes of restitution, allowed courts to use private collection agencies, and ordered the Department of Corrections to pay inmates' ordered restitution by deducting money from their personal accounts in the prison.

Comparison with Other States

With regard to restitution laws, Haynes, Cares, and Ruback (2015) looked at six constitutional and statutory provisions for all 50 states and the District of Columbia using a database maintained by the Office for Victims of Crime. A constitutional right to restitution is the strongest statement a state can make about the importance of the right. Based on the analysis of Haynes et al. and Tobolowsky et al. (2010, p. 157), 20 states give victims this constitutional right.

A second way to consider how important a state views restitution is to examine whether the state requires a judge to impose restitution by using mandatory ("shall") language or permits a judge to impose restitution by using permissive ("may") language. Haynes et al. determined that 33 states use the mandatory "shall" language, but that 3 of these states qualify this mandate. As noted, Pennsylvania changed its law in 1995 to make restitution mandatory.

A third way to determine the importance of restitution to a state is to look at whether the imposition is automatic, regardless of the defendant's financial condition, or whether the judge can, or must, consider the defendant's ability to pay. Taking into account the defendant's financial resources, vis-à-vis the victim's demonstrated losses, is thus a policy judgment about whose interests—the defendant's and the defendant's family's versus the victim's and the victim's family's—is more important. Only 6 states prohibit judges from considering the defendant's ability to pay in contrast to 23 states that allow or require judges to consider the defendant's assets and income. Because there is no mention of the defendant's ability to pay in the laws of 22 states, judges in these states can consider the defendant's resources in imposing restitution, but whether and how is unspecified.

A fourth way to determine how important restitution is viewed by the state legislature is whether the payment of restitution is to be made before the payment of other types of economic sanctions. Given the limited financial resources of most criminal defendants, payment of economic sanctions is zero-sum. That is, for example, a payment toward a fine reduces the probability that there will be a payment toward restitution. If, however, a state requires that restitution be paid first, before fines and fees/costs, the likelihood that a victim will receive restitution is increased. According to their laws, 12 states require that at least half of all payments go toward restitution, whereas 5 states prioritize other economic sanctions over restitution. The laws of the remaining 34 states do not address the order in which fines, fees/costs, and restitution must be paid. However, for-profit probation companies and collections services always take their fees first (see Chapter 8).

As an important note regarding the research reported in this monograph, Pennsylvania law requires that half of all monies received from the defendant go toward restitution, and Centre County, the location in which our experiment on increasing the payment of restitution was conducted, has a policy that all monies received go first to restitution. These policies governing the payment of restitution in Centre County likely affected the results of the experiment in terms of increasing payment (see Study 13; Chapter 5) and reducing recidivism (see Study 15; Chapter 6).

A fifth way state laws can be seen as prioritizing restitution is whether, by state law, a restitution order imposed by a criminal court automatically becomes a civil judgment if the defendant's supervision period ends before the payment of restitution is complete. Haynes et al. found that 14 states have laws that convert restitution judgments into civil judgments, whereas 37 states do not have a law that addresses the issue.

A sixth way to determine how important a state views restitution is whether state law permits the seizure of assets or property or the garnishment of wages. Eight states permit seizure or garnishment.

Overall, Haynes et al. concluded that there was wide variability in states' written policies regarding restitution. Under this framework, Pennsylvania has a definite pro-victim tilt. It mandates restitution in all appropriate cases, it does not allow judges to take the defendant's ability to pay into account, and it requires that at least half of all the defendant's payments go toward restitution.

Determining Ability to Pay

According to the Pennsylvania ACLU, "Despite numerous appellate decisions instructing trial courts to consider the defendant's ability to pay when determining the amount of fines, costs, and restitution at sentencing, Pennsylvania's appellate courts have provided almost no guidance on *how* to determine an appropriate dollar amount" (ACLU of Pennsylvania, 2020; https://aclupa.org/sites/default/files/wysiwyg/sentencing_guide_2020-03-11_1.pdf). There is some suggestion that trial courts should look only at the defendant's ability to pay in the short term. In one case the appellate court stated that the defendant's "ability to pay a fine in the immediate future was seriously curtailed by the imposition of a prison term" (*Commonwealth v. Martin*, 335 A.2d 424 (Pa. Super. Ct. 1975)). A more recent appellate case in Pennsylvania suggests that it is only the defendant's ability to pay, not that of friends or family, that is relevant. In that case, the court said, "Although Appellant indicated that he could potentially borrow money from a sibling, the court failed to find—as our law requires—that he alone had the financial ability to pay the outstanding fines and costs such that imprisonment was warranted" (*Commonwealth v. Smetana*, 191 A.3d 867 at 873 (Pa. Super Ct. 2018)).

In Chapter 8, I present suggestions from the ACLU regarding the defendant's ability to pay fines and costs.

Paying Economic Sanctions

At the time the studies described here were conducted, defendants had to pay their criminal justice debt in person and with a cashier's or certified check. Cash, personal checks, and credit/debit cards were not accepted. Now, convicted offenders can pay fines, costs, and restitution online through PAePay (https://ujsportal.pacourts.us/PayOnline.aspx). The maximum payment for any one transaction is $1,000, with a charge of $2.75 for each transaction.

In 2019, Sharpe and his colleagues looked at the imposition and collection of costs (Sharpe et al., 2018) and fines (Sharpe et al., 2019) in Pennsylvania criminal cases. In these analyses, they used 10 years of court data (August 2008–August 2018) from the Common Pleas Case Management System used by the trial courts of general jurisdiction in Pennsylvania and the Philadelphia Municipal Court (since Philadelphia has its own separate system).

Sharpe et al. (2018) examined about 1.4 million cases in which the assessed costs totaled about $1.9 billion. Of these cases, defendants were represented by the public defender or other court-appointed counsel in 906,952 cases and by private counsel in 522,318 cases. The authors assumed that defendants represented by public defenders or court-appointed counsel were indigent. Costs were imposed in 89% of public defender cases and 93% of private counsel cases. The distribution of the costs imposed was highly skewed, in that 166,658 had costs of greater than $25,000, 2,059 had costs of greater than $100,000, and 195 had costs of greater than $500,000. As a result, the authors used the median in their analyses since the median is less influenced by outliers. When costs were imposed, the median amount was $1,072 for public defender cases and $1,306 for private counsel cases. Over the 10 years examined, the median public defender client paid $441 and still owed $631, whereas the median private counsel client paid $1,306 and owed nothing.

After 10 years, 54% of the private counsel clients had paid their costs in full, compared to 24% of public defender clients.

As would be expected, the percentages of the owed costs that were paid in full are directly related to the amounts owed; for costs up to $100, 90% of private counsel clients and 84% of public defender clients paid their costs in full, whereas for costs up to $500, 68% of private counsel clients and 51% of public defender clients paid their costs in full. Based on the fact that private counsel defendants paid more costs even though there were almost twice as many public defender defendants and the total costs that were imposed on all public defender defendants were much higher, Sharpe et al. (2018) concluded that costs imposed on the typical public defender client could be reduced by more than 50% with virtually no impact on total revenue collection.

In a second related study, Sharpe et al. (2019) examined 1,719,368 cases in which the assessed fines totaled $418,314,533. Of these cases, defendants were represented by the public defender or other court-appointed counsel in 1,133,440 cases and by private counsel in 585,928 cases. The authors assumed that defendants represented by public defenders or court-appointed counsel were indigent. With regard to fines, courts imposed them in 34% of all cases, 30% of the public defender cases, and 42% of the private counsel cases. Because 99% of the fines were less than $2,500, with a few cases having extremely large amounts (54 cases with fines of more than $100,000), the authors used median fines amounts because average fine amounts can be disproportionately influenced by the outliers. The median fine amount imposed on public defender clients was $300, and on private counsel clients the median amount was $500. The median amount paid by public defender clients was $150, with the median amount still owed being $150. The median amount paid by private client defendants was $500, with the median amount still owed being $0. The total amount of fines paid by public defender clients was about $55.7 million, whereas the total amount of fines paid by private counsel clients was about $107.2 million. After 10 years, 69% of the private counsel clients had paid their fines in full, compared to 41% of public defender clients.

The difference in the imposition rates on public defender clients of costs (89%) and fines (30%) may be due to judges taking into account these defendants' ability to pay, which is a statutory factor for fines but not for costs. The fact that most public defender clients do not pay their costs and fines suggests that courts could reduce the imposed amounts without much loss in revenue (Sharpe et al., 2019). Moreover, imposed amounts that are more realistic might remove defendants' tendency to refuse to pay anything toward unrealistically large amounts and might also reduce the court resources devoted toward monitoring and collecting unpaid costs and fines.

Overview of the Research Program

The research program described in this book was designed to be a multiplistic approach to the imposition, payment, and effect of economic sanctions in the criminal justice system. *Multiplism* refers to the use of multiple methods to investigate research questions, an approach that has long been advocated by social scientists (Mark & Shotland, 1985) although rarely employed. The rationale behind the approach is that valid answers can be best achieved if answers converge across multiple dimensions.

The research program was designed to address both broad and specific questions. At the broad level, the research examined the imposition, payment, enforcement, and effect of fines, fees, and restitution. In terms of specifics, the research addressed both policy questions dealing with decisions by individuals working in government and questions of impact, looking at how economic sanctions affect offenders.

There were four specific policy questions that the research examined. One was whether the collection of the financial obligations was better realized if they were collected by probation staff or by paid staff whose sole focus was ensuring the payment of the economic sanctions. This research, which is discussed in detail in Chapter 4, compared two counties in Pennsylvania that used probation officers to collect economic sanctions against two counties in Pennsylvania that used collection agents (one county that used an outside collection agency and one county that used probation staff who focused only on collecting money rather than also supervising offenders). The results of this comparison suggest that more money is collected when probation officers rather than collection agents oversee the collection of the economic sanctions. State-level analyses (Study 1) were consistent with this result.

A second specific question looked at policy issues related to the imposition of restitution. Specifically, the research looked at whether the location of the victim and witness assistance office was related to the imposition of restitution (Study 6). The results indicate that location does matter: proximity leads to greater levels of imposition.

A third policy question related to what factors increase the likelihood that a law will be implemented. In this case, the question was what factors were related to the likelihood that judges would change their behavior regarding the imposition of restitution. In multimethod studies involving archival analyses of statewide data (Study 4) and surveys of judges (Study 5), Gretchen Cusick, Jennifer Sikorski, and I examined the percentage of cases in which restitution was ordered before and after the law was changed making restitution mandatory. Our conclusion was that, overall, the law was successfully implemented because the law was clear and judges agreed with its goal.

A fourth specific question was whether it is possible to induce probationers who owe restitution to pay more of the restitution they owe (Study 13). In addition, we wanted to know whether an experimental manipulation that increased the likelihood of paying restitution could lower the likelihood that the probationer would be arrested for committing a new crime (Study 15). Our results suggest that the manipulation was successful both in inducing more payment and reducing recidivism.

In this research program, our goal was to conduct multiplistic research across six dimensions: academic discipline, levels of analysis, actors within the system, type of process investigated, statistical techniques, and research methods. First, in terms of discipline, our research incorporated theoretical ideas and approaches from social psychology, criminology, sociology, and law. Second, in terms of levels of analysis, our research used both individual-level variables and county-level variables, which allowed us to use different types of statistical controls when we examined individuals nested within counties. We were also able to compare counties and examine one county (Philadelphia) in depth, which is unique in several ways.

Third, in terms of actors within the system, our research looked at offenders, victims, prosecutors, probation officers, and judges. Fourth, in terms of processes, our research looked at two factors: (a) people's conscious decisions and their beliefs about the policies they were implementing and (b) nonconscious factors that might also influence behavior. For example, we looked at the likelihood of imposing restitution as a function of where the victim and witness assistance office was located.

Fifth, our research used multiple statistical techniques, moving from simple to more complex research designs, and from descriptive and bivariate statistics to different types of multivariate analyses. Moreover, because the different multivariate approaches make different assumptions about the nature of the data, it is important to analyze the data with several multivariate techniques in order to test the strength of the conclusions. If a finding appears in one analysis, the question is whether that result is unique to the particular analytic technique or is a valid characterization of the patterns underlying the data. The only way to know for sure is to use multiple approaches that make different assumptions about the data in order to determine whether the finding is robust with respect to analytic technique. If the same conclusion is reached across statistical methods, then the observed finding cannot be due to the particular method used but is most likely be due to a true description of patterns in the data.

Sixth, we used four methods: (1) analyses of existing computerized datasets, (2) coding of existing data from paper files, (3) surveys of multiple individuals who have different perspectives on and roles in the criminal justice system (e.g., victims, offenders, judges, prosecutors, probation officers), and (4) a field experiment that manipulated policy-relevant variables.

Analyses of Existing Computerized Datasets

One of the most common ways that applied social scientists investigate questions is to use existing datasets. In the criminal justice system, a commonly used database comprises the court decisions made after criminal sentencing hearings. Reported here are several studies of archives: court records kept by the AOPC and sentencing records kept by the PCS.

There are three advantages to using such a dataset. First, these datasets represent actual decisions, meaning that questions of generalizability to the real world are minimal. Second, many of the factors used in these decisions—the conviction offense(s), the offender's prior conviction record, the offender's prior incarcerations and other punishments—are in the files and can be used to investigate whether they predict decisions.

Third, these files generally contain many thousands of cases, particularly if many years of data are examined. Such a large number of cases means that, for many questions, there is enough statistical power to detect real differences. That is, in statistical analyses it is important both to have confidence that differences are unlikely to be due to chance and to believe that the absence of differences means that it really is likely that two conditions are not different. A large sample size gives more confidence that detected differences are truly different and that a nonsignificant difference very likely means there really is no important difference. Another advantage of a large sample size is that it permits asking questions involving multiple variables at the same time: for example, whether fines are higher for males, for whites, for violent offenders, and for offenders in suburban than rural areas.

On the other hand, existing datasets have four disadvantages. First, real-world files often do not have important data that investigating social scientists would find helpful. In the context of economic sanctions, one type of important information is the offender's ability to pay based on assets, salary, and debts. This absence is somewhat mitigated by the fact that if the information was not in the file, the judge probably did not have it either. If the direct information is not available (e.g., bank assets), investigators use approximations. For example, one indicator of not having the ability to pay economic sanctions is that the offender did not pay money bail to be released while awaiting trial. Another approximation of inability to pay is that the offender was represented by a public defender or a court-appointed attorney, since if the judge believed the offender had sufficient funds to pay an attorney, the judge would not have allowed a public defender or court-appointed attorney to represent the offender. Although being represented by a public defender is probably a pretty good indicator of poverty, it is not perfect and is still a fairly imprecise measure of the level of poverty.

Even if the data element is present in the database, a second disadvantage of using existing datasets is that the data that are present may not have been accurately recorded. Third, for some portion of the cases, there is very likely to be missing data. Missing data can be especially problematic if it there is a systematic bias (e.g., some counties do not report a particular kind of information).

Sometimes these problems with the data mean that statistical adjustments are needed if certain questions are to be addressed. Sometimes, it is not possible to address the questions at all.

Fourth, and most seriously, analyses of actual datasets can provide information only about how variables are associated with each other. That is, researchers can talk about correlations between variables but cannot speak about causation. In recent years, statistical techniques have been developed that, given certain assumptions, allow questions of causality to be addressed. But the reality of multiple confounded variables often means that alternative explanations cannot be dismissed. Moreover, answers to questions about process (e.g., what judges were thinking when they made these decisions) can only be approximated.

Coding of Existing Data

Because computerized datasets may not exist regarding a general question (e.g., economic sanctions) or, if they do exist, often do not contain the information needed to answer specific questions, it is necessary for researchers to code information from paper files. Even with the extensive digitization of many databases in criminal justice, it is still the case that paper files are used by many actors (or at least were when the studies described here were conducted). That being the case, information relevant to an issue must be coded by individuals who have to read the files and enter the data into a spreadsheet. With large datasets, multiple coders are needed.

To make sure that these multiple coders enter the information from the paper files in the same way, they must be trained and there must be evidence that their coding is consistent. What is typically done, and what we did, was to have these coders, after receiving training, code some of the same cases that were coded by at least one other person. If the coding is the same (as measured by percentage agreement or by Kappa), the coding is said to be reliable. For example, in Study 9, three coders agreed on the coding of the 17 most important demographic, offense, sentencing, and outcome variables more than 95% of the time.

Even though researchers can have coders code information not available in digitized datasets and, assuming high reliability, can do so accurately, these coded datasets still have some of the same problems as computerized archives. That is, the information may not exist in the paper file (e.g., family assets). Moreover, even if the information exists and is accurately coded, the resulting analyses can reveal only associations, not causality. In addition, there is still a question of what factors explain the process. Although it is possible to test for statistical mediation as one way to understand process, many researchers believe that such tests to understand process should be complemented with surveys that ask individuals to explain their decisions.

Surveys

Surveys involve asking individual respondents to provide factual and opinion information. Good survey methodology requires that the sample of respondents be representative of the population to which the researchers want to generalize the results. Surveys assume that respondents understand the questions, that they are willing to give an answer, and that their answer is true. Low response rates are becoming more common across all kinds of surveys, which raises questions about the representativeness of the final sample. When respondents give an answer, their answers may be affected by the desire to look "good" or "normal," what is called *social desirability*. Moreover, research by Nisbett and Wilson (1977) suggests that, even when individuals provide explanations for their decisions, they may not have genuine insight into the factors that are actually predictive, relying instead on salient stimuli or implicit theories. Thus, one must be careful in interpreting the results from surveys.

Despite these weaknesses, surveys have three strengths that make them worth including in a program of research. First, some factual information may be possessed only by the individual who is asked, and, if that person is not asked, the answer can only be guessed at. For example, judges may be asked what factors they use to determine the imposition of restitution. Second, opinion information is the province of the individual being asked; there is no right or wrong answer. If an opinion is the desired value (e.g., "How fair do you think restitution is?"), one must ask the person. Third, sometimes researchers are interested not in facts or opinions but in how individuals perceive an event. In social psychology, this question is often referred to as an *attribution*, that is, the person's belief about why something occurred or did not occur. Regarding economic sanctions, the question often facing a judge is whether an offender lacks the ability to pay or is willfully refusing to pay despite having the ability to do so. Fourth, sometimes researchers are interested in knowing how individuals' perceptions compare to more objective measures. For example, it might be important to know how judges perceive their use of economic sanctions compared to their actual rates of use.

In the studies reported here, there are surveys of judges, offenders, and crime victims. This information is given with caveats because of the potential problems with self-reports of facts, opinions, and attributions. The key, though, is that these survey responses are used here in conjunction with other types of data.

Field Experiment

This program of research involved a field experiment. Experiments are often considered the gold standard of research, particularly in testing medical and drug interventions through randomized clinical trials. The rationale for experiments is that they can lead to statements about cause and effect as long as three conditions exist. First, the two variables of interest must vary together. Second, one variable must occur before the other variable. Third, the effect on the measured (dependent) variable must occur when the temporally preceding manipulated (independent) variable is present and must not occur when the independent variable is absent, what Mill (1843) called the *joint method of agreement and difference*. The absence of the independent variable is referred to as the *control condition*. In a true experiment, participants are randomly assigned to receive or not receive the independent variable.

This random assignment reduces selection bias as a possible explanation for the observed results. *Selection bias* refers to the fact that, in the real world, individuals who receive one type of treatment differ in a number of ways from individuals who receive a different type of treatment. Thus, if there are differences between the two groups, the difference may be due to the different treatments or it may be due to other differences between the two groups, such as education, economic status, or location.

It should be noted that the labeling of experiments in criminology as the "gold standard" has been criticized on methodological grounds by Sampson (2010), who argued that randomization does not solve the problem of omitted variable bias, that treatment assignment may interfere with outcomes, and that the internal validity of an experiment may not transfer to policy. Sampson suggested that no one method is always superior to others, the determination of what is the appropriate method being dependent on the theoretical question involved and the practical problems of research. A promising approach, Sampson suggested, is to use multiple methods, especially within the same study.

One criticism of studies in social science, especially those in experimental social psychology, which are often conducted in college laboratories or through vignettes, is that they are artificial in the sense that they do not involve actual behavior in a natural setting. The main strength of field experiments is that they have high external validity; that is, because they are conducted in a natural setting, they can be more easily generalized to other situations and populations.

The primary weakness of field experiments is that other factors might affect some participants and not others. In a laboratory, these other factors would be controlled by the experimenter so that they would not vary across conditions and could not therefore be a possible alternative explanation for the observed results. Although uncontrolled-for factors might affect participants in a field experiment, the experimenters can test whether these factors might have produced the observed results. Given that the participants were randomly assigned to a condition and that the independent variable was delivered as planned, then a difference on the dependent measure as a function of the independent variable can be tested in terms of how likely it is that this difference occurred as a result of chance (including whether some uncontrolled-for factor was the potential cause). If the observed difference could have occurred less than five times out of a hundred, then social scientists assume that the difference is a real one.

A Note on Ethical Issues

One of the issues with research involving human participants is that there are likely to be ethical issues involved. When participants are connected to the criminal justice system, review by an independent Institutional Review Board (IRB) is automatically required.

Prior to all of the studies described here, approval was granted by the Penn State IRB. Studies using archival datasets with offender-identifying information were first examined on secure computers that were accessible only by staff of the PCS. If information from multiple datasets required that the identifying information be available in all datasets, the identifying information was kept until the data files were merged. Once the files were merged, all identifying information was deleted, thus making the files anonymized.

For studies involving data collection from paper and computer files in the counties, we first received approval from the president judge of each of the counties. Before data collection began in each county, the data collection team met with someone from the Clerk of Courts office, the Director of the Probation and Parole office, and, in two counties, the director of the specialized collections unit, in order to inform them about the research project and learn about the location and handling of case files. Almost all of the data were collected by trained graduate students; in one county, probation staff coded some of the information. All of the coded data were anonymous.

For the surveys of offenders, victims, judges, probation officers, and district attorneys, information in the files used for analyses was anonymous. Because we paid offenders and victims for their participation in the study, we kept their names and addresses in a separate file so that we would be able to send them an honorarium (e.g., a Walmart gift card) for their participation.

The field experiment we conducted (Study 13; Chapter 5) required IRB approval because it involved criminal offenders and was an experiment. The survey of participants in the experiment (Study 14) required additional IRB approval and is discussed in Chapter 6.

Strengths of a Multiplistic Approach

The studies described in this book are overlapping and complementary approaches to understanding how economic sanctions are imposed, monitored, and paid. There is also research on how the payment of economic sanctions relates to recidivism. The statewide analyses allow for tests of the role of county-level contextual information on imposition and payment. Most of the studies allow for an analysis of individual-level data regarding age, gender, and race. The surveys of offenders permit an analysis of how these individuals' attitudes and beliefs relate to the payment of economic sanctions. The surveys of judges permit an analysis of how their attitudes are related to their reported imposition of economic sanctions. The surveys of victims permit an analysis of how their experience with the criminal justice agents is related to their ratings of the criminal justice system and their willingness to participate in the future. From the experimental examination of the payment of restitution and the effects of payment of restitution, causality can be investigated, although not definitively, because even field experiments can involve possible alternative explanations.

The multimethod approach of the research in this book capitalizes on the strengths of each method and permits analyses to test for convergent findings across methods. The experiment in Chapter 5 (Study 13) has the advantage of random assignment and manipulation of a policy-relevant variable (i.e., one that, if shown to be effective, could be implemented by policymakers; Ruback & Innes, 1988). The questionnaire surveys of offenders, victims, and judges enable us to look at how perceptions, attitudes, and beliefs are related to behavior, but they have the disadvantage of biased response in that highly motivated respondents are likely to be overrepresented. The statewide and multi-county studies have the advantage of large sample sizes, but they cannot directly address the issues of offenders' understanding of economic sanctions nor offenders' perceptions of the perceived legitimacy of these sanctions. Although individually the methods have weaknesses, together these studies provide a stronger framework for testing theoretical and policy-relevant ideas.

The remainder of this chapter examines economic sanctions in Pennsylvania at the state and multi-county level. The next chapter (Chapter 4) focuses on the imposition of restitution, Chapter 5 looks at the payment of restitution, and Chapter 6 looks at the effect of paying restitution on recidivism.

Study 1: Statewide Analyses of Economic Sanctions

Ruback and Clark (2011)

Among the problems with many studies of how economic sanctions are imposed is that they typically have small sample sizes, generally involve only one or a few counties, and often examine only one type of economic sanction. To overcome these problems, we examined all economic sanctions imposed in Pennsylvania over a 2-year period by the courts of general jurisdiction.

Pennsylvania has one of the most complete data collection systems in the country, including a record of virtually all economic sanctions imposed in criminal courts of general jurisdiction. To analyze the imposition of economic sanctions, Valerie Clark and I used data from three sources (Ruback & Clark, 2011). First, we used files from the AOPC). The AOPC data consist of four separate files: case information, offense information, sentencing information, and payment information. These four files are extremely large, and because the files do not have a common identifier, linking them took some time (i.e., case information is directly linked only to sentencing information, sentencing information is directly linked only to offense information, offense information is directly linked only to payment information). We used the first three files to examine the imposition of economic sanctions as a function of individual and county contextual factors across the calendar years 2006 and 2007 (Ruback & Clark, 2009, 2011). For these 2 years, there were 1,584,264 criminal offenses, 517,160 guilty pleas or guilty verdicts, and a total of 5,607,263 economic sanctions imposed.

These 5.6 million economic sanctions were imposed from 2,629 different types of economic sanctions, as coded by the AOPC. Of these 2,629 sanctions, 82 were costs/fees imposed by the state, 58 were state fines, 2,371 were county costs/fees, 79 were county fines, and 35 were restitution. Costs/fees were economic sanctions used to reimburse the state or county for costs associated with law enforcement, judicial proceedings (e.g., diversion programs, bench warrants), and probation and parole (e.g., supervision, electronic monitoring, drug tests). The total amount of economic sanctions imposed was more than $411.3 million. On average, the total assessments of all costs/fees and fines per person was $819, of which $575 was for costs/fees and $243 was for fines. Restitution was imposed in 77,417 cases for a total amount of $197.7 million, with an average of $2,554.

Two mandatory fees in Pennsylvania (Crime Victim Compensation [CVC] and Crime Commission Cost [CCC]) were imposed in more than 95% of all judicial sentencing hearings. Although the statute requires that these two fees (which totaled $60) be imposed for each conviction offense, in practice judges imposed these fees only once per judicial proceeding, regardless of the number of conviction offenses. This behavior looks reasonable and fair. Nevertheless, judges know that fees are used to reimburse counties for criminal justice expenditures, and one can wonder whether judges can be impartial if they often function as collections agents (Patel & Philip, 2012).

The AOPC data provided offense and prior record information from court files, but it did not have detail about the offender and the county context of the court. To provide that information, we combined the AOPC data with data from the PCS and the United States Bureau of the Census.

Under Pennsylvania law, judges are required to submit a computerized Guideline Sentencing Form for most felony and misdemeanor convictions in the state. This form contains information about the offender (race, gender, age), the offender's prior convictions, the offender's current conviction offenses (offense type, offense severity as measured by the Offense Gravity Score of the Guidelines), the mode of disposition (guilty plea or trial), and the sentence imposed (incarceration in jail or prison or not incarcerated, length of sentence). The PCS data for 2006 contained 134,119 offenses, and the data for 2007 contained 141,139 offenses, for a total of 275,258 offenses. We were able to link 92% of these PCS cases to the AOPC data using the Offense Tracking Number and the title and section of the offense. The remaining 8% of the AOPC cases were summary offenses, which were not included in the PCS database or were not included because some counties apparently did not completely report all of their sentenced cases. After matching the AOPC and PSC cases, information identifying individual offenders (name, Social Security Number, State Identification Number) was removed.

In the PCS data, most of the offenders were male (80%), white (67%), and between the ages of 18 and 25 (40%), 26 to 35 (27%), or 36 to 45 (21%). Most had no prior record (52%) and had committed a property crime (31%), a drug crime (23%), a person crime (17%), or a traffic crime (17%).

For our contextual analysis, we used several basic county-level characteristics and economic indicators, which came primarily from the US Census, including the population of the county, the percentage urban population within each county, the percentage of the population living below the poverty level, the percentage of males 15–24 within each county, and indicators of residential stability/mobility. These variables were included in order to test whether the size of the county, the degree of urbanization in a county, the economic climate of the county, and the number of individuals most prone to engaging in crime were related to how economic sanctions are imposed. We used this merged dataset to determine county- and individual-level factor predictors of the imposition of economic sanctions.

One of the surprising findings in our analysis was the large amount of variation between Pennsylvania's 67 counties in the use of economic sanctions. The number of uniquely different sanctions used in any one county varied from 40 to 147, with an average of 81 and a median of 75. Counties that had higher annual wages, more Hispanic residents, more total residents, and more urban residents were more likely to use more different types of economic sanctions. The average number of sanctions used per case also varied significantly between counties, from a low of 15 to a high of 200, with a mean (M) of 42.5 and a median of 34. As might be expected, counties that had more different types of economic sanctions were also likely to have more economic sanctions imposed for each case ($r(65) = .49, p < .001$), suggesting that judges were likely to impose sanctions that were legally available to them to be imposed.

Of the 2,629 sanctions in the state, most of the variation between counties was due to county level costs/fees (2,371) and county fines (79). Across the 67 Pennsylvania counties, the percentage of sanctions imposed that were county sanctions ranged from 10% to 70% (M = 48%; Mode = 41%).

In addition to the county-level analyses, we also investigated how the imposition of economic sanctions varied across individuals. In particular, we were interested in how two legally relevant variables—the type of offense the offender was convicted of and the offender's prior record—were related to the imposition of economic sanctions. There were significant differences for both variables.

In terms of type of offense, the highest average economic sanctions ($1,349) were imposed for traffic offenses (largely DUIs). Others have also noted that DUI offenders face high levels of fees (Olson & Ramker, 2001) and fines (Hillsman et al., 1984), because of both the perceived seriousness of the crime and the likelihood that offenders, who need to be able to drive for work, are particularly likely to pay the imposed sanctions. After traffic offenses, mean economic sanctions imposed were as follows: drug offenses ($881), person offenses ($701), property offenses (($669), other types of offenses ($630), and public order offenses ($624).

In terms of prior record, we analyzed the imposition of economic sanctions using the Prior Record Score (PRS) of the PCS. The PRS is a scale based on the number and severity of prior conviction offenses. We divided the PRS into three levels. At the lowest level, Level 0, which means either no prior record or 1 prior misdemeanor, and which accounts for about half of all offenders sentenced in Pennsylvania, the highest average economic sanctions were imposed ($862). Those with a low prior record (a score of 1, 2, or 3 on the PCS scale) had the next highest average economic sanctions ($825). Those with a high prior record (a score of 4 or 5 on the PCS scale) had the lowest average economic sanctions ($691). These differences still appeared even after controlling for other individual-level factors, including whether or not the offender received a sentence involving incarceration. This same pattern of higher total economic sanctions being imposed on those with lesser prior records has been found by others (e.g., Cunniff & Shilton, 1991).

In multivariate analyses, which controlled for the relationships among predictor variables, we found that type of offense had the largest and most consistent effect on total economic sanctions imposed. Traffic and drug cases increased the amount of sanctions. Being sentenced to county jail or state prison had a positive significant effect on economic sanctions. Also, having a high prior record score had a negative effect on the total amount of economic sanctions imposed. Finally, age had a relatively strong negative influence on economic sanctions, with younger offenders receiving smaller sanctions. These same effects appeared after controlling for county characteristics. In fact, county characteristics were not significant predictors of the amount of economic sanctions imposed once the characteristics of the case and the offender were taken into account.

Implications

In general, counties with larger populations and higher percentages of citizens in urban areas imposed more economic sanctions and more different types of economic sanctions. These high numbers of different types of economic sanctions are likely confusing to offenders, who likely do not know how much they owe, how much their monthly payments should be, and where the money they pay goes (see Study 12, Chapter 4). These large numbers are probably also confusing to judges, prosecutors, and probation officers, who are unlikely to understand how economic sanctions are supposed to be paid (see Study 2).

The variety and difference in number in economic sanctions is primarily due to county costs/fees. The fact that there are large between-county differences is unfair to offenders in these counties since having more different types of sanctions is related to imposing more different types on individual offenders. This relationship makes sense since judges must be responsive to the public, and county costs/fees are one way that the economic burden on citizens is shifted to offenders. One possible solution to the problem of so many different types of economic sanctions is simply to reduce the number of county costs/fees (see Chapter 8).

Rationally, longer criminal records should be related to larger amounts of economic sanctions because offenders who have committed crimes despite having been punished before should be punished more and require more deterrence. However, Study 1 found that offenders with longer criminal records were likely to receive significantly lower economic sanctions, even controlling for whether the offender was sentenced to a term of incarceration. It seems that judges believe offenders with longer records are less likely to pay any economic sanctions imposed and, therefore, judges simply do not impose them.

Study 2: Multi-County Analyses of Economic Sanctions in Adult Cases

Ruback, Cares, and Hoskins (2006)

The advantages of the AOPC and PCS databases are that there are a large number of cases in which real defendants were sentenced by actual judges to true economic sanctions. One major disadvantage, however, is that information that might be useful for testing theory and assessing policy was not included. The only way to obtain such information is for researchers to collect the information themselves. Alison Cares, Stacy Hoskins Haynes, and I did that by coding data in several counties so that we were able to examine factors related to the imposition and payment of economic sanctions in adult cases, juvenile cases, and cases where the state had given money to victims who had suffered losses.

Adult Cases

Regarding adult cases, we coded data from about 2,100 randomly selected cases in six counties in Pennsylvania (Ruback, Cares, & Hoskins, 2006). The six counties we chose, Blair, Centre, Cumberland, Delaware, Lancaster, and Westmoreland, were selected because they varied along four dimensions that we suspected would influence the use and effect of economic sanctions: (a) county population size, (b) the number of criminal cases processed by the county, (c) the methods each county uses to collect economic sanctions, and (d) geographic location in the state. In terms of population size, Blair, Centre, and Cumberland Counties have relatively small populations, Delaware and Lancaster Counties have substantially larger populations, and Westmoreland County has a population midway between the other counties. In terms of annual caseloads, the number of criminal cases processed varied closely with the population of the county; Blair, Centre, and Cumberland Counties handled fewer criminal cases than the three other counties. In terms of the method of collecting economic sanctions, all of the counties except Centre and Westmoreland Counties used specialized collections units to collect economic sanctions. Finally, in terms of geographical diversity, Westmoreland County is located in the western part of the state, Centre and Blair Counties are located in the middle of the state, and Cumberland, Delaware, and Lancaster Counties are located in the southeastern part of the state.

We created computerized data coding forms for the adult cases in each county on which we recorded the following types of information: offender characteristics (e.g., race, gender, age, and prior record), case characteristics (e.g., charge and conviction offenses, type of disposition, and sentence imposed), victim characteristics (e.g., race, gender, age, and type of injury), economic sanctions imposed and paid (e.g., fines, fees, costs, and restitution), and recidivism. We also included several variables that record the different sources of information used to collect data in each county. In each county, we collected a random sample of approximately 500 adult cases for the year 2000. We chose to collect data from cases docketed in 2000 in order to ensure that the case would have been resolved in terms of guilt or innocence, that sentencing would have occurred, and that the offender would have had some record of making or not making payments toward the amounts owed.

Summary of Findings

Variation in the Definition and Use of Economic Sanctions

One of the clearest findings in this study, consistent with what we found in Study 1, was that counties varied significantly in their use of economic sanctions. There were large differences in what was termed a cost or fee, in how restitution was used, and in the rates of imposition of all types of economic sanctions. Some of these differences among counties related to differences in practice (i.e., informal rules about the imposition of economic sanctions) rather than to differences in explicit policy (i.e., formal guidelines about the imposition of economic sanctions). There were also differences among counties in terms of the economic sanctions they imposed. For example, Lancaster imposed a $10 per month administration fee for probation on top of the $25 per month supervision fee. Other counties had only a flat supervision fee of $25. Some counties charged fees for staying in jail (e.g., Centre County had a jail maintenance fee), and counties packaged fees for DUI convictions differently.

Imposition of Economic Sanctions

In general, we found that the imposition of economic sanctions was dependent primarily on crime-related factors (the severity and type of crime) rather than on offender-related factors such as age, race, or gender. As one would expect, higher levels of economic sanctions were imposed for more severe crimes. In general, higher levels of fines and costs were imposed for traffic and DUI than for other types of crimes. Overall, crime-related and offender-related factors did not explain very well the total amount of economic sanctions ordered.

In terms of the payment of economic sanctions, we found that the percentage of economic sanctions paid was significantly lower for property offenders than for offenders convicted of personal, drug, traffic, or other offenses, possibly because property offenders often have fewer assets than do other types of offenders. Furthermore, the percentage of economic sanctions paid was, not surprisingly, significantly lower for incarcerated offenders. Even if offenders paid while they were incarcerated (which most did not), the amount of payments most could make would be very minimal. In general, however, case and offender characteristics explained little or no variation in the amount of economic sanctions ordered or the percent of economic sanctions paid across counties.

We investigated two mandatory state penalties, Crime Victim Compensation (CVC) and Crime Commission Cost (CCC). Although CVC is mandatory for adults, we found rates of imposition across six counties ranging from 86% to 97% (M = 91%). Across counties, CVC was generally less likely to be imposed for summary offenses. We found rates of imposition of CCC ranging from 84% to 97% (M = 90%). As with CVC, CCC was generally less likely to be imposed for summary offenses.

The percentage of adult cases in which CVC and CCC were paid in full was modest (M = 56% and M = 55%, respectively). The percentage of cases in which CVC and CCC were paid in full was significantly higher for offenders convicted of traffic offenses and significantly lower for offenders incarcerated in jail, paralleling the findings for economic sanctions overall.

Understanding the Actual Workings in the Counties

Although all counties emphasized that collections enforcement was a priority, no two counties handled the imposition and collection of economic sanctions in exactly the same way. All of the counties tried to enforce payment. Typically, payment plans were established so that if offenders stayed on schedule with their payments, they could complete them by the time their probation was due to expire. Many counties required offenders to pay a minimum monthly payment (e.g., $60 in one county). Although offenders were not supposed to be discharged from probation until their economic sanctions were paid in full, they could go on inactive supervision or unsupervised probation, which meant that, in practice, offenders were sometimes discharged without completing payment.

Four of the six counties examined used specialized collections units to monitor and/or collect economic sanctions. In some counties, these units were part of the adult probation department, staffed at least in part by probation officers. These specialized probation units were responsible for monitoring and enforcing payments, but they did not collect the payments directly. In Lancaster County, payments were made to the Treasurer, and in Cumberland County, they were made to the Clerk of Courts. In other counties, such as Blair and Delaware, the collections unit was separate from the probation department. For example, Delaware County had a separate Court Financial Services (CFS) office that was responsible for the collection of all economic sanctions. However, CFS staff worked closely with other departments, including probation.

The collection of economic sanctions was sometimes split between two offices. For example, in 2000, in Luzerne County, the probation office collected restitution and supervision fees, while the Clerk of Courts collected costs and fines. Additionally, offenders often had to pay for treatment that is required as a condition of their probation. Some of the programs were paid for through the payments calculated as a part of sentencing or intake to probation, but others were paid directly to the treatment provider, which was typically a private organization. There were also differences across counties in how offenders made payments. For example, a staff member in Centre County informed us that each time an offender came to the probation office to make a payment, he or she was asked which case the money should be applied to. Although offenders had payment contracts that required them to pay a specific amount of money each month, they could pay whatever amount they chose when they came in. It is important to note that what we measured in our analyses of economic sanctions may not have been the total amount an offender owed.

In many cases, if an offender was required to get counseling, participate in a safe driver program, etc., he or she had to pay for that service directly to the service provider.

In Luzerne County, restitution and supervision fees were handled by the same office, but offenders had to make two separate payments (i.e., one payment for restitution and one payment for supervision fees). Thus, if an offender were paying by check or money order, he or she would have to have two checks or two money orders each time.

The collection and distribution of restitution varied by county. In some counties, payments were made to the probation officer during regular appointments. In other counties, restitution was handled by the Victim Offender Reconciliation Program. The counties were most similar in terms of the prioritized order in which payments were applied. The law required that each time an offender made a payment, 50% would go toward restitution (until restitution was paid in full) and 50% would go toward the payment of other fines, fees, and costs. However, there were exceptions to this general rule. In Centre County, for example, offenders had to pay 100% of restitution before paying any other economic sanction (see Study 13). If the offender was in jail or on work release, however, 15% of each payment went toward jail/institutional maintenance fees and the remainder went to restitution.

In Lancaster County, offenders first paid a $10 per month probation administration fee, followed by 100% of restitution, fees and costs, and probation supervision fees. In Westmoreland County, each time a juvenile offender made a payment, the first $50 was paid to the CVC fund, followed by restitution and state and county costs.

Although restitution on older cases was generally paid before restitution on recent cases, there were no formal guidelines about how multiple cases with restitution should be handled. For example, a staff member in Blair County informed us that judges sometimes issued court orders mandating that a particular victim receive payment first. In other words, the victim who complained the most could be given priority in payment. In other counties, we heard of other alternatives, including dividing the payments proportionally across victims.

The six counties used a range of strategies in dealing with the nonpayment of economic sanctions. One strategy that many counties shared was a multistep process characterized by a gradual increase in threatened sanctions. In general, offenders who stopped making their payments received one or more warning letters asking for payment. If the offender still failed to make payments or respond to contact by the probation department, he or she was charged with contempt of court, and a judge issued a decision on the matter. While nonpayment of economic sanctions can be a violation of probation or parole, judges also had the option of setting a new payment plan, reducing the amount owed, extending probation, and/or substituting community service for fees and costs.

For instance, in Centre County, judges often reduced the total amount of economic sanctions the offender owed. These back-end reductions (as opposed to front-end decisions at sentencing) were often substantial because judges based their decision on the offender's ability to pay. In another example, in Delaware County, defendants who did not have the ability to pay (i.e., because of incarceration, unemployment, or disability) could perform community service in return for a reduction in the amount of money they owed.

Four counties (Delaware, Lancaster, Luzerne, and Westmoreland) occasionally used private collections agencies to collect money owed on old cases. Because economic sanctions cannot be forgiven without a judicial order, government agencies typically imposed an additional fee to cover the cost of private collection so as to be able to recover all of the money owed. For example, in one county the overall amount owed by the offender was increased by 25% if the case was sent to a private collections agency. The type of action taken also depended on the offender's supervision status. For example, if an offender failed to make payments while on probation, his or her probation could be revoked or extended. If an offender were no longer on probation but still owed money, he or she could be held in contempt of court for nonpayment.

A staff member in Cumberland County informed us that all collections cases were sent through one judge. If offenders were not making payments, the judge preferred that they appear in court before their probation expired so that he could extend their probation. The judge only occasionally sent someone to prison for nonpayment, mainly to send a message that it can happen. In Lancaster County, the number of cases going to court for contempt for nonpayment was drastically reduced after the introduction of the Collections Enforcement Unit.

Although Pennsylvania law requires that the first 50% of all offender payments be applied to restitution and that other economic sanctions (fines, fees, costs) be paid after that, some counties required that 100% of payments be applied to restitution until it was paid in full. At the other extreme, one county, counter to the law, required that supervision fees and DUI course instructors be paid before restitution.

Study 3: Multi-County Analyses of Economic Sanctions in Juvenile Cases

Ruback, Cares, and Hoskins (2006)
Haynes, Cares, and Ruback (2014)

Study 2 examined the imposition of economic sanctions in six counties. In a study we conducted at the same time in five of those counties, Stacy

Hoskins Haynes, Alison Cares, and I examined economic sanctions in juvenile cases (Haynes et al., 2014). We collected data primarily from both electronic and paper records from juvenile probation departments, but also relied on paper records from Clerk of Courts offices and victim and witness services. In general, juvenile case records provided only limited information about the imposition and payment of economic sanctions, particularly in informally handled cases. Typically, fines and fees were combined. Thus, we focused on the total economic sanctions.

In 2003 and 2004, we coded data from 921 juvenile cases systematically sampled from 2000 so that we could be sure that the cases had been adjudicated, that sentencing would have occurred, that the offender would have had some record of payment or nonpayment, and that there was sufficient time to measure recidivism. To analyze restitution, we created a second data set of 559 restitution-eligible cases (i.e., property and person cases with an identifiable victim, other than the state, who suffered a quantifiable loss).

We measured the imposition of economic sanctions as any economic sanctions imposed, the amount of economic sanctions imposed, any restitution imposed, and the amount of restitution imposed. We measured the payment of economic sanctions as the percentage of economic sanctions paid and the percentage of restitution paid. Recidivism was measured as any violation, a technical violation (e.g., for curfew violations, admitted drug use, truancy), a new crime, and nonpayment of economic sanctions.

Imposition

One of the factors that was an important predictor of several variables was whether the juvenile lived in a two-parent household. Thus, we controlled for type of household. Economic sanctions were imposed in 80% of the cases. Restitution was imposed in only 33% of the restitution-eligible cases. The figure could be low because stolen property might have been returned or the juvenile might have already made restitution (information generally not available in the data). Alternatively, the victims in these cases may not have submitted information about the loss. Restitution was more likely to be imposed for felonies rather than misdemeanors, and the amount of restitution was greater for felonies and for juveniles who were adjudicated delinquent.

Contrary to the low rate of restitution imposition, fees to cover the cost of administering justice were imposed in 66% of the cases, suggesting that judges cared about juveniles' accountability to the community. Fees were more likely to be imposed for females, for felonies, for juveniles who were adjudicated delinquent, and juveniles from two-parent households. The fact that fees were more likely to be imposed for felonies and for juveniles who were adjudicated delinquent (i.e., in more serious cases) suggests that judges were responding to crime seriousness with greater punitiveness.

Regarding recidivism, we found that revocations (the most serious measure of recidivism in our study) were less likely among those who paid a greater percentage of their total economic sanctions. This finding is consistent with the idea that offenders who pay more of their economic sanctions recognize that their actions were wrong. In Chapter 6, I argue that the payment of restitution is different from paying other types of economic sanctions, but in this study we were unable to separate out whether the payment of restitution matters more than the payment of other economic sanctions.

Alternatively, the juveniles who paid more of their economic sanctions may have lived in families with greater financial resources and thus would have been better able to pay the court-ordered economic sanctions and less likely to recidivate with a new crime. We did not have a measure of family income, but our indicator of two-parent families is consistent with this notion.

One of the unanswered questions from this study is who pays the economic sanctions. From the data we examined, we could not tell who was responsible for the payment, the parents or the child. This is an important issue because personal payment indicates taking personal responsibility. Following this rationale, Roy (1995) suggested that if juveniles cannot pay for themselves because they are too young to work, they should be able to pay restitution through community service. Moreover, as I suggest in Chapter 6, lumping all economic sanctions together undermines the rationale for promoting personal responsibility, which is behind making offenders pay restitution. Having juveniles make separate restitution payments may make them more accountable to the victim (Haynes et al., 2014).

The imposition of these costs for juveniles was mandatory only for consent decrees and adjudications of delinquency; costs did not have to be ordered for informal adjustments or deferred hearings. For juveniles, we found rates of imposition of CVC across four counties ranging from 19% to 82% (M = 55%). Being adjudicated delinquent was positively related to imposition in two of the four counties. We found rates of imposition of CCC ranging from 42% to 82% (M = 67%). In two of the three counties in which we collected relevant data, CCC was significantly more likely to be imposed when the juvenile was adjudicated delinquent.

The Workings of Collections in Juvenile Cases

Across counties, we found even greater variation in the types of action taken in juvenile cases. In Cumberland County, for example, probation staff could revoke probation or have the juvenile earn money through a community service program. At age 21, contempt of court proceedings could begin and judgments could be filed against the individual. In Luzerne County, juveniles who failed to pay their fines on time or who failed to make payments according to their payment plan were sent to detention until someone paid their fines. Because most juvenile cases were for nonpayment of fines, this outcome seems fairly common. However, it was at the judge's discretion to determine which juveniles were sent to detention for nonpayment of fines. In Delaware County, the case could be sent to court, community service could be ordered to cover costs not mandated by the state, or the individual could be referred to an outside collections agency. In most counties, parents or guardians were allowed to pay on a juvenile case.

In juvenile cases, the imposition of CVC and CCC costs was mandatory only for consent decrees and adjudications of delinquency. Largely because of that, across counties there was greater variation in the imposition of CVC ($M = 55\%$) and CCC ($M = 67\%$) in juvenile cases than in adult cases. Information about the percentage of cases in which CVC and CCC were paid in full in juvenile cases was generally unavailable.

In 2000, some counties did not impose some types of economic sanctions on juvenile offenders. For example, Cumberland County seldom imposed fines, fees, or costs in juvenile cases. Furthermore, in Luzerne County, juveniles were not ordered to pay court costs. In contrast to the other counties, Luzerne County required juveniles to attend school/job training or to find employment as a condition of their probation and, if they were employed, to pay 75% of their wages toward restitution and fines. The most common type of economic sanction imposed on juveniles was restitution.

In general, we found that economic sanctions were more consistently imposed on adults than on juveniles. This difference is not too surprising since many mandated fees and costs do not apply in juvenile cases. Moreover, this pattern is consistent with the fact that juvenile offenders are less able than adults to pay (because of lack of income) and with the fact that juvenile cases are more likely to be handled informally and with more individually tailored sanctions.

Our analysis of the adult and juvenile cases revealed that counties vary significantly in their use of economic sanctions, especially in juvenile cases. The variation in juvenile cases can be somewhat explained by the fact that juvenile courts appeared to be more focused on rehabilitation than on punishment, and, compared to adult courts, there was more emphasis on customizing treatment to the individual. For example, Cumberland County seldom imposed fines, fees, or costs for juvenile cases in 2000. In Delaware County, economic sanctions could be paid by the county, in which case the juvenile usually completed community service in lieu of court costs paid by the parents or by the juvenile.

Summary

This chapter set the legal context for economic sanctions in Pennsylvania. In addition, it described three studies that examined the imposition of all types of economic sanctions. The first study, an analysis using statewide archival information for adult convictions from the AOPC, found wide variation between counties in the existence and use of economic sanctions, primarily due to county-level fees and costs. The second study, which used information we coded from adult cases in six counties, found differences in the size and rates of imposition of all types of economic sanctions and differences in both explicit policy and informal practice. The third study, which used coded information from juvenile cases in five counties, found high county-level variation in the treatment of juvenile economic sanctions and large differences within counties in how adult and juvenile cases were handled.

The next chapters focus on restitution in Pennsylvania. Chapter 4 describes seven studies that look at the imposition of restitution across the state, in multiple counties, and in single counties. Chapter 5 describes three studies that look at the payment of restitution. Chapter 6 describes a single study that looks at the effect of paying restitution on subsequent criminal behavior.

4

Imposition of Restitution

The three studies described in Chapter 3 looked at the imposition of fines, costs/fees, and restitution across the state or in multiple counties. The remainder of the research described in this book focuses on the imposition, payment, and effect of paying restitution. This chapter describes seven studies that examined the imposition of restitution at the state level, in multiple counties, or in a single county. The variables examined in these studies included demographic factors, case factors, and contextual factors. These same factors were also used to predict the imposition of fines and costs so that we could determine the extent to which the imposition of restitution was similar to and different from the imposition of fines and costs. In addition, the research examined the effects of statutory changes on the behavior of judges.

These questions were examined in a systematic fashion at both the state and county levels. Study 4 used statewide data from the Pennsylvania Commission on Sentencing (PCS) for 1990–1998. Study 5 used survey responses from criminal court judges, district attorneys, and chief probation officers. Study 6 used statewide county-level analyses to investigate the role of victim-related contextual factors on the imposition of victim restitution. Study 7 used statewide county-level analyses to investigate the role of courtroom community factors on the imposition of victim restitution.

Study 8 examined the imposition and effects of restitution for 1994 and 1996 in four counties: Blair (Altoona), Centre (State College), Dauphin (Harrisburg), and Erie (Erie). Study 9 examined restitution in Allegheny County (Pittsburgh) for 1994. Study 10 examined restitution in Philadelphia for 1994–2000.

Economic Sanctions in Criminal Justice. R. Barry Ruback, Oxford University Press. © Oxford University Press 2022.
DOI: 10.1093/oso/9780190682583.003.0004

Study 4: Statewide Multilevel Analysis of Restitution Decisions

Ruback, Ruth, and Shaffer (2005)

The first study in this series analyzed 170,260 restitution-eligible cases in Pennsylvania from 1990 to 1998 in order to test two questions (Ruback et al., 2005). First, did a 1995 statutory change making restitution mandatory increase the rate at which restitution was imposed? Second, did this statutory change affect the presumed policy factors underlying the imposition of restitution, a question that could be answered based on inferences about the apparent policy reasons for restitution?

Gretchen Ruth Cusick, Jennifer Sikorski, and I defined restitution-eligible as cases in which there was an identifiable victim (other than the state) who suffered an actual loss. That meant that we dropped cases involving DUI and drug offenses and also cases from Title 18 (Crimes and Offenses) of Pennsylvania Consolidated Statutes Annotated that did not have an identifiable victim (e.g., prostitution) and cases that were not brought under Title 18. We also excluded cases in which the likelihood of actual loss was low, including retail theft (because of the high probability that the property was returned before sentencing), simple assault (because of the low likelihood that there was a need for medical treatment that could be used as the basis for quantifying harm), and all noncompleted offenses (because of the low probability of actual harm). Of course, this strategy means that the resulting cases are not perfect samples of restitution-eligible cases, but the bias would be consistent across the entire study period. Most of the sample (70%) involved property crimes.

With regard to the question of whether the statutory change making restitution mandatory had an effect, we compared 115,141 pre-statutory change cases (1990–1994) to 55,119 post-statutory change cases (1996–1998). The simple comparison indicated that the rate at which restitution was imposed increased from 37.8% to 63.5%. That increase, although not complete, was substantial. We also found that prior record and bench trials were not significant predictors of restitution orders, consistent with the idea that the mandatory law increased uniformity. However, we also found that, after the statutory change, offender gender and race were still significant predictors of the restitution decision, suggesting that, although uniformity had increased, there was still some evidence of disparity between offenders.

The second question, whether the statutory change affected the policy basis for restitution decisions, was more difficult to get at. To do so, we focused on the significant predictors of restitution imposition, reasoning that we could infer policy based on these significant predictors. This inductive approach is the opposite of what is typically done in policy studies, which examine how (often ambiguous) policy directives are translated into working policy (Wilson, 1989). Our inductive approach was especially useful for the 1990–1994 pre-statutory change period, when there was no clear general policy. After the statutory change, which was based on a mandate to consider victims' interests, we could compare this directive to factors that were actually predictive of restitution imposition.

In our examination of how state policy was implemented by individual judges, we assumed that the local context—the county in which courts were located—was a key determinant. In their analysis of how national policy is implemented at a local level, Goggin, Bowman, Lester, and O'Toole (1990) noted that pressures from both above and below interact to influence policy. In their work, they used state-level variables as the key to understanding the local implementation of national policy. Analogously, to understand individual case implementation of the state policy, we used county-level variables as the lens through which the legislative mandate was focused downward and individual cases were focused upward. To meet that assumption, we included several county-level variables that are indicative of social context (e.g., urban/rural, crime rate, poverty rate, proportion of young males), political context (i.e., percentage voting Republican in presidential elections), and criminal justice context (i.e., probation/parole resources). In general, these contextual factors were not important for restitution decisions, but it was important that we controlled for them.

Our approach to understanding policy assumed that a particular policy should be evident in the relationship between certain predictor variables and final decisions. Statistically significant relationships between predictors and outcomes that are consistent with a particular policy would be supportive of a conclusion that that policy did underlie that decision. If the relationship between a predictor and the decision was essentially zero, then that policy probably did not underlie that decision.

Based on that framework, we assumed that we could test the importance of the three most common rationales for imposing restitution: compensation to the victim, rehabilitation of the offender, and punishment of the offender. If compensation to victims was the primary consideration, then judges should be more likely to impose restitution for offenses that result in greater financial losses and for which it is easier to determine the amount of the loss. If rehabilitation of the offender were the primary consideration, then judges should impose restitution on those offenders who are more amenable to restitution: individuals with no prior records and individuals who pleaded guilty to the crime (thereby accepting responsibility and expressing remorse). If punishment of the offender were the primary consideration, then orders of restitution should be imposed more often in serious cases (person crimes and other crimes considered more serious in the Pennsylvania guidelines) and on offenders with prior records. In addition, and more generally, the two offender-focused sanctions (rehabilitation and punishment) should be associated with characteristics of the offender, whereas the victim-focused sanction (compensation through restitution) should not.

We analyzed individual sentencing decisions nested within county to account for the county-level factors. Although traditional contextual effects (e.g., poverty, political context) were not significant in our models, we did find significant variation between counties and significant random variance components, indicating that decision-level effects varied across counties. It might be that our measures of contextual effects were inadequate. For example, we did not test how context operates through proximate factors about the local court system (e.g., the way victims' losses are made known to prosecutors and judges) rather than through structural factors, such as poverty, a shortcoming that we addressed in Study 5.

In the 1990–1994 pre-statutory change period, when judges had complete discretion about restitution, results suggested that restitution was ordered to compensate victims (in that property offenses and offense severity were significant predictors), to rehabilitate offenders (in that type of plea and prior record were significant predictors), and to punish (in that offense severity and prior record were significant predictors). The fact that all three policies could be inferred from the decisions about restitution imposition suggests that restitution was intended to serve all three functions (leaving aside whether those goals were actually met).

In the 1996–1998 post-statutory change period, there was some evidence that victim compensation had become a more important purpose of restitution in that offense type and offense severity were significant predictors of the decision, and factors suggestive of other rationales (e.g., plea, prior record) were not significant. Offense severity was about 1.5 times more important after the statutory change, consistent with the mandate to make victim compensation more important.

That the statute was not perfectly implemented is evidenced by the fact that two offender factors (gender and race) and the interactions of whether fines and incarceration were imposed and the type of county were significant predictors suggests that judges were still considering offender factors. Judicial efforts to balance offender and victim needs, along with the likely differential availability of victim input on financial losses, may be the source of these continuing disparities.

Aside from assessing whether the 1995 statute affected restitution decisions, the framework we used in this study might be helpful for policy assessment in that we tried to operationally define abstract concepts in terms of specific variables. This approach might be especially useful for sentencing research in that legislatures and sentencing commissions often give multiple, ambiguous, and sometimes conflicting rationales for sentencing statutes.

After the statutory change, there was some evidence that victim compensation had become a more important reason for restitution in that offense type (property crimes) and crime seriousness (an indicator of victim harm) increased the odds of restitution being imposed 1.52 times more than was true in the pre-statutory change period. The picture is not perfect, however, in that crime seriousness is also an indicator of punitiveness, and the increase in restitution orders may have been motivated by a desire to punish the offender rather than to restore the victim. However, the fact that other factors related to punitiveness (e.g., plea, prior record) were not predictive of restitution orders suggests that punitiveness was not the primary rationale for imposing restitution.

Rather than structural factors like demographic composition and poverty, which did not affect restitution orders in our sample, it may be that more proximate factors, like factors about the local court system (e.g., the way victims' losses are made known to prosecutors and judges) and the local probation office (e.g., how monies are collected for economic sanction) may be more important. We tested these ideas in the next studies.

Study 5: Statewide Survey of Judges, District Attorneys, and Chief Probation Officers

Ruback and Shaffer (2005)

In Study 4, we found that a 1995 statutory change making restitution mandatory increased the imposition of restitution from 37.8% before the statute to 63.5% after the statute, although the level of implementation was not uniform across the state. Perhaps it is not surprising that a mandatory statute led to an increase in the imposition of restitution, but laws that have symbolism, as one supporting victim restitution does, do not always translate into actual policy, particularly if prosecutors and judges believe the laws are unjust or unworkable (Tonry, 1992). For example, mandatory sentencing laws often have little overall effect (Loftin et al., 1983) in that many cases are dismissed early to avoid those harsh laws, but offenders who are convicted receive more severe sentences (Tonry, 1992).

The results of the analyses of the 1996–1998 sentencing data were consistent with the inference that after the 1995 statutory change victim compensation was the most important purpose of restitution because offense type and offense seriousness were significant predictors of restitution decisions. That is, for property crimes it would be easier to determine the amount of loss, and for more serious crimes the amount of financial loss would be greater. Other rationales, punishing the offender or rehabilitating the offender, were less strongly supported.

The problem with concluding that the statute made judges more concerned with compensation is that such a conclusion is indirect because it is based on inferences from sentencing decisions. What is needed is a more direct test of judges' and other participants' views about the imposition and payment of restitution, a task that we addressed in Study 5 by conducting a survey of judges, prosecutors, and chief probation officers. Another question that can be answered is what factors other than the views of judges and others could explain the differences between counties in the level of implementation of the mandatory statute. We addressed that question in Study 6 to examine the role of structural factors for administering victim services in the imposition of restitution.

Study 5, a statewide questionnaire survey of judges, prosecutors, and chief probation officers, was intended to investigate whether policy agreements/disagreements and practical limitations are likely reasons why the level of restitution imposition increased after the 1995 statute but was not higher. To examine both broad policy questions and specific questions regarding implementation, Jennifer Sikorski and I conducted a statewide survey of criminal court judges, district attorneys, and chief probation officers in each of the 67 counties in Pennsylvania (Ruback, 2002; Ruback & Shaffer, 2005). We included district attorneys and chief probation officers because these individuals often make recommendations to judges and, at least for chief probation officers, because they are more likely than judges to know the effects of restitution orders (e.g., who pays and how much).

In September 2001, questionnaires were sent to all 454 criminal court judges in Pennsylvania, whose names were obtained from a list maintained by the PCS. Questionnaires were also sent to the 67 district attorneys and 67 chief probation officers in the state (one for each of the 67 counties in the state). Of the 454 judges, 322 (72%) were judges in urban counties and 132 (28%) were judges in rural counties. The determination of a county as urban or rural was based on the distinction made by the Center for Rural Pennsylvania, which uses Census variables to make that determination. The location of the numbering on the questionnaire (centered or bottom right) was an unobtrusive indicator of whether the respondent was from an urban or rural county. All responses were anonymous, although 150 respondents (66%) did identify their county.

Samples

The final sample consisted of 225 individuals, 147 judges (33% response rate), 30 district attorneys (45% response rate), and 49 chief probation officers (73% response rate). The overall response rate (39%) is low, although similar to other studies of judges. Although the percentage of judges responding from urban counties (72%) was significantly higher than district attorneys (37%) and chief probation officers (35%) responding from urban counties, the proportions from urban and rural counties were not significantly different from their proportion in the population.

Questionnaire

The questionnaire contained items related to the goals of restitution, specific factors that judges might use when deciding whether to order restitution, the appropriateness of giving restitution to specific types of victims and third parties, and the types of information that judges might use to determine the amount of restitution owed. Additionally, there were questions on the types of background information available, the effect of restitution on fine orders, the importance of restitution for three types of victims, the amount of contact with victims, responses to slow payment, and enforcement difficulties (adapted from a national survey of judges regarding their use of fines; Cole et al., 1987). All of the ratings of these items were made on 7-point scales. In addition, there was one item assessing the degree to which respondents believed collecting restitution was a problem, which used a 4-point scale. There were also five questions relating to specific responses to nonpayment which called for yes/no responses.

Results

By a wide margin, compensation was ranked significantly more important (more than 6 on the 7-point scale) than punishment and rehabilitation (which were rated at about the midpoint of 4), all three of which were rated significantly more important than deterrence, which was rated quite low (below 3 on the 7-point scale). The fact that judges rated compensation as the primary rationale for restitution is consistent with what had been inferred from the statewide analysis in Study 3 of the predictors of judges' restitution decisions.

Respondents said that for determining whether to order restitution they relied primarily on victim input, the extent of the victim's injury, somewhat less on the type of offense, less on the type of sentence imposed, the offender's employment, and the offender's ability to pay, and least on the offender's family obligations and the offender's prior record. In general, all three groups of respondents agreed on the relative ranking of these factors and, generally, did not disagree with each other. The exceptions were that judges said they were more likely than district attorneys and probation officers to rely on the offender's ability to pay, the offender's family obligations, the offender's employment, and the type of sentence imposed (probation or prison). This information that judges said they relied on is specifically prohibited by law.

Judges' ratings of factors used to determine an order of restitution indicated that victim input and the extent of the victim's injury were much more important than factors about the case (the type of offense, the type of sentence imposed) and factors about the offender (employment, ability to pay, family obligations, and prior record), all four of which were rated below the midpoint 4 on the 7-point scale. That the victim-related factors were the most important determinants of whether restitution should be imposed is consistent with the compensatory purpose of restitution, and the relative objectivity of these two indicators is consistent with fairness. Related to the amount of restitution set, judges were asked whether fines should be lowered in order to reduce the total economic burden on offenders. Of the respondents, 63% said yes.

With regard to the type of victim for which restitution is appropriate, in general responses were consistent with the statute, in that individuals and businesses were ranked higher than the Victim Compensation Board, and insurance companies were ranked very low. This ranking was captured by the remarks of one judge, who said, "Although I order restitution is every case where it is claimed, I believe it is far more important that an individual, rather than a corporate entity, is made whole. Such losses are a part of doing business. For insurance companies, I do not see an insured getting a rebate because a defendant reimbursed the company."

Respondents were asked to indicate the extent to which eight factors (five system-related and three offender-related) accounted for difficulties in enforcement or collection of restitution orders. The three highest rated reasons were all offender-related: offenders do not think anything will happen to them if they do not pay, offenders cannot afford to pay, and offenders cannot be located. Judges were significantly more likely than chief probation officers to believe that the county had inadequate collection methods, that too much time elapses before payment, and that there is inadequate notification. Judges and district attorneys were more likely than probation officers to believe that offenders do not think anything will happen to them if they do not pay and that offenders cannot be located.

Urban counties had more problems than rural counties with four of the five system difficulties: inadequate warrant services, too much time elapses, inadequate collection methods, and inadequate notification. There was one factor (inability to locate the offender) that was more problematic in rural counties than in urban counties.

Conclusion

Overall, criminal court judges', district attorneys', and chief probation officers' perceptions about the imposition and payment of restitution in Pennsylvania suggested that the failure to implement the policy at a higher rate may have resulted from both disagreement with the policy and from practical factors affecting the way the policy is enforced. Although judges, prosecutors, and probation officers all agreed that the primary goal of restitution is victim compensation, they also said that it serves both to rehabilitate and punish the offender. Given that punishment is not supposed to be a goal of restitution but that decision-makers believe that in fact it is, they may be inclined to avoid imposing restitution in order to avoid punishing the offender further. Consistent with this explanation for why restitution was not imposed in all situations where it might have been, one judge wrote the following on his survey: "Many judges give stiff sentences in lieu of restitution, less stiff sentences if restitution is ordered. This practice is incompatible to the given situation and dissatisfies the victims and breaks down the reasons for restitution and its effective collection."

Aside from policy disagreements, judges might not impose restitution in all cases because of practical limitations on the system's ability to collect it. Or, as one judge from a large city put it, "I hear only major crimes where 90+ percent of the time the offenders are indigent. You can't get blood out of a stone. When you have rapes, aggravated assaults, gun-point robberies [by] those with no skills [and] who have never held a job, what good is restitution? They will be in jail for 5 to 10 years and have no assets. It's the exception, not the rule, in the major cases in a large city."

There is a symbolic aspect to restitution, aside from the actual monetary amount imposed. One judge wrote that "Many judges in my county feel criminals are not capable of paying restitution. My experience has been they will pay if they face jail." Even so, it was much more common for judges to indicate that they had no real expectation that the restitution would be paid. For example, one judge said, "This court expends significant resources, including regularly scheduled collection court proceedings, to collect limited amounts of ordered restitution due to low income levels and poverty. Nevertheless, even collection of small amounts reinforces the restorative nature of the judicial system and the need to reinforce accountability to offenders."

This recognition that much of the imposed restitution will not be paid suggests that judges' purpose in ordering it is primarily symbolic. The fact that restitution was made mandatory is similar to other victims' rights actions taken by state legislatures, such as victim compensation and victim impact statements, that many believe are more aimed at giving the appearance of concern for victims rather than actually improving their condition (Elias, 1986; Erez & Tontodonato, 1990). If this symbolism is the case, then the legislature's attempt to control judges' decision-making by making judges order restitution and leading victims to believe that they will receive it does more than simply limit judges' discretion. It may also set victims up as targets for dissatisfaction with the system if the promises of mandatory restitution were not realistic to begin with.

The survey results suggest that judges are following the law by imposing restitution for appropriate victims and comply with the law because it is primarily victim-centered. That is, the intent of the statute appears to be to compensate victims rather than, as with mandatory incarceration laws, to punish offenders. Thus, this focus on victims may explain judges' willingness to follow the law.

However, we also found that judges said they relied somewhat, and significantly more than district attorneys and chief probation officers said, on factors about the offender (e.g., ability to pay, employment, family obligations), even though these factors are not supposed to be considered. Even though judges said they relied on victim input and the extent of the victim's injury, the fact that judges also seemed to rely on offender factors may be because they have relatively little contact with victims.

Judges' responses indicated that they are generally following the law by imposing restitution for appropriate victims. Moreover, it may be that they said they complied with the mandatory statute because it is victim- rather than offender-centered. That is, the focus of the law is to compensate victims, not to punish offenders, and it is this focus on victims rather than offenders that explains judges' willingness to follow the law.

However, this study involved a questionnaire, and beliefs about willingness to act do not necessarily indicate actions in fact. To test whether victim-related services and whether community-level factors supportive of victims facilitate the imposition of restitution, we conducted a follow-up study, a statewide analysis of restitution decisions that examined county proximal contextual factors.

Study 6: The Role of Victim-Related Contextual Factors in the Imposition of Victim Restitution

Ruback and Shaffer (2005)

Study 5 suggested that judges' general agreement with the mandatory statute might partly explain the large increase in the imposition of restitution after the law took effect. However, the increase was not uniform across counties. It could be that the judges in different counties disagreed with each other, but we found few differences between judges in urban counties and judges in rural counties. Rather than look at judges' attitudes, an alternative is to look at the structures necessary to implement the law, such as obtaining the needed information about victims' losses. This examination is especially relevant in light of one implication from the survey—that judges have relatively little contact with victims.

Study 6 investigated whether victim-related contextual factors matter in restitution decisions (Ruback & Shaffer, 2005). Jennifer Sikorski and I looked at factors proximal to the restitution imposition decision (i.e., the location of the victim and witness services office) and distal county-level factors (support for victims in the county as evidenced by the number of funded victim programs).

The location of the victim and witness advocacy office and its position within the court community, we expected, would be important
factors in the day-to-day implementation of the mandatory restitution
law. Specifically, we expected that victim and witness advocacy offices
located within the courthouse, compared to those located in some other
building, would be more efficient at collecting and distributing information about restitution to judges. Although restitution is supposed to be
ordered in every case in which victims suffered quantifiable damages,
these losses are unlikely to become known to the judge unless victims
are made aware of this provision and receive help filing the paperwork.
Thus, we thought that victim and witness advocacy offices located in the
courthouse would make it more convenient for victims and more likely
that victims would request restitution.

We also investigated the nature of the relationship between the
victim and witness advocacy office and other criminal justice offices in
order to examine the position of the victim and witness advocacy office
within the court actors' workgroup. The idea of the workgroup is that the
different actors in a courtroom constitute a community (Eisenstein et al.,
1988) that has norms about the appropriateness of different decisions (see
Study 7).

We examined the effect of four different types of victim and witness
offices: (1) part of the district attorney's office, (2) part of the probation
office, (3) independent and located in the courthouse, and (4) independent and located outside of the courthouse. The effect of these different
types of victim and witness advocacy could be in one of two directions.
On the one hand, victim and witness offices that are housed within the
district attorney's office or within the probation and parole office may
increase restitution orders because, relative to independent victim and
witness advocacy offices, they are probably more tightly integrated into
the courtroom community and thus better able to influence other actors'
perceptions of victims' needs and rights. Being part of the courtroom
community might mean that advocates can better make victims' needs
and concerns salient to other court actors.

Alternatively, because independent victim and witness advocacy
offices probably have more autonomy than those housed in court offices,
it may be more difficult for judges and other court actors to influence the
implementation of victim policy and therefore more difficult for them to
preserve established court routines and the "going rates" for sentences
(i.e., the typical amounts imposed in most cases). Given that restitution
was traditionally awarded to only a minority of eligible victims, restitution orders were probably not an established component of court routines.
If this reasoning is correct, then independent offices would probably be
better able to resist pressure from other court actors to disrupt established routines and sentences.

Aside from the nature and location of the victim and witness advocacy office, we also looked at another proximate contextual measure: how economic sanctions were collected in the county. We expected that judges would be more inclined to impose restitution if the county had a special office for collecting restitution, as well as other sanctions, because judges in these counties would have greater confidence in the courts' abilities to enforce restitution orders. Moreover, many specialized collection units implement additional fees and costs, making them self-supportive. Thus, judges would have fewer concerns that managing restitution orders would drain county criminal justice resources needed elsewhere.

To obtain these two proximal system-related contextual measures, we called the probation offices in each of the 67 counties of the state. We asked whether there was a victim and witness assistance office in the county and, if so, whether it was located in the courthouse or somewhere else. We also asked how economic sanctions were collected in the county, which we considered in two categories: (1) by the probation office or (2) by some other governmental office or an outside collections agency.

In addition to these two proximal system-related contextual measures, we included three more distal measures. First, we included the rural/urban nature of the county, since rural counties are generally found to be more punitive, such as with the imposition of probation fees (Olson & Ramker, 2001). Second, we controlled for the percentage of each county's population living below poverty since there is some limited evidence that socioeconomic status of a jurisdiction affects sentencing decisions. Finally, we included the number of grants to each county from Victims of Crime Act (VOCA) funds over a 3-year period. VOCA funds represent federal money passed through a state agency to support programs for victims. We assumed that counties with more grants were more interested in supporting victims. VOCA funding did not have any direct effects on restitution, but there were some complex interactions that suggest VOCA grants have only indirect, and small, effects.

To test our hypotheses, we used 55,119 sentencing decisions for the years 1996–1998 from the PCS. The cases all involved convictions for restitution-eligible offenses, selected as in prior studies (e.g., Study 4). We looked at the imposition of restitution, controlling for the imposition of fines and for whether the offender was sentenced to incarceration since both variables are generally negatively related to restitution. We also controlled for the type of crime, the severity of the crime (based on the Offense Gravity Score of the PCS guidelines), the offender's prior record, the type of conviction (plea or trial), and offender demographics (gender, race, and age).

Sample Description

Most of the offenders in the sample were male (83%) and white (62%), and their average age was 29. Most of the cases in the sample (72%) involved property crimes, and almost all of the offenders (94%) pleaded guilty. At the county level, on average 40% lived in urban areas and 12% lived below poverty. In 52% of the counties, the probation office was responsible for collecting economic sanctions. In terms of the location of the victim and witness assistance office, 72% were part of the district attorney's office, 8% were part of the probation office, 15% were independent offices located in the courthouse, and 5% of the counties had victim and witness advocacy offices or other victim service providers that were independently located outside of the courthouse.

We conducted our analyses using multilevel logit models, which simultaneously test for variations in the effects of both offender/case characteristics and social context. Multilevel models are appropriate when cases are nested within a jurisdiction since such cases are probably more similar to each other than to cases in other jurisdictions. In our analyses, restitution decisions were nested within county.

Imposition of Restitution

Analyses indicated that restitution was ordered more for property offenders, for offenders who committed more serious crimes, for female offenders, and for older offenders. In terms of contextual effects, restitution was significantly more likely to be imposed in counties where the probation office collects economic sanctions. The location of the victim and witness advocacy office had marginally significant effects on the likelihood of a restitution order. Compared to counties in which the victim and witness advocacy office was part of the district attorney's office, judges were less likely to order restitution in counties where the victim and witness advocacy office was an independent office located outside the courthouse and when the victim and witness advocacy office was part of the probation office. These effects make sense in light of the statute requiring the district attorney to recommend the amount of restitution.

Regarding the amount of restitution imposed, the PCS dataset included information for 16,435 cases from 66 counties. The distribution of the amounts imposed was highly skewed by some offenders who were ordered to pay millions of dollars, but only 395 (2%) had amounts greater than $20,000. To reduce this skewness, we capped the restitution amount at $20,000 and transformed the variable by taking its natural log + 1. Using a hazard rate (the probability of an order to pay any restitution), we also controlled for the sample selection bias that arises from the fact that the amount of restitution ordered followed an initial decision imposing restitution.

Judges ordered higher amounts of restitution for older offenders, for white offenders, for offenders with no prior record, for severe offenses, and for property offenses. Some of these factors (e.g., age, race) are likely related to the ability to pay, a factor that is statutorily prohibited. Judges ordered lower amounts of restitution for offenders who had also been ordered to pay fines. This result is consistent with the survey finding in Study 5 that most judges said that when imposing restitution they would lower fines in order to reduce the total economic burden on offenders.

There was one significant contextual factor. Judges ordered lower amounts of restitution in counties in which the victim and witness advocacy office was an independent office located outside the courthouse, suggesting that this arrangement disadvantages victims.

Conclusions

This study suggests that the structure for delivering victim services can influence judges' decisions regarding restitution. Specifically, independent victim and witness advocacy offices located outside the courthouse appear to be less functional than offices with other structural arrangements in that they are associated with significantly lower odds of a restitution order. In light of the finding from Study 5 that judges and district attorneys rely primarily on information that victims provide in making decisions about restitution, this finding makes sense and suggests that victims are either unable (e.g., because of a lack of information) or unwilling (e.g., because it is inconvenient) to follow the procedures necessary to request restitution.

Contrary to expectations, but consistent with other research we conducted (see Study 8), judges in counties with a special collections office were less likely to impose restitution. It may be that judges in such counties impose restitution in all typical cases because collections are more routinized, but not in the most difficult cases. In contrast, where there is no special collections office, judges might impose restitution in all cases, routine and difficult, and simply rely on the probation officers to do their best to collect it.

Taken together, Studies 5 and 6 suggest that judges are motivated to order restitution because they agree with its goal of compensating victims for direct, tangible losses. Both studies also indicate that judges rely most heavily on information about victims' losses in making decisions about restitution. Furthermore, the two studies suggest that whether judges have this information—and perhaps the content of the available information—may be a function of how well integrated victim and witness advocacy offices are into the courtroom community, how well informed victims are about their rights, and how convenient it is for victims to exercise their right to restitution.

One of the strengths of Study 6 is that it combined information about individual-level variables (the offender and case information) with two types of contextual information: the larger context (operationalized as county-level variables) and the immediate context (operationalized as courthouse-level variables). At the very least, consistent with the rationale for multiplism, controlling for multiple types and levels of information is likely to provide a clearer picture of decision-making.

Policy Implications

Study 6 suggests that the structure for delivering victim services affects what judges know about victims' losses and influences judges' decisions about whether to order restitution and how much restitution to order. Where victim assistance offices are located and how they are linked to court actors have clear implications for whether or not restitution is ordered.

These results suggest two reasons why housing victim and witness advocacy offices within the judiciary may be an effective organizational structure for delivering victim services. First, in addition to reducing victims' burden of having to travel to multiple locations, this arrangement positions victim and witness advocates at the heart of the court community. Moreover, this arrangement addresses all of the Office for Victims of Crime's (1998) recommendations concerning the role of the judiciary in facilitating victims' rights. Second, housing victim and witness advocacy offices within the judiciary may help to reduce judges' concern about offenders' ability to pay restitution (found in the survey of judges in Study 5) by increasing their awareness of victims' losses. Furthermore, such a move emphasizes the importance of victims to the operation of the criminal justice system.

Study 6 suggests that it is important to consider context in the analysis of legal decisions. For restitution decisions, this research suggests it is important to know factors about the crime (type, seriousness), the individual defendant (e.g., prior record), and both the immediate context (operationalized here as courthouse-level variables) and the larger context (operationalized here as county-level variables) in which the decision is made. We also found in this statewide analysis that judges in counties with a specialized collections office were less likely to impose restitution.

What we think is most likely in terms of why judges are not ordering restitution is that the restitution is not being requested. What is clear from both Study 5 and Study 6 is that judges rely heavily on victim input when making decisions about restitution. If victims do not provide the district attorney with this information, then judges are probably unlikely to order restitution even though, under the statute, prosecutors are obligated to make this order even when victims do not provide estimates of their damages. Victims who are unaware of their right to restitution are unlikely to criticize a sentencing order, district attorneys who do not have the necessary information are unlikely to challenge a sentence, and offenders who escape without having to pay restitution are unlikely to complain. Assuming this scenario is correct, in some percentage of cases in which restitution is not ordered, nothing is done because there is no one to object.

Study 7: The Role of Courtroom Community Factors in the Imposition of Victim Restitution

Haynes, Ruback, and Cusick (2010)

One of the assumptions of Study 6, and a finding consistent with that assumption, was that victim and witness advocates are likely to be more effective if they are physically near the courtroom community and particularly if they are part of the district attorney's office. The reason that physical closeness might matter is that it is one factor relating to the cohesion of a courtroom workgroup that shares a common task environment and works together to sentence offenders.

In a subsequent study (Haynes et al., 2010), Stacy Hoskins Haynes, Gretchen Ruth Cusick, and I examined three aspects of courtroom workgroups: similarity, proximity, and stability. We predicted that there would be higher cohesion among groups if there was higher similarity, closer proximity, and greater stability.

We defined *similarity* as the level to which workgroup members share demographic characteristics, educational background (Pennsylvania colleges/universities or not; Pennsylvania law schools or not), and political beliefs, and we operationalized it in terms of information we coded from *The Pennsylvania Manual* (Commonwealth of Pennsylvania), the *Martindale-Hubbell Law Directory* (Martindale-Hubbell, 2003), the Pennsylvania District Attorneys Association (2004), and personal communications with court personnel in all 67 Pennsylvania counties. Within each county, similarity was high in terms of race (99%), gender (90%), and political party (68%). Compared to the remaining 65 counties, the two largest counties in the state, Philadelphia and Allegheny (Pittsburgh), had lower race similarity, gender similarity, and political party similarity, but higher college similarity and law school similarity.

We defined *proximity* in terms of whether the president judge (the chief judge) and the district attorney had offices in the same building. Across counties, 75% of judges and district attorneys did share the same building. We defined *stability* as the number of years that the district attorney worked together with judges in the jurisdiction. Across counties, the average stability was 3.8 years, but it was higher in Philadelphia and Allegheny (Pittsburgh) Counties.

We tested whether these three social psychological aspects of courtroom workgroups affected sentencing decisions and, particularly, the imposition of economic sanctions. We used sentencing decisions in 211,153 restitution-eligible cases from the PCS dataset for the 11-year period 1990–2000. Across this 11-year time period, there were 599 judges and 125 district attorneys. In both groups, most were white and male and had attended Pennsylvania colleges and Pennsylvania law schools. Slightly more than half (59%) of judges were Democrats, but about three-fourths (71%) of district attorneys were Republicans. As in our prior analyses of sentencing decisions, we used hierarchical models to account for the fact that decisions were nested within counties.

Here, I focus only on the results concerning how the courtroom workgroup characteristics affected the imposition of economic sanctions after the 1995 statute making restitution mandatory. Fines were more likely to be imposed when the president judge and the district attorney had offices in the same building. Fines were also likely to be higher when judges and the district attorney had both gone to college in Pennsylvania.

In terms of restitution, generally the more similar the workgroup in terms of law school (i.e., both the judge and the district attorney had gone to a Pennsylvania law school), the lower the odds that restitution would be imposed. Similarly, the longer the judge and the district attorney had worked together, the less likely restitution was to be imposed.

Conclusions

Although crime seriousness and offense history were the most important predictors of sentencing outcomes, the imposition of both fines and restitution were affected by workgroup characteristics. That we found significant effects given the relatively small number of counties, the large number of variables that we controlled for, and the fact that Pennsylvania has guidelines that structure sentencing decisions suggests that the effects are real and meaningful.

In general, workgroups had high similarity (white males who attended both Pennsylvania colleges and law schools). In general, high similarity in groups probably means that they function better since homogeneity leads to more communication overall, particularly informal communication, and high value similarity leads to less misunderstanding. In their work with courtroom workgroups, Eisenstein et al. (1988) found homogeneous workgroups were more likely to resolve cases through consensus. In our sample, greater law school similarity led to a lower likelihood of incarceration and a lower probability that restitution would be imposed.

Stability was associated with a lower likelihood of imposing fines and, after the 1995 statutory change, a lower likelihood of imposing restitution. More stable workgroups may have been less likely to impose economic sanctions because workgroup members had more experience with offenders, particularly with offenders' (in)ability to pay. With regard to restitution, more stable workgroups may have been less likely to impose restitution because they were more resistant to the statutory change making restitution mandatory. Such resistance would be consistent with Eisenstein et al.'s (1988) conclusion that entrenched groups are less likely to adopt new laws.

Study 8: County-Level Analyses of Restitution: Four-County Study (Blair, Centre, Dauphin, and Erie)

Ruback, Shaffer, and Logue (2004)

Studies 4, 6, and 7 relied on data from the PCS, which, as noted earlier, contains much detailed information about offenders and sentencing. One of the weaknesses of this dataset, however, is that some information is not captured in the computerized files. The only way to obtain that information is to code it from paper files, which is what Jennifer Sikorski, Melissa Logue, and I did (Ruback et al., 2004). If the results from studies using the Commission files are consistent with the results using the paper files, then we can have more confidence in conclusions based on the results from both methodologies.

Study 8 examined the paper files contained in court records, probation records, and collection office records in four counties in central and northwestern Pennsylvania: Blair (Altoona), Centre (State College and Bellefonte), Dauphin (Harrisburg), and Erie (Erie). These counties were chosen because they vary along two dimensions: (a) population size (Dauphin and Erie are relatively large, whereas Blair and Centre are relatively small) and (b) the use of specialized units for the collection of monetary sanctions (Blair and Erie have them, whereas Centre and Dauphin do not).

Population size could matter in the imposition of restitution in that in small counties individuals are likely to have both more acquaintances in their community and a higher percentage of all their acquaintances who live in the community than are individuals in more populous counties (Weisheit et al., 1995). One likely effect of this acquaintance density is that actors in the criminal justice system are more likely to know personally a higher percentage of individuals in the county, to be more aware of victims' needs and offenders' problems, and thus to be more responsive to those conditions under which restorative sanctions would work best.

In contrast, in more populous counties, where criminal justice personnel are simply trying to process cases and where they are less likely to know victims personally, victims' needs and offenders' problems would be expected to have less effect on decisions about restitution. Based on this reasoning, we hypothesized that smaller counties would impose restitution more frequently than larger counties because of the closer social ties between all of the actors involved, as compared to the greater anonymity in larger counties.

In addition to the population of a county, we suspected that whether or not there was a specialized collection unit would affect the imposition and payment of restitution. In organizing a probation office, it is possible to make probation officers responsible for all aspects of probation supervision or to divide those responsibilities such that, for example, some workers are responsible for monitoring the payment of economic sanctions and others are responsible for the remaining aspects of probation supervision. Whether to assign workers to perform specific tasks that are coordinated hierarchically or to make workers responsible for a large cluster of tasks is a central decision in the design of organizations (Scott, 1992, p. 264). In particular, the division of labor is assumed to make individual workers more productive because workers hone their skills for a narrow task, becoming experts through learning and repetition (Scott, 1992, p. 154). Weber (1947) believed that the ideal bureaucracy, like the ideal industrial organization, involved technical expertise and a division of labor in that this professional bureaucracy would be the most efficient, precise, and reliable.

With respect to probation supervision, the question is whether the component tasks are independent, in which case dividing the tasks among groups would lead to optimal performance or whether they are overlapping, in which case dividing probation supervision tasks would be suboptimal. More specifically, the question is whether separately monitoring and collecting restitution payments from offenders facilitates the goals of getting money to the victim (in order to repair the harm) and increasing the offender's awareness of the victim's harm (in order to rehabilitate the offender) or whether monitoring offenders' payments separately from their other probation responsibilities interferes both with offenders' actual payment of the ordered sanctions and with their ability to avoid future crime.

In terms of restitution collection, we found the general belief about specialized collections units to be very positive, as one judge from a county with a specialized collection unit wrote on the survey reported in Study 5: "We have instituted a very active and aggressive collections bureau as an offshoot of our probation department and have collected millions in restitution." In fact, there are two good reasons why specialized collection units should be better than having probation officers monitor and enforce collection as part of their overall responsibilities.

First, specialized collection units should decrease the overall burden on probation officers and allow them to focus more time on monitoring other aspects of offenders' supervision conditions (e.g., employment, substance use). Second, probation officers' role can be difficult because there is likely to be ambiguity about whether their primary responsibility is counseling, supervision, or the collection of fees (Olson & Ramker, 2001). Thus, specialized units would lessen the conflict that many probation officers face when they attempt to build a working rapport with an offender in an effort to establish trust and, at the same time, demand monetary payments.

Despite these potential advantages of separate collection units, there are also reasons why specialized units might be worse. First, because specialized collections officers must continue to show that they are useful, in terms of both total monetary collections and collections that support the office, they may be unwilling to accept small "good faith" payments in the short term, even if doing so would increase the likelihood that the offender would remain in the community and ultimately pay more in the long run. They may also be more likely to subvert the rules governing the allocation of offenders' payments among restitution, court costs, fines, and supervision payments by diverting more of the payment toward supervision costs.

Second, specialized collection officers are probably less able to respond to the needs of individual offenders than are probation officers. The rules governing specialized collection units generally permit less discretion in decisions about when to penalize an offender for failing to pay than those governing probation offices. In general, specialized collection agents' knowledge about offenders is limited to factors related to the monetary penalties owed, whether they have paid these penalties, and offenders' capacity to pay them. But specialized collection officers are probably unaware of whether offenders are in compliance with their other supervision conditions and of whether probation officers have complaints about offenders. Consequently, it may be difficult for specialized collection officers to judge when an offender is sincerely trying to meet the terms of his or her probation but is simply having difficulty making the payments versus when an offender is simply failing at community supervision altogether.

Third, the establishment of specialized units separates restitution and other economic sanctions from the other components of an offender's supervision and, consequently, from the larger goals of rehabilitation and deterrence that restitution is intended to meet. Specifically, specialized collections units are generally not concerned with an offender's successful completion of his or her probation or parole condition other than full payment of costs, fines, restitution, and supervision fees. Instead, the collections unit continues to monitor and enforce the payment of monetary penalties even if all other conditions have been met. Thus, there may be a disconnect between the punishment of the crime (e.g., payments, community service, or supervision) or the treatment of the offender (e.g., increasing the offender's awareness of the victim's harm, substance abuse programs, counseling) and the payment of monetary penalties, ultimately making it difficult for restitution to achieve rehabilitation goals.

Taking into account these conflicting rationales, we initially hypothesized that judges would impose restitution more often in counties with specialized versus nonspecialized units due to the presumed belief that specialized units would have higher rates of collection.

Prior to data collection, which began in 1998, approval was granted by the Penn State Institutional Review Board and the president judge of each of the counties. Before data collection began in each county, the data collection team met with someone from the Clerk of Courts office, the Director of the Probation and Parole office, and, in two counties, the director of the specialized collections unit in order to inform them about the research project and to learn about the location and handling of case files. Almost all of the data were collected by trained graduate students; in Erie County, probation staff coded some of the information.

From each county, restitution-eligible cases were randomly sampled from both 1994 and 1996. A case was included if it involved an identifiable victim, either an individual or a business, and if the offense involved some harm to the victim for which restitution was possible. The final sample size for these analyses was 1,785 cases: 547 cases from Blair County (262 cases from 1994 and 285 from 1996), 340 cases from Centre County (149 cases from 1994 and 191 from 1996), 450 cases from Dauphin County (246 cases from 1994 and 204 from 1996), and 448 cases from Erie County (173 cases from 1994 and 275 from 1996).

For each case, we coded directly from the court records all of the data relevant to the crime (e.g., charged and conviction offenses, crime severity, judge's sentence, mode of conviction). Defendants' demographic information (e.g., race, education, marital status, criminal history) and information about the offender's behavior after sentencing (e.g., probation/parole violations) were coded from the court file and the probation file. Finally, data about whether and how much defendants paid were coded from the records of the office in charge of collecting and recording defendants' costs, fines, and restitution payments. In Centre and Dauphin Counties, this information came from the probation records. In Blair and Erie Counties, this information came from the records of the special collection units that are responsible for ensuring that defendants pay the monetary penalties imposed by the courts.

To determine the reliability of the coding, in three of the counties, three coders independently coded the 17 most important demographic, offense, sentencing, and outcome variables from a total of 186 randomly selected cases. As a percentage of agreement, interrater reliability ranged across counties from 94% to 97%.

Multivariate models indicated that restitution was significantly more likely to be ordered for property crimes, offenses that were more easily quantified, offenses against businesses, and offenses after the statutory change. We found that restitution was more likely to be ordered when the harm was quantifiable, when the victim was a business, and when the offense was a property crime (see consistent results in Study 9).

Aside from these case and offender factors, both the population size of the county and whether the county had a specialized collection unit affected the imposition of restitution. Offenders in the two counties with smaller populations were more likely to have restitution imposed. These results are consistent with the idea that criminal justice agents in counties with smaller populations are more likely to respond to the needs of victims. In terms of specialized collection units, we found that offenders in the two counties with these special units were less likely to have restitution imposed in 1996 (following the 1995 statute making restitution mandatory).

In addition to analyzing the effects of the type of collections office in a county, in this study, we were able to test the idea that judges' decisions about the imposition of restitution depend primarily on information from victims. That is, victims who are aware of their right to an order of restitution or who become more upset might be more likely to receive restitution than victims who just want to move on. If so, orders of restitution may reflect victims' reactions to crime more than judges' behavior. To examine that possibility, we looked in more depth at Dauphin County, the only county in this study in which information about victims' estimates of their monetary damages was readily available. Analyses of these data indicated that cases in which victims provided the court with an estimate of their losses were significantly more likely to result in an order of restitution than were cases in which the victim did not provide an estimate. In a multivariate analysis, whether the victim provided an estimate of damages was the strongest predictor of whether or not restitution was imposed, consistent with what was found in the survey of judges in Study 5.

This finding in one county about the importance of victims' actions in providing an estimate of damages suggests that active victims are the ones most likely to receive restitution. Our informal interactions with probation and collections officers suggested that some victims follow-up on judges' orders of restitution with phone calls to the office responsible for collecting monetary sanctions and with letters to judges and other court actors. In Study 11 (Chapter 5), we asked victims some of these questions regarding whether and how they learned about restitution in their case.

Study 9: County-Level Analyses of Restitution: Allegheny County (Pittsburgh)

Outlaw and Ruback (1999)

Focusing on one county is often a good way to learn about an issue in depth, which Maureen Outlaw and I did in examining the imposition of restitution in Allegheny County (Pittsburgh). Data for the study came from Allegheny County (Pittsburgh) probation records, court records, and Integrated Court Information System files, which provide payment information on each defendant for both restitution and fines. We systematically sampled 903 probation records from 1994, when the imposition of restitution was discretionary (Outlaw & Ruback, 1999).

Information on all of the relevant measures was coded directly from the files of the sampled cases. Background data for the cases, such as the offender's sex, race, prior record, employment, and type of crime, were obtained from the fact sheet contained in the probation records. Prior record was indicated by the number of prior convictions in Allegheny County. The offender's employment score was based on evidence in the file that the offender was employed during the probation period. Type of crime was coded directly from the court and probation records. Additionally, sentence length (in months) was recorded as a proxy for seriousness.

Finally, a variable was created based on the type of crime in order to capture the ease in quantifying the harm to the victim. For each case, this measure, called *quantifiable damage*, was coded into one of three levels: not quantifiable (e.g., indecent exposure; 16% of victim cases), potentially quantifiable (e.g., assault; 42% of victim cases), or definitely/ easily quantifiable (e.g., robbery, forgery; 42% of victim cases). In order to assess the reliability of this coding, a second independent rater coded a random subset of 100 cases. As measured by both percent agreement (92%) and kappa (.87), the reliability was good.

The measure of whether there was a restitution order was dichotomous. The amount of restitution and/or fines ordered was measured in dollars and was obtained through the Integrated Computer Information System (ICIS), a computer database used by the probation office and the clerk of courts to track payment records of defendants. Payment of restitution was recorded from ICIS in terms of the amount and the percent of the total order paid.

Results

The majority of probationers were young, single, and male; had little or no prior record; and were not ordered to pay restitution. This pattern holds for both the entire sample and the subsample of cases involving victims. For the 481 cases in which there was a victim, quantifiable damage was the only significant predictor of restitution being imposed. Results indicated that offenders were most likely to make payment when they were able to pay and when the victim was a business. The payment of restitution, but not of fines, was related to lower recidivism (see Chapter 6).

Study 10: County-Level Analyses of Restitution: Philadelphia County

Ruback (2006)

Philadelphia, a city of about 1.5 million people, accounts for more than one-quarter of the crime in Pennsylvania (Federal Bureau of Investigation, 2019). We analyzed 84,970 cases from Philadelphia during the 7-year period 1994–2000, for which restitution was possible (i.e., an identifiable victim, not a DUI, not a drugs case). For each of the restitution-eligible cases in the dataset, which were taken from computer files maintained by the Philadelphia courts, 20 items of information were coded. Analyses were conducted separately for crimes in which private individuals and businesses were the victims ($n = 79,555$) and for crimes in which the state was the victim ($n = 5,415$). Restitution was significantly more likely to be ordered and for higher amounts when the victim was the state rather than a private individual or business (Ruback, 2004).

For private victims, restitution was significantly more likely to be ordered for younger individuals, whites, individuals who had private attorneys, cases in Common Pleas court, cases after the 1995 statute was imposed, probation cases, and cases in which costs were imposed, and were significantly less likely to be imposed for cases in which fines were imposed. For state-victim cases, restitution was significantly more likely to be ordered for welfare fraud cases than for other types of cases (e.g., tax violations, Medicaid fraud), individuals who had private attorneys, and cases after the 1995 statute was imposed, and was significantly less likely to be ordered for male offenders, cases in which fines were imposed, and cases in which costs were imposed.

One of the clear findings from this study was that the 1995 statute making restitution mandatory had effected change: both restitution imposition rates and restitution amounts ordered were higher after the statute than before. However, the imposition rate was greater for crimes against the state than for crimes against private individuals and businesses. The increase in imposition rates for crimes against private individuals and businesses after the statute was probably not greater for three reasons. First, despite the mandatory nature of the statute, it is probably the case that, in practice, restitution is ordered only if the victims request it. It is likely that in Philadelphia, where many victims are poor and the victim assistance agency is overworked, these requests were not always made. Second, most of the offenders are probably poor, and the odds are low that they would be able to make payments. Third, the amounts of money involved were relatively small, and judges, prosecutors, and probation officers may not have believed that the money was worth the effort to impose and that, if imposed, they would be unlikely to collect it.

In contrast to private victims, offenders of most crimes with the state as the victim were ordered to pay restitution. This difference is probably due to the fact that the state agencies involved asked for restitution, the offenders in the non-welfare fraud cases probably did have money (since they were relatively more likely to have private attorneys), and the average amounts of money involved were relatively large.

This study also found, consistent with prior research, that there is a "going rate" for the imposition of economic sanctions. That is, judges appeared to make tradeoffs between restitution and fines for both individual/business victims and state victims. Thus, when the statute required higher rates of restitution, judges appeared to balance that increase with a decrease in the imposition of fines. Costs, however, seemed to be imposed if either restitution or fines were imposed.

The analyses of payment of restitution and fines/costs were restricted to those individuals who were ordered to make the payment and who were on probation because, although some incarcerated individuals may be able to make payments, most cannot. These results suggest the obvious: individuals who were ordered to pay both restitution and fines/costs had difficulty paying both.

In September 2001, we sent an anonymous statewide survey to all criminal court judges in the state (Study 5). Of the 147 responses, 17 judges identified their county as Philadelphia. Typical of these judges' views of restitution is the statement of one: "Except in fraud and theft/burglary cases, we rarely see requests for restitution. Most of our offenders are too poor to pay anything substantial." Another judge wrote, as referred to earlier, "You can't get blood out of a stone."

Based on the results from Study 5, compared to the judges in the rest of the state, Philadelphia judges were more likely to take type of offense into account, more likely to lower fines in order to reduce the total economic sanctions, less likely to say they impose restitution for violent victims, more likely to say collecting restitution is a problem, more likely to impose indirect criminal contempt charges for failing to pay, more likely to believe too much time elapses before payment is made, more likely to believe there is inadequate contact with offenders, more likely to believe there is inadequate priority given to warrants, and more likely to believe that offenders think nothing serious will happen to them. Thus, as we suspected, economic sanctions in Philadelphia are different from those imposed in the rest of the state.

Conclusions About the Imposition of Restitution

Across studies, we found that restitution was more likely to be imposed for property offenses, for offenses for which the loss could be easily quantified, and for whites than for nonwhites. There was also evidence that the imposition of restitution was influenced by contextual factors. Statewide analyses indicated that rural counties were more likely than urban counties to impose restitution. Among urban counties of approximately the same size, more populous counties were less likely to impose restitution but more likely to impose restitution of larger amounts.

In general, the survey results indicated that judges' ratings were less consistent with the mandatory statute than were those of district attorneys and chief probation officers. This pattern was especially evident in connection with factors used to determine restitution. That is, judges were significantly more likely than the other two groups to rely on information, such as the offender's ability to pay and the offender's family obligations, that is specifically prohibited by the law. Relatedly, judges were more likely than the other actors to believe it is appropriate to make more adjustments for failing to pay.

Whereas chief probation officers were likely to report knowing all of the information except the offender's assets, judges were likely to report knowing only the offender's criminal record, family status, employment status, and aggravating or mitigating factors of the offense, and district attorneys reported knowing only the offender's criminal record and any aggravating or mitigating factors about the offense.

Restitution has widespread support because many people believe that it can compensate victims and both punish and rehabilitate offenders. Consistent with this general belief, the judges, district attorneys, and chief probation officers who responded to our statewide survey believed that victim compensation was the most important goal of restitution but that punishment and rehabilitation were also important goals. Our analysis of the statewide data from the PCS suggests that the primary purpose of restitution is punishment.

Restitution is broadly supported because it is believed (1) to help victims by addressing their financial losses, (2) to help offenders with rehabilitation by forcing them to recognize both the losses that they caused and their responsibility for repairing those losses, and (3) to help society by punishing offenders in that the required payments put more burden on offenders than straight probation or incarceration (McGillis, 1986). Whether restitution is punishment is the source of much debate, particularly in the legal literature, as that determination has implications for whether the offender's ability to pay must be considered when restitution is imposed.

According to the Office for Victims of Crime (1998, p. 355), restitution is not punishment; it is simply a debt that the offender owes the victim. In Pennsylvania, the first two rationales, compensation and rehabilitation, are considered the primary reasons for restitution, although courts have also acknowledged that restitution can also have deterrence and punitive effects (*Commonwealth of Pennsylvania v. Kline*, 1997).

Policy Implications

Aside from providing a general understanding of how judges impose restitution and of how judges respond to mandatory legislation, this set of studies has three specific policy implications: one relating to the imposition of restitution, one concerning the efficacy of specialized collection units in terms of payment and recidivism, and the last concerning the effects of economic sanctions on two measures of recidivism.

Imposition of Restitution

Results from three studies indicated that business victims are more likely to get restitution than are individual victims and that the state is more likely to get restitution than private victims. It is likely that neither of these outcomes was the intended result of the restitution legislation. In both instances, restitution is more likely because requests for restitution are more likely to be made and the amounts of loss are more easily determined.

Judges' and chief probation officers' responses on the survey confirmed what we had learned from conversations with probation officers (Study 2) that, despite the mandatory statute, restitution is imposed in many cases only if the victim requests it. In practice, many victims do not know of this requirement and the victim and witness assistance agency in many counties is probably so understaffed that contacts with victims and, consequently, requests for restitution are not always made. Our research suggests that there should be stronger links between the victim and witness assistance office and the probation office so that victims' restitution needs can be better tied to the sentencing process. Moreover, the consistent finding that quantifiability is strongly related to the imposition of restitution suggests that helping victims document their losses will increase the likelihood that restitution will be ordered.

Specialized Collection Units

With regard to specialized collection units, qualitative information suggests that there is a generally positive view of such units. On their questionnaires, judges from the two counties with special units commented on the amount of money that their units collected. Moreover, in informal discussions, probation officers in these counties indicated that they believed the specialized collection units reduced the burden on them. Despite these positive qualitative remarks, our quantitative analyses suggested that such units are no more effective and may, in fact, be less effective than having probation officers perform this responsibility.

We found that offenders in the two counties with these special units were less likely to have fines imposed overall, more likely to have lower amounts of restitution ordered, and more likely to pay a smaller proportion of the ordered restitution. These generally counterintuitive results are consistent with our position that specialized collections units may be less effective at collecting economic sanctions because special collection unit officers, relative to probation officers, have fewer resources to encourage offenders to pay and less information about how well the offender is managing community supervision overall. The finding that offenders in counties with specialized collections are less likely to be rearrested is also consistent with our perspective. Specifically, the apparent positive effect of special collection units on recidivism is probably an artifact of the fact that offenders in these counties can successfully be discharged from their probation supervision even though they have not completed payment of their monetary sanctions. Thus, offenders in these counties can avoid close criminal justice supervision, which means that any subsequent offenses may not be discovered.

These results suggest that *probation officers should supervise all aspects of probationers' behavior, including the payment of economic sanctions.* As suggested earlier, when probation officers handle economic sanctions, they are likely to know more about the entire case and can make adjustments if problems arise, as they inevitably do. Probation officers have a working rapport with their clients in that offenders know that probation officers have the power to invoke further mechanisms of formal control and ease current formal controls. In short, probation officers typically have more resources to bargain with than do collections officers. It might also be the case that, like doctors managing individual lines rather than a pooled line at an emergency room (Armony et al., 2021), probation officers are more efficient because they have a sense of ownership over their clients.

Probation officers can use discretion about such matters as whether and when to arrest offenders for a technical violation, whether and when to revoke offenders' probation/parole, whether to allow the offender to travel out of the county, and whether to facilitate or hinder offenders' access to treatment and training programs. Given that probation officers have such broad discretion, it should not be surprising that offenders would make payments to garner favor with their probation officers. Alternatively, if probation officers do not have responsibility for the entire case, including the payment of economic sanctions, collections units might be tied more closely to probation units, collections officers and probation officers might be asked to work more closely together, or collections officers might be given more discretion and resources.

A related implication of the results concerns what happens to the economic sanctions offenders pay. Specialized collection units require money to operate. Thus, we found that in one of the counties that had special units, the monthly supervision fees were rarely waived, and, in the other county, there was an additional fee in order to make the special collections unit self-supporting. In contrast, in one of the counties without the specialized collections unit, the probation office routinely waived supervision fees so that the money that had been paid could be applied to the restitution debt.

Summary

The results of these studies indicate that the imposition of restitution varies across counties (rural more than urban), across offenses (property offenses more than person crimes), across offenders (whites more than nonwhites), and victims (businesses more than individuals). Restitution was more likely to be imposed after a statute making it mandatory, largely perhaps because judges and prosecutors agreed with the aim of the statute.

Across studies, we found that restitution was more likely to be ordered when the harm was quantifiable, when the amount of damages could be easily estimated and proved (e.g., by a receipt), when the victim was a business, and when the offense was a property crime (Study 8—Four-County Study; Study 9—Allegheny County). But even though restitution is ordered, payment is not guaranteed. The next chapter presents survey studies of victims and offenders and examines factors that decrease the likelihood that restitution will be paid. It also presents an experimental study designed to increase payment.

5

Payment of Restitution

A Review and Field Experiment

The imposition of restitution is the first step in restoring victims to where they were before the crime occurred. The second step, payment, does not necessarily follow from the first. Indeed, collection rates for restitution are often low. In one national study, the rate was 45% (Smith et al., 1989). An analysis of felony probation in 32 counties found that the average restitution order imposed per probationer was $3,368, of which on average only 54% was paid when the probationers had completed their sentences (Cohen, 1995).

In this chapter, I summarize the relevant findings regarding payment from the studies presented in Chapter 4 that examined the imposition of restitution. Then I describe three studies that looked at factors related to the payment of restitution. Study 11 is a survey of victims, which investigated victims' experience with the criminal justice system. Study 12 is a survey of offenders, which investigated their perceptions of economic sanctions generally and their responses to questions about why they were often unable to make their restitution payments. Study 13 is a field experiment, which examined whether it is possible to communicate with offenders about the restitution they owe in such a way as to increase the amount of money they pay.

Restitution Payment in Pennsylvania

In our analyses of sentencing data from the Pennsylvania Commission on Sentencing, we found that restitution was imposed in only about two-thirds of the cases where it was appropriate (Study 5), a decision that depends on factors about the crime, the offender, and the county context (Study 1).

Economic Sanctions in Criminal Justice. R. Barry Ruback, Oxford University Press. © Oxford University Press 2022.
DOI: 10.1093/oso/9780190682583.003.0005

At the time of our studies, in most jurisdictions, offenders make their payments in person with a check (many jurisdictions require a certified check) to an officer of the court, typically the clerk of courts office and the probation office. The fact that payment had to be made in person during office hours can make it difficult for defendants who cannot get away from work or other responsibilities. Moreover, requiring a certified check made paying the economic sanction more expensive for the poor, who will have to make more such payments than wealthier defendants who can pay off their economic sanctions with fewer payments. Possible policy changes to these matters are discussed in Chapter 7.

In Study 2, we learned how six counties handled the payment of restitution. Paying restitution is straightforward if a defendant owes restitution to only one victim. The problem is much more complex if a defendant owes restitution to more than one victim at a single judicial proceeding. Assuming payments are limited, how should the monies be divided among the victims? The largest amount owed first because the harm is greatest? The smallest amount first in order to satisfy at least one defendant? All victims receiving exactly the same amount, regardless of their injuries? The problem becomes even more complex if there are multiple judicial proceedings in multiple years, each one involving multiple victims.

In one county, we found that victims from the oldest cases were paid first. In another county, the defendants' payments were divided equally among all of the victims. In some counties, individual victims were favored over business victims, insurance companies, and the state. We return to these policy issues in Chapters 7 and 8.

In our four-county study (Study 8), we looked at the effect of population size and the presence of a special collections unit on the payment of restitution. Regarding population size and payment, we hypothesized that offenders residing in smaller counties would pay more of their restitution than would offenders in larger counties because probation officers in those counties would be more likely to respond to the needs of both the victim (in terms of ensuring payment) and the offender (in terms of making accommodations so that the offender would be able to pay). Regarding specialized collection units, we expected that offenders would pay higher rates of restitution in counties with nonspecialized rather than specialized units. Because they are largely isolated from the other components of offenders' community supervision, specialized units may seem to many offenders to reflect another bill collector they seek to avoid, whereas nonspecialized units in which probation officers are responsible for all aspects of clients' supervision, including collection of monetary sanctions, may invoke fear of more criminal penalties because of the direct link between clients' payment and the legal system.

Results indicated that offenders in the two counties with smaller populations, where restitution was more also likely to be imposed, were more likely to pay a higher proportion of the ordered restitution. These results are consistent with the idea that criminal justice agents in counties with smaller populations are more likely to respond to the needs of victims and the prob- lems of offenders. In terms of specialized collection units, in the four-county study (Study 8), we found that the two counties with special collections units did not collect higher proportions of ordered restitution and did not col- lect higher proportions of ordered fines, although they were marginally more likely to collect higher proportions of ordered costs (i.e., the funds that enable them to be self-supporting).

In our study of restitution in Allegheny County (Pittsburgh; Study 9), we examined the payment of restitution of 127 restitution orders, with a mean (M) amount of $1,642 and a median (Mdn) amount of $315. About half (48%) of the sample paid their restitution in full, 36% paid some of their restitution, and 16% did not pay any of their restitution. Of those who paid some of their restitution, 69% (25% of the total sample) paid less than half of the restitution ordered.

There were three significant effects in the multivariate analyses of pay- ment/nonpayment in Allegheny County. First, as is consistent with pre- vious work, females were significantly less likely to pay their restitution, presumably because they have fewer resources. Second, business victims were more likely than individual victims to receive restitution payment. This result could reflect the fact that many of the cases that received res- titution orders involved white-collar offenses, the perpetrators of which may be more able to pay. Alternatively, it is possible that businesses were more persistent in pursuing restitution payment or that the system pro- vides more consideration to business victims. Third, rearrest was sig- nificantly related to payment, such that those who were rearrested were less likely to pay restitution. This last effect is not surprising, especially for offenders who may have been jailed as a result of the new offense (see Chapter 6, Study 15).

Conclusions About the Payment of Restitution

One of the purposes of this series of studies was to determine how well the goal of compensating victims was being met. Overall, the evidence was mixed for each of the three goals. With regard to compensation, our research suggested, consistent with prior studies, that only about half of all restitution ordered is in fact paid. In general, restitution was more likely to be paid by those who would be expected to be able to pay—particularly employed indi- viduals. In some of the findings, we found that characteristics expected to be related to the ability to pay were related to payment: older individuals, males, and whites were, depending on the analysis, more likely to make payment. Contrary to the expectation of individuals in Blair and Erie Counties, the two counties we investigated that had specialized collection units, we found that these units were related to lower likelihood of making full payment.

Study 11: Survey of Victims

Ruback, Cares, and Hoskins (2008)

Victims are important to the criminal justice system because they are generally needed to prosecute the crime they suffered, and they can report future crimes against them. To test whether crime victims' satisfaction with the criminal justice system related to their perceptions of the fairness of the process and their outcomes in their case, Alison Cares, Stacy Hoskins Haynes, and I surveyed 238 individual victims in two Pennsylvania counties (Cumberland and Lancaster) whose cases resulted in an order of restitution (Ruback, Cares, & Hoskins, 2008).

In both counties, we worked with county victim and witness services personnel to obtain a list of all individual victims who received orders of restitution in 2002 and 2003. After obtaining the two samples, we mailed victims packets containing a cover letter from the victim and witness services office, two consent forms, a survey, and a $1 incentive. After we received the completed survey and a signed consent form, we paid the victims an additional $10 for their participation. After eliminating those surveys that were returned as undeliverable, the response rates for Cumberland and Lancaster Counties were 31% and 20%, respectively. These rates are low, but consistent with other studies of victims (e.g., Orth, 2003) and with studies using a single contact, as we did here, because we wanted to minimize the intrusiveness to victims. In all, the survey included 49 questions and was pretested on victims who, after completing the survey, participated in structured cognitive interviews.

Results

Because only 2 of 70 comparisons between counties were significant, below what would be expected by chance, we pooled responses across counties. The sample was primarily white (94%), male (59%), married (67%), and fairly well educated (91% high school graduates, 35% with at least a college degree). Of the 238 respondents, 24% were victims of burglary, 42% were victims of theft, 4% were victims of robbery, 12% were victims of assault, and 30% were victims of other crimes, most of which were vandalism (19%) or automobile accidents (7%). Most of the crimes (54%) occurred at the respondent's home.

Slightly more than half of the crimes involved one offender (54%). The offender was known to the victim in 37% of the cases. Almost all of the offenders (88%) were male, with an estimated median age of 22. Most of the cases (69%) were resolved by guilty plea, although 25% went to trial. About 61% of the samples in the two counties said the offender in their case was ordered to pay restitution, although more than a quarter said they did not know whether restitution had been ordered.

About 43% were notified about the trial by the district attorney's office, and 17% were notified by the victim and witness services office. Of the sample, 16% said they testified at trial. Respondents said they learned they were eligible for restitution primarily from the victim-witness advocate (45%) and the police (23%). Of the respondents, 70% said they were asked to fill out a form in order to request restitution, and 59% of the entire group said they did complete it.

Victims reported that restitution had been ordered in 61% of the cases, most for stolen property or for repair to property. However, it is important to remember that the entire sample had been selected from a group of victims whose cases were known to have involved an order of restitution. Thus, as mentioned in Chapter 2, we need to be a little skeptical of such self-reports. For example, Erez and Tontodonato (1990) found that 20% of victims who reported that they had not completed a victim impact statement had actually done so, as evidenced by the statement in prosecutors' files.

In general, individuals reported contacting the victim and witness advocate significantly more often about restitution payments than they were contacted by the victim and witness advocate. Similarly, individuals reported that they were more likely to have to contact the court themselves about the status of the restitution order than they were to be contacted by the court. Contacting the victim and witness advocate and being contacted by the victim and witness advocate were unrelated, suggesting that victims' actions regarding the victim and witness advocate's office were unrelated to what the victim and witness advocate did.

The fact that only 61% of the victims for whom restitution had been ordered actually knew that it had been ordered suggests that victims may not be told about the outcomes in their cases. We also found that 23% of respondents did not know who had determined the restitution owed them, and victims on average were below the midpoint on a 7-point scale indicating how much they understood the restitution process. We found generally that those responsible for collecting and paying restitution generally did not keep victims informed about restitution, other than when they sent victims payments.

We found that victims reported their restitution orders ranged from $0 (some victims said they did not remember that restitution had been ordered) to more than $61,000, with a mean of more than $7,000 and a median of $500 (Ruback et al., 2008). The reported restitution orders ranged from $0 to $61,800 (M = $7342; Mdn = $500). Only 27% of victims believed the court had taken their estimate of losses into account when ordering the amount of restitution the defendant owed. Not surprisingly, victims often believed that the restitution amount ordered did not cover their losses (see also Davis et al., 1992).

We found that 24% of the victims in the sample received all of the court-ordered restitution, 28% received some, and 48% received none.

These numbers are similar to what others have found. We also found that 60% of victims disagreed or strongly disagreed with the statement that they had been kept up to date about their restitution. Not surprisingly, then, victims were generally not satisfied with the restitution process. Davis et al. (1992) found that only 37% of victims were satisfied with the timeliness of restitution payments and only 33% were satisfied with the amount paid.

One of the important dependent variables in this study was whether respondents would be willing to report crimes in the future. Respondents who said they understood the restitution process, said they were satisfied they with the amount of contact they had had with the victim-witness advocate, and perceived the procedures used to determine the amount of restitution in their case to be more fair were more likely to say they would report crimes in the future. As victim satisfaction with the criminal justice system is one of the goals of criminal justice, it is apparent that procedural justice concerns need to be addressed, a point that I return to in Chapter 8.

Study 12: Survey of Offenders

Ruback, Hoskins, Cares, and Feldmeyer (2006)

Because there are increased pressures to collect more money from offenders in order to punish them, make them pay at least part of their costs to the criminal justice system, and restore victims to their pre-crime condition, we were interested in the extent to which offenders were able to make the court-ordered payments.

Stacy Hoskins Haynes, Alison Cares, Ben Feldmeyer, and I conducted a survey of 122 offenders in two counties, Blair and Westmoreland, in order to obtain basic descriptive information about the offenders' economic situation, including their total debts and total payments due to the criminal justice system (Ruback, Hoskins, Cares, & Feldmeyer, 2006). In addition, this study explored four possible reasons for the low rate of payment of these sanctions: (a) lack of understanding of the sanctions, (b) disagreement with the rationale for the sanctions, (c) perception that the sanctions are unfairly applied, and (d) lack of money to pay the sanctions.

Lack of Understanding

Supreme Court decisions since *Miranda v. Arizona* (1966) have indicated that before offenders can be convicted of a crime, they must understand the nature of the proceedings against them so that they can contribute to their defense. After being convicted, however, offenders have fewer rights and their understanding of the system is less important. However, in the context of economic sanctions, offenders' understanding is important, the assumption being that offenders will pay only if they understand what they are paying for. Moreover, understanding that their payments go to victims has implications for rehabilitation in that restitution is assumed to be effective only if offenders understand that they are taking responsibility and making reparations for their wrongdoing (Outlaw & Ruback, 1999).

Disagreement with the Purpose of the Sanctions

A second possible rationale for nonpayment is that offenders disagree with the purposes of the sanctions and therefore choose not to pay. Allen and Treger (1994) interviewed 82 probationers in the Northern District of Illinois about fines and restitution and found that probationers believed fines and restitution primarily served the goal of punishment, followed by the goal of justice. They did not believe these sanctions served the goal of either deterrence or rehabilitation.

Perception that the Sanctions Are Unfair

Individuals care about both the outcomes they receive (distributive fairness) and the process by which those outcomes were reached (procedural fairness). Thus, a third possible rationale for nonpayment is that offenders believe that economic sanctions are unfair because the amounts are too large or the procedures used to determine the amounts are unfair. There is some research to support these ideas. For example, probation officers typically have some flexibility in terms of payment schedules for fines and restitution, and thus offenders may be treated inequitably (Alexander et al., 1998). Our survey of victims (Study 11) indicated that victims were generally more satisfied with procedural fairness than outcome fairness in terms of their treatment by agents in the criminal justice system, particularly regarding restitution, since about half received nothing and another quarter received only some of the restitution owed. As with victims, we expected that offenders' perceptions of both distributive and procedural fairness would be related to their behavior, specifically their payments toward their economic sanctions.

We explored these three possible reasons for offenders' low rate of payment of economic sanctions: (a) lack of understanding of the sanctions, (b) disagreement with the rationale for the sanctions, and (c) perception that the sanctions are unfairly applied, together with a fourth possible reason, (d) lack of money to pay the sanctions. Although there was some support for the first three explanations, offenders' reported lack of money was the best predictor of nonpayment.

Method

The sample consisted of 75 males and 47 females who ranged in age from 20 to 67 (M = 34.1; Mdn = 33). Of the sample, 93% were white, 4% were black, and the remainder described themselves as belonging to other racial groups. In terms of marital status, 39% had never been married, 41% were married or living with someone, and 20% were divorced. In terms of education, 25% had not completed high school, 28% had graduated from high school, and 38% had at least some college or advanced technical training, 5% had a college degree, and 4% had some graduate training. In terms of work, 30% were employed full time, 13% were employed part time, 20% were unemployed, 21% were disabled, and the remainder included students, retirees, homemakers, and occasional workers. In terms of income, 49% reported annual incomes of less than $10,000, 31% reported incomes between $10,000 and $20,000, 13% reported incomes between $20,000 and $30,000, and the remaining 7% reported incomes greater than $30,000. We recoded the crimes respondents said they were convicted of into five categories: (a) property (burglary, theft), (b) personal (robbery, assault), (c) drugs, (d) DUI/traffic, and (e) other (which consisted of firearms violations, gambling, fleeing from police, and false ID). When a respondent listed more than one conviction offense, we coded the most serious crime (e.g., personal more serious than property).

Economic Sanctions Imposed

Overall, 79 respondents said they had been ordered to pay some type of economic sanction, with the total amounts ranging from $101 to $25,000 (M = $2,848; Mdn = $1,400). Of the group, 28 had been ordered to pay jail fees, 72 had been ordered to pay court costs, 58 had been ordered to pay supervision fees, 34 had been ordered to pay other fees and costs, 72 had been ordered to pay fines, and 29 had been ordered to pay restitution. An additional 42 respondents said they did not know the total amount they owed.

A total of 87 respondents said they were ordered to make monthly payments that ranged from $1 to $2,000 (M = $104; Mdn = $68). An additional 27 respondents said they did not know what their ordered monthly payments were. Of the respondents, 61 said they had been given a sheet to keep that indicated the specific fees and costs they owed. Of these individuals, most rated that having been given a sheet was very important. An additional 48 individuals who said they had not been given a sheet indicated that they would have liked to have been given a sheet listing the specific amounts they owed.

In terms of objective measures of difficulty in making payments, we found that 53 offenders said they had missed making any type of payment at least once, 13 offenders had had their monthly payments reduced, and

2 offenders had been allowed by the court to stop payments. However, consistent with Petersilia and Deschenes (1994), who found that about 70% of their sample of offenders said that they would pay all of the restitution they owed, we found that 103 of our respondents (80%) said they expected to pay all of the money they owed.

We had hypothesized that offenders do not pay a higher percentage of their ordered economic sanctions both because they are not motivated to do so and because they are unable to do so. This survey of offenders found some support for all four reasons that we investigated, both the three reasons pertaining to motivation to pay and the one reason relating to ability to pay.

Motivation to Pay

We hypothesized that offenders might not be motivated to pay their economic sanctions because they do not understand them, do not agree with them, and do not believe the sanctions were fairly applied. We found some support for all three rationales.

First, there was strong evidence that offenders did not understand how fines, fees, and costs were imposed. Respondents were asked how well they understood how the amounts of five economic sanctions (court costs, supervision fees, other fees and costs, fines, and restitution) were determined. In general, respondents indicated that they did not understand how the amounts were determined. Analyses indicated that restitution was understood better than all of the other economic sanctions, which did not differ significantly from each other. Property offenders understood the determination of restitution significantly more than the four other types of economic sanctions. Personal, drug, and DUI/traffic offenders indicated that they understood the determination of all five economic sanctions at a fairly low level. Although offenders, and particularly property offenders, said they understood how restitution decisions were imposed, the absolute number (a mean of 4 on a 7-point scale) was in fact not very high.

Second, there was evidence that offenders did not agree with the rationale for economic sanctions. Our results indicated that the offenders did not rate any of the goals of punishment very highly. And, as compared to victims (Study 11), they rated all of the goals as less important, especially those related to concern for victims (including making restitution to them). Third, there was evidence that offenders did not perceive the amounts of the economic sanctions or the procedures used to determine them to be very fair.

Inability to Pay

Although there was support for all three reasons pertaining to motivation to pay, the strongest explanation related to inability to pay. We used four measures of the extent to which the economic sanctions posed a hardship to respondents: (a) their reported difficulty in making their monthly payments, (b) their responses to two questions about whether paying economic sanctions interferes with offenders being able to complete probation or parole successfully and to provide for their families, (c) their expectations about paying off their ordered economic sanctions, and (d) two behavioral indicators of hardship: whether they had missed any payments and whether they had had their monthly payments reduced. Most respondents indicated that it was difficult for them to make their monthly payment. As would be expected, difficulty in making payments was negatively related to income ($r(117) = -.28$, $p < .01$) and positively related to the total amount owed for economic sanctions (for this crime and prior crimes) ($r(105) = .18$, $p < .07$). However, difficulty in making payments was not related to monthly payments for other expenses or to the number of dependents.

Difficulty in making monthly payments for economic sanctions was also related to reactions to the system. Respondents who said it was difficult to make their monthly payments said they understood sentencing less, believed the amounts of economic sanctions were less fair, and believed the procedures for setting the economic sanctions were less fair. As would be expected, difficulty in making monthly payments was positively related to respondents' beliefs that paying economic sanctions interferes with offenders successfully completing probation or parole and that paying economic sanctions interferes with offenders being able to provide for their families. That is, offenders who had more difficulty in making monthly payments were also more likely to say that making the payments interferes with successfully completing probation or parole and with being able to provide for their families.

Our multivariate analyses of an objective indicator of nonpayment (having to miss payments) indicated that our indicators of motivation to pay were not significantly related to missing a payment, whereas indicators of ability to pay (e.g., total economic sanctions owed, total monthly payments) were significant indicators.

Alternative Explanation for Nonpayment

A rationale for nonpayment that we did not investigate is that there are no perceived penalties for nonpayment. Many probationers do not comply with their court-ordered conditions, and there are often no sanctions for failing to comply (Langan, 1994). For economic sanctions in particular, research suggests that often no punishments are imposed for nonpayment of court-ordered fines and restitution (Petersilia & Turner, 1993).

Offenders learn that threats (e.g., meetings, letters of reprimand, warnings) often have no repercussions, and probation revocation for failure to pay is unlikely (Wheeler et al., 1990). Nonpayment of restitution is rarely the basis for revocation of probation (Lurigio & Davis, 1990).

A study of probationers in Illinois illustrates these points (Allen & Treger, 1994). The survey suggested that offenders start out believing that payment is required but then learn this is not true. About half of the offenders believed their probation officer would report nonpayment to the court but would not recommend incarceration. About a quarter believed their probation officer expected them only to make a good faith effort at making full payment, and more than a tenth believed their probation officer did not expect them to make full payment.

In our study, we did not find any support for this idea. In fact, open-ended responses, coded with high reliability by individuals blind to hypotheses, to a question about whether paying economic sanctions interferes with offenders being able to complete probation or parole successfully indicated evidence that our respondents did fear nonpayment. The most common response of those individuals who answered the question (27%) was that failure to make the payments meant that they could not complete probation/parole. An additional 12% said that failure to pay resulted in going to jail.

A possible reason why we found that offenders feared the repercussions of nonpayment is that our respondents were a self-selected sample of individuals who could be reached by mail, who were not in prison, and who were probably more conscientious than those who did not respond. The high rate of nondelivered questionnaires 2 years after conviction (17%) suggests that our initial pool of individuals was highly transient. Those individuals who responded not only were probably less transient (and therefore probably had more ties to the community) but also were more concerned about earning money.

Implications

One of our key findings was that, with the possible exception of restitution, most offenders did not understand how the amounts they owed were determined. Nor did they understand where the money they paid went. Correctional scholars believe that by making payments on a regular basis, offenders can learn to take responsibility for their crimes. However, particularly with regard to restitution, this belief is premised on the assumption that offenders know where their payments go. Thus, it is important to learn how best to convey this information to offenders and whether this information gives offenders a better understanding of economic sanctions, makes them feel more responsible for their crimes, and reduces their likelihood of committing a new offense.

Study 13: Field-Experimental Analysis of Restitution Payment

Ruback, Gladfelter, and Lantz (2014)

The payment of restitution is important for two reasons. First, for the criminal justice system to work, victims need to be treated better, including receiving higher rates of payment of court-ordered restitution (Office for Victims of Crime, 1998; Study 11). Second, if economic sanctions can be shown to reduce recidivism, they might be more likely to be seen as credible alternatives to incarceration (Lurigio & Davis, 1990).

What we learned in Study 12 (the survey of offenders) is that, in general, offenders do not understand economic sanctions, do not know how much they owe, and do not know where their payments are directed. It could be that offenders would become more motivated to pay economic sanctions if they understood where their payments go. Moreover, because offenders have a more positive view of restitution than of fines and fees/costs, they may be more inclined to pay restitution. Such a conclusion would be consistent with research on distributive and procedural fairness (Tyler, 2006).

Aside from the perceived legitimacy of the system, another reason why making payments toward economic sanctions might lead to internalized motivation is that it affects reintegrative shaming. As suggested by the findings in Study 9 (Allegheny County), restitution can be rehabilitative if offenders understand that, because their payments go to victims, they are taking responsibility for their crime and making reparations for their wrongdoing. In that study we found that the effect of paying restitution was stronger among married individuals and somewhat stronger among employed and older individuals, which is consistent with Braithwaite's (1989) notion that marriage, employment, and age are indicators of integration. After reviewing the literature on policies that affect payment, we turn to the field experiment we conducted.

From Studies 4 and 8 we learned that the amounts of economic sanctions paid were generally higher when monitored by probation officers rather than specialized collections offices. Given that local conditions matter, can the probation office change its policies to increase the payment of restitution?

Prior Studies on Payment of Restitution

Four studies by other researchers have examined whether it is possible to improve the payment of restitution. Davis et al. (1991) surveyed 75 restitution offices across the country and found that jurisdictions in which restitution programs monitored offenders more closely had higher rates of restitution payment, as indicated by the amount of restitution paid within 2 years of the court order. However, this research reflects the estimates of directors of restitution programs rather than the actual level of compliance. Thus, the research is only suggestive about the importance of monitoring.

In a second study, an experimental investigation of the enforcement of economic sanctions, Lurigio and Davis (1990) sent letters to probationers, chosen at random, who were delinquent in paying restitution. These letters did three things: reminded probationers of how much they owed, informed them about how to make payments, and threatened them with serious sanctions if they did not comply. Overall, the notification procedure brought in money that was owed. However, the research indicated that it was the threats, regularly enforced through incarceration and other punitive measures, rather than the information provided that explained why the letters seemed to be effective.

A third study, also an experiment, looked at how different levels of enforcement affected the payment of restitution (Davis & Bannister, 1995). The study, conducted in Kings County (Brooklyn), New York, involved 449 misdemeanor probationers who owed between $12 and $1,990 in restitution (Mdn = $263). Probationers received one of three levels of enforcement:

1. *Maximum enforcement*, which included initial invoices, payment schedules, reminder letters sent out monthly, phone contact for those who did not pay, and, after 3 months of nonpayment, a warning that they would be returned to court if they did not pay;
2. *Moderate enforcement*, which included all of the actions of the maximum enforcement condition except for the phone call; and
3. *Minimum enforcement*, which included only the initial invoice and, if payments were not made, a second demand letter containing a warning that they would be returned to court if they did not pay.

After 9 months, offenders in the maximum enforcement condition (53%) and moderate enforcement condition (48%) had paid more of their restitution than those in the minimum enforcement condition (33%). At the end of 1 year, all three groups had paid between 50% and 60% of the restitution they owed, and there were no significant differences between groups.

These results are encouraging, but it should be noted that all of the participants were misdemeanants, which means that the crimes were generally not too serious and the amounts of money relatively small. It is likely more difficult to obtain payments from individuals who owe much higher amounts.

The fourth study, an experiment in New Jersey (Weisburd et al., 2008), randomly assigned low-risk probationers who were delinquent in payments (fines, fees, and restitution) to one of three conditions:

1. An intensive program involving four steps (being served with a violation, performing community service for every missed payment, intensive supervision combined with job training and placement, and termination from the program and a recommendation for incarceration in jail);
2. A violation of probation condition in which offenders' probation was revoked for failure to pay their financial obligations; and
3. Regular probation.

More money was paid in the first two conditions (which threatened probation revocation) than in the regular probation condition. Weisburd and his colleagues termed this result "the miracle of the cells," because the threat of incarceration was enough to force offenders to find the money somewhere. However, the cost-effectiveness of the procedure must be examined. On average, the amount of additional money that was paid was $100, probably less than the cost of processing such additional amounts.

All three of the experiments involved threats, which cannot be empty if they are to have an impact. That is, threats are effective only as long as the punishment is perceived to be credible (Tyler, 2006). And credible threats of jail may be inefficient in that the cost of processing and incarcerating delinquent offenders may not justify the additional amounts paid. This requirement of credible threats restricts what can be done with an experiment.

Another restriction on an experiment is that it should address possible reasons for nonpayment. Our survey of offenders found that offenders revealed that they do not understand the imposition of economic sanctions in Pennsylvania, do not know how much they owe, do not know what their payments are for (Study 11). The offenders also indicated that they believe economic sanctions are unfair, although restitution was seen as less unfair than fines, costs, and fees.

Social Influence to Change Behavior

Changing behavior through some combination of punishment, deterrence, and rehabilitation is a central goal of the criminal justice system. Usually, this goal is thought of in terms of preventing or reducing future criminal behavior. But, as with paying restitution, changing behavior may be aimed at the short term, in terms of payment, and the long term, in terms of reducing recidivism (see Chapter 6).

Our concern in Study 13 was to test whether written communications can be used to increase the amount of restitution paid. In general, written communications can be somewhat effective in changing attitudes if the communications present only one side and are linked to positive feedback about the sought-after behavior. There is also some research suggesting that giving people information about injunctive norms (what people should do) can lead to behavior consistent with socially acceptable norms (Mahler et al., 2008).

Our goal was to produce changes in behavior that would not be dependent on the credibility of a threat. To do that, we sought to induce change by increasing perceived procedural justice. Procedural justice refers to being treated with politeness, dignity, and respect (Tyler & Lind, 1992). It also includes what Colquitt (2001) called *informational justice*: that is, receiving explanations for decisions and procedures that are complete, truthful, timely, and tailored to the level of the person's understanding (Shapiro et al., 1994).

We hoped these communications high in informational justice would lead to behaviors that were intrinsically rather than extrinsically motivated. *Intrinsic motivation* refers to behavior done for internal reasons, such as enjoyment or the belief that the behavior is the correct one. *Extrinsic motivation* refers to behavior caused by external conditions, such as social pressure or the threat of punishment. Behavior motivated intrinsically is likely to be long-lasting, whereas behavior motivated extrinsically is likely to be present only as long as the external force is present.

More generally, research in social psychology suggests that attempts to change behavior can produce one of four outcomes: compliance, internalization, reactance, or no change. *Compliance* refers to a change in behavior as a result of receiving rewards or avoiding punishments (Kelman, 1958). Compliance is effective only as long as the target of these efforts at behavior change is aware of being observed and aware that rewards or punishments will actually follow. This is the approach taken by the three experiments just described, which relied on threat to induce behavior change. Although cues to being monitored might be effective in some cases (Bateson et al., 2006), the mere threat of punishment in the criminal justice system is not enough (Hollin, 2002; Ray & Kilburn, 1970), especially if punishment does not follow the threat.

Internalization refers to a behavior change that occurs because the target of the attempt actually believes that the reasons for changing behavior are correct (Kelman, 1958). Internalization is the most long-lasting type of behavior change because it does not require any type of monitoring by the source of the communication. Another type of internalization can occur through a change in self-image, as people come up with their own reasons to justify their changed behavior (Cialdini, 2001).

Both compliance and internalization result in a change in the target's behavior to that behavior preferred by the person communicating the change. However, there is a difference in the permanence of the change. Behavior change in response to compliance is contingent on monitoring, whereas behavior change in response to internalization is not.

In contrast to compliance and internalization, behavior change efforts can sometimes cause people to behave in the opposite way of what was intended by the influence attempt. This process, called *reactance* (Brehm, 1966), refers to a person's reassertion of freedom after that freedom had been impinged by a change agent that tries to limit the target's freedom of choice.

The fourth possible outcome of an attempt at behavior change is no change in behavior. It is the most common result in research studies because changing behavior, particularly for pleasurable activities (e.g., smoking, drinking, overeating), is so difficult. From most research on social influence attempts, the typical conclusion is that intervention alone is not sufficient to change behavior (e.g., Burger et al., 2010).

We expected that probationers who got information about the restitution imposed on them (how much they paid and how much they still owe) would be more likely to pay the restitution they owed than would probationers who did not receive this information. We also expected that probationers who received a rationale for why they should pay restitution (help victims, acknowledge the harm they caused) would be more likely to pay the restitution they owed than would probationers who did not receive a rationale. We also expected that probationers who received both information and a rationale would be the most likely to pay restitution.

Before beginning the experiment, we posted the experimental design with the Criminological Protocol for Operating Randomized Trials at Cambridge University in England. The document included information about how the experiment would be conducted, the specific hypotheses that were being tested, and the types of analyses that would be conducted.

Method

Study 13 was a true randomized experiment (Ruback, Gladfelter, & Lantz, 2014). The purpose of randomly assigning cases to experimental condition is to ensure that any extraneous factors that might be related to the dependent measure are not more likely in one condition than another (Aronson et al., 1990). If that condition is met and if there are differences as a function of the independent variable, then it is reasonable to conclude that the independent variable, rather than some other factor, caused the observed differences between conditions.

Participants, probationers who were at least 3 months delinquent in paying their court-ordered restitution, were randomly assigned to one of four conditions, including a control condition that reflects the status quo. Because the study was an experiment in the real world and because it involved convicted offenders, it underwent full board review and was approved by the Penn State University Institutional Review Board.

Andrew Gladfelter, Brendan Lantz, and I conducted the experiment in Centre County (the county in which Penn State is located). As of the

2010 census, Centre County had a population of about 154,000, and Penn State had a student population of about 43,000. The county is 88% white. For four reasons, Centre County was an appropriate place to conduct the experiment. First, prior research indicated that it has a good rate of collecting economic sanctions (a range of 31% to 81%, depending on the sanction; Ruback, Cares, & Hoskins, 2006). Thus, using it provides a fair test of the manipulations in the study. That is, if a county with a low rate of collection were used, the manipulations might prove to be effective, but only because almost any intervention would be effective. Second, Centre County is small enough that the experiment could be managed effectively within the budget constraints of the proposed grant but big enough to provide a large enough sample of offenders. Third, in Centre County, by court rules, payments are made first to satisfy restitution orders, even though by statute only half of the payments must go toward restitution. This fact means that, for individuals who owe restitution, the payment is largely going to just one category. Finally, we had a long and productive history of working with the Centre County Probation Department, including studies of restitution (1998–2000) and economic sanctions (2003–2006).

The study had also been approved by the President Judge of Centre County Court of Common Pleas and was conducted with the cooperation of the Director of the Probation and Parole Department of Centre County.

At the time of sentencing, offenders are told about the conditions of their probation, including the economic sanctions they owe. However, according to probation officers, the probationers are often overwhelmed immediately after the sentencing hearing and do not remember what they were told at the time.

In Centre County offenders were told that failure to pay their fines, costs, fees, and restitution could result in the revocation of their probation, a finding of contempt that could result in time in jail, a sheriff's sale of their property, and assignment of their case to a collection agency. Such actions typically occurred only if the judge believed that the offender was not making "a good faith effort" to pay his or her economic sanctions (generally, this means making a monthly payment and a minimum of at least $20 a month). A series of three increasingly threatening letters was sent to offenders who were not making payments. If payment were still not made, one or more of the threatened actions could be taken.

The experiment was a 2 × 2 (Information × Rationale) between-subjects design. The first between-subjects variable, Information, refers to information about economic sanctions. Half of the research participants were given information monthly for 6 months about what they owed originally (in total and by type of economic sanction), how much money they still owed (in total and by type of sanction), how much their monthly payments were, and the category or categories to which these payments have been and would be sent. Information is important because, at the time of sentencing and subsequently, based on our survey study, offenders generally do not know how much money they owe. At sentencing, judges typically order that all applicable economic sanctions be imposed rather than listing all of the individual sanctions that were imposed.

The manipulation of information represents an aspect of procedural justice. Information about economic sanctions owed is analogous to dynamic speed-activated feedback systems that provide information to car drivers about their speed relative to the speed limit. Traffic studies suggest that providing this feedback can reduce average speeds (Hallmark et al., 2015).

However, information alone may not be sufficient to cause people to change their behavior (e.g., knowing the number of calories in food at restaurant chains does not reduce the number of calories that patrons eat; Elbel et al., 2009). Nevertheless, information should lead to better understanding of the penalties, which is an important aspect of perceived legitimacy. This manipulation was delivered through letters, one per month for 6 months. We relied on Probation Office files for contact information.

The second between-subjects variables, Rationale, refers to the type of explanation research participants were given. Half of the research participants received no rationale for why they should make their payments. The other half of the participants received a letter monthly for 6 months describing why the economic sanctions are legitimate. The wording of the rationale letter pointed to the need to recognize the harm caused to the victims and take responsibility for repairing the harm caused. The letter also indicated that paying restitution was related to a lower likelihood of committing a crime while on probation.

About 80% of experiments on the criminal justice system yield null findings, in part because there are not enough participants in the study, a circumstance that is referred to as *low statistical power* (Farrington & Welsh, 2005; Mears, 2010). In this study, for the two main effects, there were about 400 participants in each of the two conditions, and there was power to detect an effect of $f = .20$ at $\alpha = .05$ at greater than .99 and an effect of $f = .10$ at $\alpha = .05$ at .82 (Cohen, 1977).

Consistent with the implications of reintegrative shaming theory, Lurigio and Davis (1990) found that notification had a stronger effect for probationers who had jobs and Outlaw and Ruback (1999; Study 9) found higher payment rates and lower recidivism among those with greater community ties. Similarly, we expected the effects of information and legitimacy to be stronger for those with stronger ties to the community (e.g., marriage, employment, age).

Sample

We began the process of selecting a sample by creating a list, provided by the Centre County Probation Department, of the entire population of offenders who had been placed on the delinquent case list at the probation department as of January 2012. To be on the delinquent list, a probationer had to owe outstanding economic sanctions on at least one docket and the probationer had not paid any economic sanctions for a period longer than 3 months. From this list, we selected all 932 individuals who were delinquent in paying restitution in Centre County. We eliminated juvenile dockets if the offender was still a juvenile. All adult dockets owing restitution were included.

Every remaining individual had at least one court docket number indicating a criminal conviction for which he or she owed restitution. However, several individuals owed restitution on more than one docket. We collected data on a maximum of nine dockets. For the two individuals, clearly outliers, who each owed restitution on more than 20 dockets, we wrote them letters pertaining to their most recent nine docket numbers.

At the beginning of the experiment, we identified several cases that were ineligible for one of the following reasons: (1) addresses were not in the probation database and could not be located; (2) offenders were currently incarcerated for another offense and were being housed in prison, jail, or other institutions; (3) offenders had paid all of their restitution owed between when we received the initial list of delinquent payments and when data collection began; or (4) individuals were no longer in the probation database (i.e., the docket had been expunged). After excluding the 157 cases that met one of these conditions, we had a total of 775 cases that could be assigned to experimental and control groups. At the end of the study, we wrote individuals who participated in the experiment and gave them the opportunity to withdraw their data. Four individuals, from three of the four experimental conditions, withdrew consent, and their data were destroyed.

Most of the cases (74%) of the 771 individuals who participated in the experiment dated from 2007 or later, and 95% were from 2003 or later. The year of the sentence was marginally related to the total amount of restitution owed ($r = -.07, p = .052$), meaning that older cases were somewhat more likely to involve larger amounts of restitution owed. However, because this correlation was small and because the year of sentence was never significant when used as a control variable in multivariate analyses, we concluded that year of sentence was not an important factor.

Assignment of Participants to Condition

The experiment involved the manipulation of Information and Rationale. In addition, we included gender as a factor in the study because men commit more crimes and more serious crimes than do women (Steffensmeier & Allan, 1996), and, given evidence of differences in moral development (Gilligan, 1982), we wanted to be able to test whether women would be more likely than men to pay restitution and whether women might be more responsive to the manipulations, particularly the manipulation of rationale for paying restitution. To be able to analyze the data by gender of the participants, we blocked on gender to ensure that there were equal proportions of women to men in each of the four experimental conditions. Blocking ensures that there is as much statistical power as possible to test main effects and interactions. As it turned out, our initial analyses indicated that gender was not a significant predictor, either as a main effect or in interaction with other variables. Thus, we dropped the gender variable from the subsequent analyses, and it is not discussed further.

Participants were randomly assigned to one of the four conditions by randomly generating a number (1–4) for each participant and then using batch assignment to produce equal numbers in the four conditions. The experiment began in April 2012, and, because there were not enough participants in the initial mailing (due to letters that were returned as undeliverable), we continued to enroll participants for two additional periods. When a letter was returned, we attempted to obtain a new address. By the final treatment period after 6 months, 89 cases were lost because addresses could not be updated.

A problem with this attrition due to undeliverable mail is that returned letters indicated no treatment was delivered; but for the control condition, which did not include letters, no attrition was possible. To deal with differential attrition, the treatment groups were analyzed using an intent-to-treat approach since there could be substantial differences between those dropping out of the sample and those who remained at the same address. For example, those who moved without updating their new address with the probation office were probably at greater risk of recidivism than those who did update their address.

Measurement

Each month, coders looked up offender docket information on the Pennsylvania Unified Judicial System website and recorded any payments made in the prior month in the category (restitution, fees, fines) to which the money was applied. If the probationer made a payment, we used that information in the next letter and gave positive feedback if there was a payment.

Each treatment group received a total of six letters. Payments were coded on each docket on the 12th to 15th of each month. Letters were printed and prepared for mailing on the 16th through 18th and mailed on the 19th of each month, or the Monday immediately following the 19th if it was on the weekend. The last letter was sent in December 2012, but we collected additional information about payments into 2013.

Data Collection

For each case, we recorded the initial amount of each type of economic sanction assessed. Then we recorded any adjustments to the amount of each sanction, in terms of increases (e.g., penalties) or decreases (e.g., canceling a sanction). At the beginning of the experiment, we noted the baseline amounts for each offender docket based on the total amounts assessed, total adjustments (if any), and total payments (if any). The two dependent measures were the total amount of restitution paid (which, since Centre County puts all economic sanctions payments toward restitution, should equal the total amount paid) and the number of monthly payments made.

Results

Description of the Sample

Most of the individuals in the sample (75%) were male, 81% were white, and the average age at conviction was 34. The average amount of restitution owed was $7,261; the median amount owed was $891. The fact that there was such a large difference between the mean and the median indicates that the distribution of restitution owed was not normal (i.e., it was highly skewed). Similarly, the distribution of the amounts of restitution paid was highly skewed; amounts ranged from $0 to $39,603 (M = $388; Mdn = $25).

The skewness of these two variables was largely the result of outliers. In terms of the amount of restitution owed, the top three amounts were $527,084, $639,032, and $947,639. Four tests used to indicate whether these outlying cases were overly influential all indicated that they were. In terms of amount of restitution paid, one case was an outlier ($39,603) based on three of the four outlier tests. Analyses of the two dependent measures (restitution paid and number of payments) were conducted both including and excluding the outliers, as well as with square root, logarithmic, and reciprocal transformations of the data. In general, regardless of which type of analysis was used, the results were fairly robust.

The amount of restitution paid was analyzed in two different ways, both of which indicated that more restitution was paid in the Information

Only condition (M = $652) than in the Rationale Only condition (M = $261), the Control condition (M = $248), and the Information and Rationale condition (M = $213), which did not differ significantly from each other. Additional analyses indicated that, over the 12-month period that payments were monitored, payments increased in the Information Only condition but remained constant in the other three conditions. Comparisons involving only the Rationale manipulation indicated that providing a rationale was generally counterproductive in that individuals who were given the rationale paid less money than did probationers who did not receive a rationale for paying restitution.

In sum, the results from all of the analyses indicated that the manipulation of information about restitution paid and still owed had a positive effect on the payment of restitution. Probationers who received information monthly for 6 months about how much they still owed tended to pay more money over the 12 months of the study (including 6 months after the last letter had been sent) than did probationers who did not receive such information, whereas probationers who received a rationale for payment tended to pay less. In terms of the number of months of restitution payments, analyses indicated that probationers in the Information Only condition made significantly more payments than probationers in the other three experimental conditions.

Cost-Effectiveness

The significant effects of information on amount of restitution paid and the number of payments made are a first step in determining whether there should be a policy change that incorporates this intervention. This judgment about policy must consider the cost of implementing that policy and then comparing it to the benefits (i.e., the increase in restitution paid).

The experimental treatment of delivering the information was relatively cheap. It took about 40 hours to set up the data file and format the letters to the probationers. Collecting data from the website regarding payment and preparing letters took about 240 hours over the 12 months of the study. Another 50 hours was needed to track cases for which letters were marked undeliverable. If we assume the labor cost is $20 per hour, the total estimated labor costs would be $6,600 over 330 hours. Supplies included postage, paper, and envelopes, which were about $3,000. The total estimated cost of labor and supplies was $9,600.

To compute the cost-effectiveness measure, we compared the cost of delivering the treatment in the Information Only condition to the Control condition: $9,600 versus $0. Then we compared the amount of restitution paid by probationers in the Information Only condition to the amount of restitution paid by probationers in the Control condition: $116,028 versus $54,235. We then compared the difference in restitution collected ($61,793) to the cost of the treatment ($9,600), for a ratio of 6.44. That is, for every dollar spent delivering the treatment in the Information Only condition, there was a return of $6.44, which would not have been paid in the absence of the treatment. This improvement in payment is consistent with work in the United States (Thaler & Sunstein, 2008) and Britain (Benhold, 2013) suggesting that small-scale interventions can be cost-effective ways to change behaviors in ways that benefit society (e.g., paying taxes, quitting smoking, donating to charity).

Conclusions

The results of the study indicated that the provision of Information led to reliable increases in both the amount of restitution paid and the number of restitution payments made. But the Rationale manipulation seemed to result in significantly lower payments. These results fit within the larger framework of research from social psychology and communication, presented earlier, about the possible effects of attempts to change attitudes and behaviors.

Earlier, I noted that such attempts could produce four possible outcomes: (1) Compliance, whereby targets of persuasion attempts change their behavior to receive rewards and avoid punishments; (2) Internalization, whereby targets change their behavior because they believe the new behavior is correct; (3) Reactance, whereby targets change their behavior in the opposite direction of the influence attempt; and (4) No effect. In our study, we found evidence of all four possible outcomes.

First, the evidence for compliance appeared as an initial spike in payments after the first letter. After the first letter, 208 of the full sample of 771 (581 who received a letter) made a restitution payment ranging in size from $.30 to $39,603. Across all eight observation points, the payments made after receiving the first letter were the highest (M = $106), primarily because of the single large payment of $39,603, which paid off the amount this person owed and which, as noted earlier, was a clear outlier. The fact that this outlying payment was made after the first letter is consistent with the notion of compliance after the person became aware that he was being monitored. However, even when we excluded this outlier, the effect of a large payment after the first letter was still present, although it was no longer the largest amount of restitution paid.

Second, evidence for internalization came from the probationers in the Information condition, who paid more restitution and made more monthly payments than did probationers in the other three conditions. In support of the notion that their payments reflected internalization is the fact that participants in the Information condition paid significantly more at 6 and 9 months, and marginally more at 12 months, than did participants in the No Information condition. If the effect were merely the result of compliance, then the effect should have occurred only during the first 6 months of the study, when letters were being sent, not after the letters had stopped. Consistent with the internalization explanation, it may be that once the probationers started making restitution payments, their self-image changed (Cialdini, 2001), such that they came to see themselves as recognizing the harm they had caused and as assuming responsibility for repairing that harm.

Third, reactance likely explains why probationers in the Rationale condition paid significantly less than participants in the No Rationale condition. Consistent with a reactance explanation, participants who were told how they should behave may have resented the forced rehabilitation—that they should acknowledge the harm they had caused and that they should take responsibility for correcting that harm. A study aimed at using moral persuasion to elicit tax compliance from corporations in Israel found a similar backfire effect (Ariel, 2012).

Fourth, our finding of no effect in the Both Information and Rationale condition is the common finding in most studies of attempted behavior change. In this study, the Both Information and Rationale condition did not differ from the Control condition, quite possibly because while the Information manipulation might have increased restitution payment, the Rationale manipulation reduced payment.

Summary and Implications of the Study

This study found that providing information to probationers about what restitution they have paid and how much they still owe leads to more money paid toward restitution and more payments of restitution. The effect could be due to simple monitoring, as feedback on not performing a task (in this case not paying restitution) might motivate delinquent probationers into paying. For example, a study of mask-wearing in Bangladesh during the COVID-19 pandemic found that gentle intervention was a key factor in increasing the use of masks (Abaluck et al., 2021). However, we found that payments continued in the Information condition even when the probationers were no longer being monitored. Thus, we interpreted the results as being due to a change in internal motivation, although future studies need to better test whether the mechanism is fear of punishment because of increased monitoring or simply more information about what is owed.

In an experiment in Kenya designed to increase savings, Ariely and his colleagues found that having something that served as a reminder of payment was the most effective technique, more than bonuses paid for saving. The reminder (a coin on which they marked whether they had saved that week or not) helped make savings salient and helped shape "memory, attention, and thinking" (Ariely & Kreisler, 2017, p. 244). One reason that our experiment was effective may have been that the letter served to make payment salient. Another reason that our experiment was successful is that the letters also acknowledged prior payments, since research suggests that acknowledging a job well done increases workers' satisfaction and productivity (Ariely, 2010, p. 80).

At the very least, our field experiment and prior research (Davis et al., 1991) suggest that sending letters to offenders with information about amount of restitution paid in the past month and the amount still owed can be effective in increasing restitution payments. This intervention is relatively inexpensive to implement and could be computer-generated, as Davis et al. suggested 30 years ago. Earlier intervention, before probationers become delinquent in payment, might be especially cost-effective. Even if it served only as a reminder, that would be beneficial. Texting clear reminders to New Yorkers about upcoming court dates reduced failure-to-appear rates by 26% and thus the arrest warrants that can follow a failure to appear (Ottaway, 2018).

The major strength of this study was that it was a true field experiment, in which research participants in a real-world context were randomly assigned to condition. In addition, there were enough participants in the study to ensure adequate statistical power for most of the tested main effects and interactions. However, we do not know very much about the probationers who participated in the study, including such factors relevant to payment as employment, income, financial assets, and financial obligations.

Study 14: Survey of Offenders Who Participated in the Field Experiment

Gladfelter, Lantz, and Ruback (2018)

In our survey of 122 offenders (Study 11), we learned that, as expected, inability was the primary reason why offenders were unable to pay the restitution they owed, but that offenders often did not understand how their court-ordered economic sanctions were imposed, how much they owed, and what their payments were for. The experimental study investigating the effects of information on payment (Study 13) addressed this lack of knowledge about restitution and found that information led to increased payments.

Our next question was whether this information changed offenders' conscious beliefs and attitudes. But, even if they did not, were any system factors related to payment? In particular, Andrew Gladfelter, Brendan Lantz, and I were interested in whether procedural justice—fair treatment from probation officers—was related to participants paying more of their outstanding court-ordered restitution and making more payments toward restitution. Procedural justice includes being treated with politeness, dignity, and respect (Tyler & Lind, 1992) and what Colquitt (2001) calls informational justice. Informational justice refers to receiving complete and truthful explanations for decisions and procedures (Shapiro et al., 1994) and incorporates explanations that are timely and tailored to the level of understanding of the specific person. A system that imposes economic sanctions that offenders do not understand is unlikely to be seen as legitimate, and, indeed, our survey of offenders found that they do not understand economic sanctions and think most of them are unfair (Study 11).

Individuals who are treated fairly by authorities are more likely to believe that they are valued members of society and more likely to obey the law because they believe it is the right thing to do (Tyler, 2006). In the criminal justice system, offenders who are treated fairly are more likely to follow rules and comply with orders (Jackson et al., 2012). This willingness to comply has been supported by research on individuals' interactions with the police (Slocum et al., 2016), courts (Kaiser & Holtfreter, 2016), and prisons (Beijersbergen et al., 2016; Sparks et al., 1996).

According to Tyler's (2006) theoretical model of procedural justice, the perceived fairness of treatment by legal actors leads to more positive views of legal authorities (Tyler & Huo, 2002) and increases the perceived legitimacy of the criminal justice system, which in turn increases behavioral compliance with the law. Longitudinal research on the effect of informational fairness on tax payments is consistent with this notion (Murphy & Tyler, 2008; Wenzel, 2002).

To answer the question about the effect of procedural fairness on the payment of economic sanctions, we sent a survey to individuals who had participated in the experimental research (Gladfelter et al., 2018). Of the 771 participants in the experiment whom we contacted about the survey, 241 letters were returned as undeliverable, meaning that we were able to successfully contact 530 (68%). To maximize the number of respondents who participated in the survey, we used the Dillman (2007) survey method, which involved up to four mailings: (1) an initial contact letter briefly describing the study, (2) a survey with a $1 incentive attached, and, if necessary, (3) two follow-up mailings. The survey, which took about 30 minutes to complete, consisted of questions about ability to pay; intentions to pay; attitudes toward probation that might affect payment, with a focus on the perceived duty to obey probation officers; and prior payment of restitution. Respondents were mailed a $20 Walmart gift card upon completion.

Five months after the survey, participants received a debriefing letter about the combined experiment and survey research and were informed that they could withdraw their data if they wished. Of the 149 respondents who returned the survey, four chose to withdraw their data and were eliminated from the data files. Before we analyzed the data, we used multiple imputation to correct for missing data and survey weighting to correct for survey nonresponse for the remaining 145 individuals.

As in the experimental sample, offenders were primarily white, male, and in their mid-30s. In general, they had low incomes (on average, a little more than $20,000), meaning that paying restitution would have been difficult for most of them after housing, food, and other expenses.

Results from multivariate analyses, in which all of the predictors were tested holding the other variables constant, indicated that the respondents paid more restitution if they had paid more prior to the experiment, if they had a higher income, and if they believed their probation officer was more fair. This effect for procedural fairness was not affected by the probationers' income level. That is, even offenders with lower incomes were likely to pay something toward the restitution they owed if they believed they were being treated fairly. Fair treatment by probation officers was also related to offenders making more restitution payments.

Although the perceived legitimacy of the probation officer was related to paying restitution, the perceived duty to obey the probation officer was not. This finding is consistent with Tyler's (2006) suggestion that authorities' perceived legitimacy encourages individuals to regulate their own behavior. Moreover, consistent with Jackson et al.'s ideas that inducing people to follow the law through procedural justice and legitimate authority (leading to internalized beliefs) rather than through fear of punishment (which is effective only as long as the threat is real), our research indicates that getting people to pay restitution is likely to result more from the perceived legitimacy of the probation officer than from the perceived duty to obey the officer.

This study is limited by the size and representativeness of the sample. Moreover, our measure of ability to pay—household income—was inadequate because we did not capture outstanding debts and necessary monthly expenses. Nor were we able to separate the individual probationer's ability to pay from external sources of support (e.g., family and friends who provide housing or other aid). Neither were we able to determine whether restitution payments were made by the offender or by someone else.

A final weakness was the cross-sectional nature of our study. In order to preserve the integrity of the experiment, the survey was not sent out until after the experiment had ended and restitution payments had been collected. Tests indicated that the experimental conditions did not significantly affect the attitudes of the probationer respondents, which suggests that the changes observed in our experiment (Study 13) were not reflected in the measures we used in this survey study or, perhaps, that we did not have enough statistical power to detect differences if they did exist.

Conclusion

In this study, probationers who perceived their probation officers to be fair paid more restitution and made a greater number of payments toward fulfilling their obligations. This effect occurred independently of the amount of resources the offender had. The study is consistent with other research in criminal justice showing the importance of justice system actors' procedural fairness in reducing criminal behavior. In addition, fair treatment by probation officers may be one reason why payment rates are higher when probation officers, rather than special collection units, are in charge of collecting payments (Study 8).

In the context of police–citizen interactions, Nagin and Telep (2020) argued that procedurally just treatment of citizens is normatively and socially important but that there is no convincing evidence that procedurally just treatment is causally related to perceived legitimacy and compliance with the law because the causal process may be reversed or third causes may be involved. Our results here are consistent with the correlational work found with police–citizen interactions, as our findings suggest only a correlation between the perceived fairness of the probation officer and the payment of economic sanctions. Future experimental research needs to address whether greater procedural justice by probation officers might lead offenders to increased payment of economic sanctions.

Summary

This chapter reviewed the results from the studies we conducted that included measures of payment of restitution. Those studies indicated that restitution was generally not paid in full. The correlational results indicated that older individuals and employed individuals were more likely to make payments. From the victim survey, we learned that many victims said they did not know that restitution had been awarded, and most were not satisfied with the restitution process and with their restitution outcomes. From the survey of offenders, we learned that offenders said they were unable to pay economic sanctions and that they did not understand their sanctions or, with the possible exception of restitution, think they were fair.

In the final part of the chapter, our field-experimental analysis of restitution payment indicated that a randomly assigned group of probationers delinquent in paying restitution who received information about what they owed paid more restitution and made more payments than did delinquent probationers who received reasons why they should pay restitution and delinquent probationers who did not receive letters. A survey completed by some of the participants in the study indicated that the perception of having been fairly treated was related to the payment of restitution.

In the next chapter, I turn to the follow-up question: whether paying restitution is related to subsequent criminal behavior.

6

Effects of Paying Restitution

The primary purpose of restitution is to reimburse victims for the losses they sustained as a result of the crime. The experiment described in Study 13 indicated that providing information to probationers about the amount of restitution they have paid and how much they still owe led individuals to pay more restitution and make more restitution payments as compared to individuals in the other conditions of the experiment.

A secondary purpose of restitution is to help offenders recognize the harm they have caused and take responsibility for correcting that harm, both of which would presumably lower the likelihood that they would commit crime in the future. The purpose of Study 15 was to test that idea by following participants in the experiment to determine whether their subsequent criminal behavior, as indicated by whether or not they were arrested, was affected by their payment of restitution and, ultimately, by the experimental condition that they were in.

In this chapter, I discuss the research literature investigating how paying restitution relates to recidivism. Then I summarize the relevant findings from the Pennsylvania studies presented in Chapters 4 and 5 that examined recidivism after payment. Finally, I describe Study 15, the recidivism follow-up of the offenders involved in the field experiment.

Restitution Payment and Recidivism

Two competing hypotheses can be made regarding the effects of restitution payment on recidivism. On the one hand, *paying economic sanctions could increase crime*, consistent with the general link between joblessness and crime (Wilson, 2008). Harris et al. (2010) suggested several reasons why there might be a link between economic sanctions and crime: (a) lost income and

Economic Sanctions in Criminal Justice. R. Barry Ruback, Oxford University Press. © Oxford University Press 2022.
DOI: 10.1093/oso/9780190682583.003.0006

the resulting financial stress of having less money; (b) the fact that these legal financial obligations limit opportunities through poor credit ratings and the resulting constraints on housing, education, and employment opportunities (Bannon et al., 2010); and (c) the legal penalties for not paying these economic sanctions, including continuation on probation supervision, warrants, and reincarceration. These arguments make sense, in that offenders report having little money (Study 12). And, there are anecdotal accounts of people stealing to make payments on their economic sanctions (e.g., Harris et al., 2010; "Man Accused," 1997), although the prevalence of such instances is unknown.

Moreover, there are often broader negative consequences from not paying economic sanctions. The adverse effects on credit, borrowing, housing, and employment may reduce offenders' chances to be successfully reintegrated into society (Harris et al., 2010). And there are often negative effects of economic sanctions on families, especially minority families. Campos-Bui et al. (2017) found that administrative fees imposed in the juvenile justice system in California caused financial hardship to families, particularly black and Hispanic families.

One of the problems with determining whether paying economic sanctions leads to probation revocation is that probation is likely to be revoked for several reasons, and the failure to pay restitution is often simply one (Ruback, 2011). In an examination of cases handled by a public defender's office in Florida, Iratzoqui and Metcalfe (2017) found that legal factors (e.g., new charges, drug possession, weapon possession), not fees or restitution had the largest effect on recidivism. In a study of juveniles, Piquero and Jennings (2017) found that higher amounts of costs imposed (on 94% of the sample) and of restitution imposed (on 36% of the sample) and higher amount of costs and restitution together still unpaid were related to recidivism. Importantly, because the two types of economic sanctions were merged, it is likely that the costs sanctions had the larger effect.

Although there is reason to believe that facing a sentence of economic sanctions could increase crimes, it is also possible that *paying economic sanctions could decrease crime.* This nonintuitive notion assumes that, to the extent that these payments are made voluntarily (i.e., not just because of the threat of jail), they might lead to the internalization of responsibility through processes of self-perception (Bem, 1972) and cognitive dissonance (Festinger, 1957). This internalized behavior, in turn, might lead to perceptions of legitimacy and procedural justice, consistent with Tyler's (2006a) call for psychological approaches to activate internal values.

Even though collection rates for restitution are generally low (Cohen, 1995; Lurigio, 1984; Smith et al., 1989), several studies of adult offenders suggest that paying restitution is associated with positive outcomes (Heinz et al., 1976). Miller (1981) found that the 54% of the 419 offenders in his study who paid their restitution in full had significantly fewer revocations than did offenders who paid none or only some of their restitution. However, these 419 offenders ordered to pay restitution had higher revocation rates than those who had already made restitution. One of the problems with such comparisons is the selection bias inherent in the comparison groups, in that the offenders who had paid their restitution in full might have been systematically different from offenders who did not make full restitution payment. One of the advantages of experimentation (see Study 15) is that selection bias is eliminated as a plausible explanation for the findings.

The rehabilitative potential of restitution hinges on both offenders' ability to pay and their willingness to pay (Galaway & Hudson, 1975). Offenders who lack adequate resources to pay restitution are generally unwilling to even attempt payment (Galaway & Hudson, 1975). This obstacle can be overcome by emphasizing the benefits of paying restitution, supervising probationers closely, and providing employment opportunities to offenders to help with payment (Rubin, 1988; Schneider, 1990; Van Voorhis, 1985). Thus, it may be that the likelihood of payment can be increased by emphasizing the importance of restitution payment and providing opportunities to fulfill the obligation.

By accepting responsibility and repairing the damage to the victim in a tangible way, offenders may reap benefits that remain long after the criminal sanction has ended, including taking responsibility in other aspects of their lives and avoiding criminal behavior in the future. Both reintegrative shaming theory (Braithwaite, 1989; Braithwaite et al., 2006) and defiance theory (Sherman, 1993) provide insight into the potential of victim restitution as an effective means of reducing subsequent criminal behavior.

Reintegrative shaming theory is based on the proposition that sanctions shame offenders either in a stigmatizing way, which increases crime, or in a reintegrative way, which reduces crime. Stigmatizing sanctions increase crime by shaming the offenders as people (i.e., through formal court proceedings and labeling sanctions), causing them both to feel like outcasts and to continue offending. Reintegrative shaming, on the other hand, reduces crime by shaming the act rather than the individual; it allows offenders to make amends for their crimes and be reintegrated into the community (Braithwaite, 1989).

Consistent with this theory, some researchers (Schneider, 1990; Van Voorhis, 1985) have reported that restitution works because the process makes amends for one's actions. That is, recidivism rates are lower among offenders who recognize the reparative benefits to the victim. Moreover, paying restitution allows offenders to take responsibility for their actions without stigmatizing them. Likewise, research indicates that successful completion of a restitution order is generally one of the strongest predictors of lowered recidivism (Ervin & Schneider, 1990).

Such positive effects of restitution payment may be especially likely for individuals who are more fully integrated into the community: that is, those who are older, married, and employed. According to reintegrative shaming theory (Braithwaite, 1989), those who initially are more fully integrated will be reintegrated more easily through the appropriate sanctions. In fact, according to *defiance theory*, such integration is essential if any type of sanction is to reduce subsequent offending (Sherman, 1993). Specifically, reintegrative sanctions should have a positive effect on all offenders, but the effect should be stronger for individuals who are more fully integrated into the community. Other research has also shown that commitment to social institutions (marriage, employment) and a sense of community are powerful insulators against crime (Sampson et al., 1997).

Most studies examining the effect of paying restitution on subsequent recidivism have been conducted with samples of juveniles, which makes sense given that the primary emphasis of the juvenile justice system is reha- bilitation rather than punishment. Most of these studies of juveniles have found that paying restitution is associated with lower recidivism (Farrington & Welsh, 2005; Roy, 1995; Shichor & Binder, 1982). In a study using data from Utah, 7,233 juvenile cases handled informally and 6,336 adjudicated cases resulting in formal probation in Utah, Butts and Snyder (1992) found that juveniles who paid restitution, whether as part of the informal disposi- tion or of formal probation, were significantly less likely to recidivate. In a four-site experimental study, Schneider (1986) compared restitution orders to traditional dispositions (detention, counseling, or probation). In two sites (Washington, DC, and Clayton County, Georgia), juveniles ordered to pay restitution had lower recidivism, and in the other two sites (Boise, Idaho, and Oklahoma County, Oklahoma) recidivism rates were not significantly different. In a correlational study of 183 juveniles ordered to pay restitution in Lincoln, Nebraska, Jacobs and Moore (1994) found a significant nega- tive correlation between the proportion of restitution paid and subsequent offending: more restitution was related to less crime. These results also fit with Lipsey's (2009) meta-analysis, which found lower recidivism for juve- niles ordered to pay restitution or perform community service.

Overall, based on these studies conducted in jurisdictions other than Pennsylvania, paying restitution appears to be an effective means of reducing recidivism. In particular, although formal restitution (as a condition of pro- bation or assigned by the court) may be less effective than less formal restitu- tion arrangements (residential programs or court diversion), it is still more effective than straight probation or incarceration (Rowley, 1990; Schneider, 1990) because it leads offenders to take responsibility. In general, stud- ies examining the effectiveness of restitution among juveniles (Schneider, 1990) have shown that rearrest rates are lower among juveniles who pay res- titution than among those who receive other sanctions.

Restitution Payment and Recidivism in Pennsylvania

Aside from these studies conducted in other jurisdictions, all of them corre- lational and some conducted 30 or 40 years ago, research that we conducted in Pennsylvania is also consistent with the general conclusion that paying restitution is associated with lower recidivism. In Study 3 (five-county study of juveniles; Haynes et al., 2014), our analyses of 921 juvenile cases found that the percentage payment of total economic sanctions imposed was negatively related to the revocation of sentences. As noted earlier, however, one problem with analyzing payment data from juvenile cases is that the payments may have been made not by the juveniles themselves, but by the juveniles' parents, particularly parents in more stable and affluent families. Moreover, the juveniles' attempts at compliance, rather than actual reductions in juveniles' criminal behavior, may have been what led judges to be less likely to revoke sentences (Greenwald et al., 2014). A second problem with generalizing from studies of juveniles to the adult system is that the juvenile justice system is more oriented toward treatment and rehabilitation, and thus, programs aimed at restoring justice to victims are probably a better fit there (Lipsey, 2009).

In Study 8 (the four-county study of restitution in which the counties varied in terms of population size and whether or not the county had a specialized collections unit), we found that the greater the proportion of restitution paid, the lower the likelihood of a new arrest, an effect that was not present for the payment of fines or costs. The absence of a finding supporting an effect of payment of fines on rearrest suggests that there is something distinct about restitution orders that affects rearrest.

In Study 9 (Allegheny County), we found that restitution payment was negatively related to rearrest, controlling for time at risk, and this effect was especially strong among married persons and somewhat stronger among employed and older individuals, consistent with Braithwaite's (1989) notion that marriage, employment, and age are indicators of integration. Thus, this study suggested that restitution was particularly effective for individuals who were better integrated into the community. The payment of fines was not significantly related to rearrest, implying that the salutary effect was due to the payment only of restitution.

Across these three correlational studies, which combined imposition, payment, and recidivism data, we found that individuals who paid a higher percentage of their ordered restitution were less likely to commit a new crime. Obviously, however, the causality could work the other way. That is, individuals who did not commit a new crime were more likely to pay more of their ordered restitution because they had more time and perhaps money from employment to make those payments. Or, some third factor, like individual change, might have led offenders both to be more likely to pay the restitution and be less likely to commit a new crime. To test these possible causal explanations for whether paying restitution leads to less recidivism, we added recidivism information to the data from the experiment we conducted earlier (Study 13).

Study 15: Recidivism Follow-up of Offenders Involved in the Field Experiment

Ruback, Knoth, Gladfelter, and Lantz (2018)

This follow-up of the individuals who had participated in the earlier experiment (Study 13) had three purposes. First, Lauren Knoth, Andrew Gladfelter, Brendan Lantz, and I wanted to replicate our and others' findings from correlational studies that paying restitution is significantly related to lower recidivism. Second, we tested whether the experimental intervention regarding information about restitution paid and still owed was related to lower recidivism. Third, we tested for the time order of effects in order to get at the question of spurious causation, which might account for the relationship between payment and lower recidivism found in prior studies. Our goal was to determine whether or not increasing the number of economic sanctions payments and the proportion of economic sanctions paid precedes recidivism and mediates the relationship between experimental condition and recidivism (Ruback et al., 2018). If it does, then we could be more confident that nonpayment has a causal relationship to recidivism. If it does not, then it is likely that some third variable leads to both the payment of economic sanctions and lower recidivism.

The data for the study came from the experiment (Study 13), from which we had data from 771 probationers who had been randomly assigned to one of four conditions and data from the Pennsylvania State Police regarding arrests after the experiment. The State Police data included information on each arrest of an individual for which there was a charged offense, regardless of whether the charge resulted in a conviction. We created a 685-day follow-up period for each individual in the sample, which, because it was equal for all offenders, meant that there was no need for additional statistical controls for different exposure times (Shadish, Cook, & Campbell, 2002). Recidivism was measured as an arrest for a new crime.

We merged recidivism data from the State Police using four identifiers: name, date of birth, State Identification Number, and Offense Tracking Number. Once the files were merged, we removed these identifiers. The final sample size was 712 individuals (539 men; 171 women) who had an average age of 34.1 years. More than half of the sample had been convicted of a property offense, and on average they had 4.35 arrests prior to their conviction offense. Most ($n = 43$) of the 59 cases that were dropped did not have matching State Police files; the remainder were excluded because they had been incarcerated at the beginning of the experiment (unknown to the experimenters), because they involved amounts of restitution that were outliers, or because the amount owed in restitution had later been reduced by the judge to zero. There were no significant differences in attrition among the four experimental conditions in terms of gender, age, conviction crime, prior arrests, or amounts owed for restitution, fees, or fines.

Of the 712 individuals, 159 were arrested for a new crime. Recidivists were more likely to be male and younger and to owe more total fees. Those who paid some of their economic sanctions, compared with those who paid nothing, owed significantly more fines, fees, and restitution; had a significantly higher income; were significantly more likely to be female; and were significantly more likely to be white. Individuals who were not rearrested were more likely to have paid something toward their restitution and more likely to have made more monthly payments toward economic sanctions.

To test whether these bivariate relations showing that paying restitution was causally related to lower recidivism, we conducted multivariate analyses in which we controlled for the experimental condition in which individual offenders had randomly been assigned. We found that offenders in the Information Only experimental condition (i.e., those who were told how much they had paid and how much they still owed) were significantly less likely to be rearrested. Given this finding, we conducted mediation analyses, which tested whether this link between being in the Information Only experimental condition and lower recidivism could be explained by the prior finding that individuals in the Information Only condition were significantly more likely to pay their economic sanctions.

We used a method for testing the mediation effect of payment in nested, nonlinear models. Our interest was in testing two aspects of payment—the frequency of payments and the size of payments—to determine whether either or both mediate the relationship between the manipulation of information and subsequent recidivism. We expected that the number of monthly payments would be more important than the amount of the payments because we believed that the repeated act of making payments toward economic sanctions would be more likely to lead offenders to resolve potential dissonance and internalize the attitude change, leading to changes from the behaviors that lead to a new crime.

We focused on the Information Only condition as this was the only experimental condition that was significantly related to recidivism in the multivariate analyses. The experimental condition had an independent effect on recidivism, and this condition also significantly increased the frequency and amount of payments. Almost all of the mediation effect (83%) was the result of the frequency of payments (the number of months paid).

In addition to analyzing whether offenders were rearrested, we also looked at time to failure. First, we looked only at the 159 individuals who were rearrested. The effect of the two experimental manipulations (Information and Rationale) was not significant. Second, we looked at the entire sample of 712 individuals, using 685 days (the time when we collected the recidivism data) for the 553 individuals who did not recidivate. An analysis of the means (M) for the four conditions in the experiment found a significant effect: the Information Only condition (M = 626.3 days) was significantly longer than the Both Information and Rationale condition (M = 570.6 days) and the Control condition (M = 578.8 days). The Rationale Only condition (M = 591.0 days) was not significantly different from the other three conditions.

These findings very likely underestimate the effects of the Information Only condition in that this condition had the fewest individuals who recidivated. Thus, the time to failure used in this analysis (685 days) understates time to failure since most individuals did not fail (i.e., were not rearrested) in our time period and would have been unlikely to fail had we used a longer time period.

In addition to these analyses using rearrest records, we also merged the responses from those individuals who completed the survey (Study 14) with their recidivism data. The only significant effect we found was that offenders who indicated greater agreement with the statement that their "own feelings about what is right and wrong usually agree with the law" were less likely to recidivate. This one data point is limited, however, because only a small percentage of all participants in the experiment completed the survey, the question was asked more than a year after the experiment had ended, and this measure of Moral Alignment was not affected by the experimental manipulation.

Cost-Benefit Analyses

Among the 159 individuals who were rearrested, the difference in time to failure between the Information Only condition (M = 328.3 days) and the other three conditions (M = 248.7 days) was 79.6 days. At a cost of $64.19 per day for jail in Pennsylvania, the savings on average could be as much as $2,978.42 per offender (based on figures from a VERA Institute study; Henrichson et al., 2015). Prison costs would be higher because of the higher expenses for security, medical and mental health care, and treatment. Moreover, it is important to consider "trips through the criminal justice system," which involve police, prosecution, court, and community supervision costs, in addition to incarceration costs (Washington State Institute for Public Policy, 2017). There are also costs to victims of these crimes (Cohen, 2005).

Balanced against these possible benefits are the costs of monitoring and enforcing restitution orders, which an estimate in 2009 put at $2,000 (Dickman, 2009). For offenders who do not have incomes, there would be costs to finding probationers jobs or providing community service in lieu of jobs (Greenwald et al., 2014). It should be noted that the costs of the experiment were minimal (about $20 per person), independent of the restitution follow-up.

Conclusions

This follow-up analysis of the experimental study overcomes the problems of correlational data, confounded variables, and uncertain time order that characterize prior research on the link between paying restitution and lower recidivism. In our study, the payment of economic sanctions, all of which went to restitution for 94% of the sample but some of which went to fees for 6% of the sample (in contravention of county policy), reduced recidivism, consistent with the idea that paying economic sanctions could decrease crime. However, the fact that offenders who faced higher fees were more likely to be rearrested for a new crime is consistent with the idea that paying economic sanctions could increase crime (Harris, 2016).

Explanation for the Finding

The technique we used in our experimental study is consistent with research on other behavior-change topics on how to induce people to change their behavior. Cialdini (2001) argued for four aspects of commitment to achieve long-term behavioral change. To create initial behavior change, Cialdini suggested that there needs to be an active commitment (e.g., a signature on an official form), the commitment needs to be public, and the commitment needs to require effort. If these conditions are met, then the fourth aspect comes into play: it is difficult for the actor to deny having made the commitment. If the behavior is performed and is perceived by the actor to be voluntary, then the behavior is likely to lead to a change in internal motivation.

These techniques have also proved useful in studies designed to encourage citizens to act in ways that are more friendly to the environment (Lokhorst et al., 2013). In their meta-analytic review of studies in which the effect of experimental interventions to create more pro-environmental behaviors was evaluated, Lokhorst et al. found evidence that programs that made the aimed-for behavior salient by reminding individuals of their commitment and telling them how well they are doing were effective.

More generally, the manipulation used in our field-experimental study is similar to work in behavioral economics in which "nudges" (Thaler and Sunstein, 2008) have been used to increase low-income high school graduates' enrollment in college, military service members' participation in the federal employees' savings plan, and noncustodial parents' payments of child support (Porter, 2016). For those programs, however, poverty places a true limit on what the targets of these nudges can do. In the case of owing economic sanctions, nudges will not be effective if probationers do not have the funds to pay anything (Gladfelter et al., 2018).

Despite the advantages of field-experimental research, there is still the possibility that factors we could not control for (such as employment or family stability/support) were important reasons for our results. Future research should look for ways to test how income and assets affect offenders' ability and willingness to make restitution payments.

I need to note that our findings are modest. That is, even though the Information Only condition led to more payments, the average number of payments was small (M = 1.79; Median [Mdn] = 1.00) and only 29% of the participants made more than two payments. We also need to test explicitly the mediating mechanisms that we assumed were operating. That is, we need to make sure that the probationers who made payments really understood that their payments went to restitution and not to fines or fees. We also need to determine the extent to which probationers felt responsible for causing and correcting the harm. These presumed mediational processes need to be assessed while probationers are making these payments. Along this line, it would also be important to test how a broader view of reparation than monetary restitution, which includes apologies and community service (Walsh, 2014), might facilitate the effects of paying restitution.

Mental Accounting

The most important point to note about this research is that paying restitution was effective in reducing recidivism because the economic sanction was restitution, not fines and not fees. That is, it is important to emphasize that the obligation is to the victim, not the government.

This separation can be thought of as a form of mental accounting. Ariely and Kreisler (2017, p. 42) argue that we tend to mentally compartmentalize the money we spend. That is, rather than seeing money as completely fungible (see Chapter 1), we tend to put money in categories (e.g., rent, food) and account for money within these budget categories. Thus, if we spend the budgeted money only for food and not for entertainment, essentially we are saying that the money is not fungible.

In terms of economic sanctions, some of this mental accounting may be undermining the effectiveness of particular categories. In many jurisdictions, probation offices will initially list all of the different sanctions imposed on offenders. However, in terms of payment, the offenders will simply make a payment, and, hidden to them, there will be a computer algorithm that allocates the paid amount to the different types of sanctions. Thus, from the offender's perspective, there is only a single category of economic sanctions, not the different types of economic sanctions originally imposed on him or her.

If, as is suggested by our field experiment on restitution, restitution is a different type of economic sanction, putting it together with fines and fees/costs, although possibly easy to administer, may undermine the rehabilitative impact of paying restitution. Moreover, it may be that lumping fees (which are generally seen as unfair) with restitution (which is seen as more fair) generates resentment for all of the economic sanctions.

Thaler's (1985) research indicates that people keep different mental accounts. His research shows that people are happier if they have two gains, one for $50 and one for $25, than if they have a single gain of $75, even though the total amount of gain is the same. By the same token, three losses are seen as producing more negative value than a single loss, even though the total amount of the loss is the same. Given this mental accounting, the impact of the numerous fees and costs governments impose at sentencing, although ordered no doubt to fully inform offenders of their punishment, actually may lead to further negative emotions.

One of the ways to make mental accounting easier is to have decisions made automatically, as, for example, when individual retirement account (IRA) savings are automatically deducted from a paycheck. With regard to economic sanctions, one could ask whether these payments should be automatically deducted from offenders' accounts, or should we make offenders pay themselves? Based on Thaler's research, offenders would adapt to the fact that they do not have the money. But that may not always be the best idea. In the case of restitution, it might be best to make offenders pay restitution consciously rather than automatically, so that they would be more aware of the harm they caused, the amount they owe, and their effort to correct the harm.

Summary

This chapter reviewed the research, from both adults and juveniles, that shows fairly consistently that paying restitution is associated with lower subsequent criminal behavior. Because Study 13 was an experiment, we could test whether payment was related to lower recidivism and could eliminate alternative explanations for our finding, consistent with that prior research, that payment is related to less criminal behavior. Because of the experiment, the results suggest that the relationship may be causally related.

7

Research Summary and Implications

As described in Chapters 1 and 3, our research program was designed as a multilevel, multimethod investigation of the imposition, payment, and effects of payment of economic sanctions in Pennsylvania. The rationale for the multimethod approach is to look for convergent findings across methods because such convergence provides evidence for the validity of conclusions. In this chapter, I summarize the findings across the 15 studies about which we can be most confident and suggest how these findings can be used to address policy questions. I also present a few specific policy questions that were not addressed in the research. In Chapter 8, I look at larger policy issues that go beyond the research we conducted in Pennsylvania.

Convergent Findings Across Studies

This summary of convergent findings is organized into three larger topics: (1) economic sanctions in general, (2) offenders and their experiences with economic sanctions, and (3) the imposition and effects of paying restitution. Under each of these topics, I present the convergent findings across studies and then suggest what implications the findings have for policy.

Economic Sanctions in General

There are two consistent findings regarding economic sanctions in Pennsylvania. The first relates to the large number of economic sanctions imposed in Pennsylvania and the variation between counties in the number imposed. The second relates to the payment of economic sanctions.

Economic Sanctions in Criminal Justice. R. Barry Ruback, Oxford University Press. © Oxford University Press 2022.
DOI: 10.1093/oso/9780190682583.003.0007

A Large Number of Economic Sanctions Can Be Imposed on Defendants and the Actual Number Imposed Varies Greatly Across Counties

The one clear finding from all of our studies was that any one defendant is likely to have several different economic sanctions imposed at sentencing. Most of these economic sanctions are fees and costs that are payable to reimburse local and state governments for expenses related to the administration of the criminal justice system.

In 2006, we noted that there were 36 different county fees and costs that could be imposed in addition to state-mandated fees and costs (Ruback & Bergstrom, 2006). Of these 36 county costs/fees, 5 were authorized in only one county, and 1 (monthly supervision fee) was authorized in 64 counties.

Five years later, in Study 1, we examined the actual implementation of the different types of economic sanctions. We found there were 2,629 different types of economic sanctions across the 67 counties in Pennsylvania: 82 costs/fees imposed by the state, 58 state fines, 2,371 county costs/fees, 79 county fines, and 35 related to restitution. On average, the total assessments of all costs/fees and fines per person was $819, of which $575 was for costs/fees and $243 was for fines.

As is clear, the variation between counties in terms of the number of economic sanctions imposed on offenders was due virtually completely to the different number of fees imposed by the different counties, and essentially the system as it presently stands awards counties that are more creative in initiating new costs/fees. Costs/fees that are unique to a county raise a question of unfairness if the burden of paying for the costs of criminal justice is shifted to offenders only if the county believes that offenders should pay what taxpayers in those counties consider to be user fees. It would be difficult to argue that offenders who live in certain counties should have to pay higher costs/fees merely because of where they live, not because of their actual offense.

The number of uniquely different sanctions used in any one county varied from 40 to 147, with an average of 81 and a median of 75. The average number of sanctions used per case also varied significantly between counties, from a low of 15 to a high of 200, with a mean of 42.5 and a median of 34. Counties that had more different types of economic sanctions were also likely to have more economic sanctions imposed for each case.

Across counties, and even within counties, there is a high level of variation in how economic sanctions are handled. In conversations with different staff members, we received different information about procedures and policies. As evident from our qualitative analyses in Study 2, there are clear differences among counties in terms of how economic sanctions are paid and tracked. Part of the reason offenders do not understand the economic sanctions they are expected to pay is that, in each of the counties, there are probably few individuals who know everything that needs to be known about economic sanctions. In our conversations with staff, we received multiple answers regarding what a certain economic sanction was (especially for many of the ones that were acronyms) and whether it was paid to the state, county, municipality, or private agency. The incomplete and conflicting information we received suggests that offenders who wanted to know what a payment was for would not be able to receive a correct answer.

Given the large number of fees and costs we found in Pennsylvania, it is reasonable to ask whether they are justified. Several scholars have called for the abolition of costs/fees for three reasons: (1) they lack a clear penological rationale; (2) they raise questions of fairness because they make sentences too severe, they reflect class bias, they reflect disparity, and they have a large impact on families; and (3) they are not cost effective (Harris et al., 2011). Bannon, Nagrecha, and Diller (2010) called for lawmakers to consider the total debt burden on offenders before adding new fees or increasing fee amounts and argued that indigent offenders should not have to pay these fees. According to Patel and Philip (2012), states should examine the costs and benefits of fees in the criminal justice system. Their analyses suggest that these fees impose costs on both individuals and society and that these fees do not raise enough revenue, and, in fact, often are costly. In Alameda County, California, one study found that the County spent more than $250,000 to collect about $420,000 (Valle & Carson, 2016, cited in Martin et al., 2018).

From our follow-up recidivism study (Study 15), there was evidence that individuals who faced higher fees were more likely to be rearrested for a new crime. The negative effects of fees may be the result of the financial and collateral consequences of the additional debt and because offenders believe these costs are unfair (Study 12; also see later discussion). In addition, payments for fees probably do not have the rehabilitative potential that restitution payments have because they lack the assumption underlying restitution: that payment requires a recognition of both the harm caused and the need to restore justice to the victim. In Chapter 8, I argue for the elimination of costs/fees.

Payment of Economic Sanctions Was Higher in Counties Where It Was Supervised by Probation Officers Rather Than Specialized Collections Units

Our research indicates that offenders are likely to make greater payments if probation officers rather than collection agents monitor and enforce the payment. Although some have argued that it is not appropriate for probation officers to set up payment plans, monitor payments, and punish those who do not pay (Patel & Philip, 2012), our research suggests it is better that probation officers handle these duties.

From Study 4 and Study 8, we found that more restitution was collected when probation officers have this and other supervision responsibilities, rather than when there is a specialized collections office. In fact, in Study 8, we found that specialized collections units did not collect higher proportions of ordered fines, although there was some evidence that they did, marginally, collect higher proportions of ordered fees and costs. This finding suggests that specialized units are better at collecting funds that enable them to be self-supporting rather than economic sanctions that serve other purposes. Our results about specialized collections units suggest that, if restitution is to have the positive results on offenders that our Studies 13 and 15 suggest occur when restitution is paid, probation officers should supervise both general probation conditions and the collection of economic sanctions.

Thus, our results suggest that relying on specialized collections units to collect economic sanctions are not as effective as relying on probation officers. A long line of research indicates that communication increases cooperation, trust, and trustworthiness (Charness & Dufwenberg, 2006; Kerr & Kaufman-Gilliland, 1994; Sally, 1995). One reason that probation officers handling restitution payments seems to be more effective than credit agencies may be that offenders can communicate with the monitoring person. Communication leads to trust, and trust increases the likelihood that a promise will be kept. Our finding that probation officers were more effective than collections agents in eliciting payment is consistent with research showing that probation officers are likely to be able to make the best use of incentives and sanctions because they know the offenders (McLean & Thompson, 2007, p. 36). In Chapter 8, I argue on other grounds that special collections units are inappropriate.

Brett, Khoshkhoo, and Nagrecha (2020) have argued that probation officers should not monitor or enforce the payment of economic sanctions because they can impose significant consequences on offenders (e.g., electronic monitoring, periods of incarceration, drug testing) without meeting due process requirements. Based on their multistate analysis of statutes and interviews with judges, probation officers, and defense attorneys, Brett et al. concluded that many probation offices either have no policies for imposing sanctions for failing to follow probation guidelines or have polices that are not binding and thus, as a result, probation officers have a great deal of control over probationers' lives, particularly the quality and quantity of time on probation.

The issue of whether economic sanctions should be monitored by probation officers or by someone else goes directly to the question of the confusion of roles, being a counselor or a police officer. As I noted in Chapter 2, probation officers generally believe that collecting fees takes too much time and infringes on their ability to do what they consider to be more important duties (Morgan, 1995). One clear rule is that probation officers should not be collecting fees since their interest and the interest of a probation office that relies on the collected funds for support conflicts directly with those of the probationers. For restitution, however, there may be less conflict, and perhaps even a convergence of interest, if probation officers oversee the payment of restitution.

Offenders

The two consistent findings regarding offenders relate to their understanding of economic sanctions and their perceptions of the fairness of economic sanctions.

Offenders Have Little Understanding of Economic Sanctions

Our survey of offenders (Study 12) indicated that they had little understanding (a) of how the economic sanctions they were ordered to pay were set and (b) of where their payments were directed. They also seemed to have little understanding of how much they owed in total. One of the assumptions of rational sentencing is that the goals of sentencing—punishment, deterrence, rehabilitation—can be accomplished only if offenders understand the sanctions imposed on them.

One rationale behind some economic sanctions is that offenders understand that the money they are paying is going for a specific purpose. In the case of restitution, the economic sanction for which understanding is assumed to be most important, offenders learn that they have caused specific harm to a specific victim and that their monthly payments are directed at restoring the victim to his or her pre-crime state. Economic sanctions whose purpose is punishment (e.g., fines) also assume that offenders understand the underlying purpose. Despite the implicit assumption that offenders understand the economic sanctions, our survey of offenders indicated that they had little understanding (a) of how the economic sanctions they were ordered to pay were set and (b) of where their payments were directed. They also seemed to have little understanding of how much they owed in total.

As noted earlier in connection with the large number of different types of economic sanctions imposed in Pennsylvania, no one we interacted with—probation officers, judges, clerks—understood all of the different types of sanctions, with some suggesting that they relied on computer programs to determine how payments were to be distributed.

Understanding could be increased if offenders were reminded of what they owe for each type of economic sanction. It might be helpful if each county had a list explaining all of the possible economic sanctions that could be imposed, as well as a clear description of the policies and procedures operating in the county. However, because there are so many different types of economic sanctions, a full list may well be more confusing than helpful.

Centralized Information

Part of offenders' lack of understanding relates to how much they owe, an issue addressed by the Model Penal Code: Sentencing and recent court cases. The Model Penal Code: Sentencing suggests that there needs to be a centralized agency concerned with collections in order to ensure that the rules for collection are followed (p. 186).

States do not have centralized datasets containing information about whether and what offenders owe in terms of fees, fines, and restitution. Thus, the only place to find it is in the records of county clerks of court. Martin and Spencer-Suarez (2017, p. 11) suggested that the state should be obligated "to track all outstanding debt, [so that] debtors could more easily understand and manage their CJFO [criminal justice financial obligations] debt." Moreover, as events in Florida in 2020 showed (Campos-Flores & Kamp, 2020), without such a centralized agency, offenders cannot know what they owe.

This issue arose after Florida passed a constitutional amendment in 2018 overturning a 150-year-old law and restoring voting rights to individuals with felony convictions. In 2019, Florida passed a law requiring, before voting rights are restored, that felons pay all fines, fees, and restitution they owe (see Cammett, 2012). Because Florida did not have centralized records for these economic sanctions, that requirement meant that these ex-offenders would have to go to counties whose records may not include decades-old documents relating to the economic sanctions (Campo-Flores & Kemp, 2020).

In the case of *Gruver v. Barton* (subsequently consolidated with other cases as *Jones v. DeSantis*, 2020) Daniel Smith, a professor of political science who served as an expert in the case, analyzed data from 48 counties concerning offenders with a felony conviction who were released from Florida Department of Corrections supervision from 1997 to 2019.

Smith (2019, p. 5) stated that in those 48 Florida counties he analyzed, 66,108 (17.6%) of 375,256 offenders with felony convictions completed payment of their legal financial obligations, leaving 309,148 individuals (82.4%) who did not complete payment . Florida does not have a "publicly available unified, up-to-date, centralized database or repository that reports those persons with a felony conviction who . . . might be permitted to obtain their voting rights in the state."

In May 2020, a federal judge held in *Jones v. DeSantis* that the Florida law requiring convicted offenders to pay all court fines and fees before they can register to vote is unconstitutional because it violates the 24th Amendment, which prohibits the denial of the vote "by reason of failure to pay poll tax or other tax" (Mazzei, 2020). The judge held that these economic sanctions, regardless of how they are labeled, cannot be used as a condition of voting if the person is unable to pay them.

The judge was also concerned about the state's failure to establish a process by which felons could determine what they owe (Breslow, 2020), a problem found in the absence of a centralized database.

According to the decision, between 2013 and 2018, courts in Florida imposed fines and fees of more than $1 billion but did not expect 80% of that amount to be paid. The judge concluded that, because there are no centralized records, it is virtually impossible to determine what a person owes.

By Florida's own estimates, it will take nearly 6 years to determine who owes what. None of this accounts for all the additional expenses associated with paying court debts. Want a copy of your original judgment of conviction? It will cost you. Maybe you'd prefer to pay your fees directly? Watch out for the 4 percent surcharge. How about setting up a payment plan? That'll be $25—better, at least, than being sent to a collection agency, which will skim 40 percent of your payment off the top. Florida has, in short, "shown a staggering inability to administer the pay-to-vote system," Judge Hinkle wrote. He noted that he gave lawmakers ample warning and opportunity to fix the problems in a preliminary ruling last fall, and yet they have done essentially nothing." (New York Times, Editorial Board, 2020)

In September 2020, an appellate court reversed the district court decision allowing ex-felons to vote. The appellate court held that all legal financial obligations, including fines and restitution, would have to be paid before an ex-felon would be eligible to vote (*Jones v. Governor of Florida*, 2020, https://www.scotusblog.com/wp-content/uploads/2020/09/9-11-20-Jones-v-Florida-11th-Opinion.pdf). As a result of this decision, about 800,000 ex-felons were disqualified, including about 69% of ex-felons who had registered to vote but were not able to do so (Jones & Kamp, 2020).

Regarding the same issue in Iowa, the governor restored voting rights to most felons who had completed their sentences, but without requiring full payment of fines, fees, or restitution (Reynolds, 2020).

Offenders Generally Think the System Regarding Economic Sanctions Is Unfair

Study 12 indicated that offenders do not understand how economic sanctions are imposed, how much they owe, or where the money goes. Although offenders rated the fairness of restitution only at the middle of a 7-point scale, this was significantly greater than the judged fairness of fines and fees. Beyond the fairness of economic sanctions per se, our research suggests that individuals, both victims and offenders, are more satisfied with the criminal justice system if they believe that police and probation officers listen to their ideas and opinions (Study 14). Offenders who believe that they have been treated fairly by their probation officer also pay more restitution. In our experiment, we found that probationers who said they received more fair treatment by their probation officers were likely to pay more (Study 14). One reason why probation officers get more economic sanctions paid than do collection agents (Study 8) may be that they treat probationers with more procedural justice.

Restitution

With regard to restitution, our research revealed five consistent findings.

Most Victims Do Not Receive the Restitution They Are Owed

All studies of restitution indicate that only a small proportion of victims receive all of the restitution that is ordered. Like that prior research, we found in several studies that most victims do not receive what they are owed. That conclusion was found in Study 11 (the survey of victims) and in all of our studies investigating restitution payment (Studies 2, 3, 8, 10, and 13).

Few studies have investigated, as we did, the imposition of restitution. Victim organizations had argued for years that restitution was not always imposed when it should have been. In our statewide studies (Studies 1 and 4), multi-county study (Study 8), and single-county study (Study 10), we found that restitution was not imposed when it should have been.

One implication of this consistent finding in our research and in others' research is that the state needs to seriously consider covering the costs of restitution for those victims who do not receive recovery from the offender or third parties. This societal duty to restore the victim may arise through society's responsibility because it may have contributed to the offender committing the crime (Minow, 2019), because society is responsible for not protecting the victim, and because of a general obligation to provide for the social welfare of citizens. Expanding restitution may be difficult because offenders have a limited ability to pay. However, expanding state compensation may be possible because some states have a surplus of these funds (Newmark & Schaffer, 2003). Moreover, because crime victims tend to be disproportionately poor, the societal welfare function of victim compensation may be especially important.

A Statutory Change Making Restitution Mandatory Can Change Judges' Behavior

The 1995 Pennsylvania statute mandating the imposition of restitution significantly increased the rate at which restitution was imposed from 38.5% of the restitution-eligible cases before the statute to 63.5% of the cases after the statute. In Study 5, we found that the imposition of restitution was generally supported by judges, prosecutors, and probation officers.

More generally, our research suggests that changes in the law are likely to be implemented, and changes can be identified if the law is clearly written, the dependent measure can be assessed in the same way both before and after the change in the law, and the decision-makers whose decisions are affected (judges in our case) agree with the law.

Two Contextual Factors Affected Imposition of Restitution: Location of the Victim-Witness Assistance Office and Nature of the Courtroom Community

Our research suggests that restitution is more likely to be ordered if the relevant information (the amount and proof of loss) can easily be transmitted to the decision-maker. In the case of restitution for victims, this information is more likely to reach the district attorney—and therefore the judge—if the victim and witness assistance office is in the same building as the district attorney and the judge. In Pennsylvania, this meant that restitution was more likely to be ordered if the victim and witness assistance office was located in the courthouse.

Both Study 5 (the survey of judges) and Study 6 (the statewide analysis of the imposition of restitution using county-level and court-level contextual factors) found that judges rely heavily on victims to provide information about losses. Thus, one policy suggestion is to reduce the administrative inconvenience that might deter victims from seeking an order of restitution.

Our results suggest two reasons why housing victim and witness advocacy offices within the judiciary may be an effective organizational structure for delivering victim services. First, in addition to reducing victims' burden of traveling to multiple locations, this arrangement places victim and witness advocates at the heart of the court community, consistent with the recommendations of the Office for Victims of Crime (1998) regarding the role of the judiciary in facilitating victims' rights. Second, housing victim and witness advocacy offices within the judiciary may help to reduce judges' concern about offenders' ability to pay restitution by increasing their awareness of victims' losses. Such a move also emphasizes the importance of victims to the operation of the criminal justice system.

Communicating with and informing victims and courts is likely to be facilitated by placing victim and witness services within courthouses and better integrating those services within prosecutors' and probation offices (Ruback & Shaffer, 2005).

The Amount of Restitution Paid Can Be Increased If Delinquent Offenders Receive Information from the Probation Office About How Much Has Been Paid and How Much Is Still Owed

Our experimental research indicated that offenders were more likely to pay, pay more often, and pay more money toward the court-ordered restitution they owed if they received letters indicating how much money they had paid and how much they still owed. Although this was only one study, we can have some confidence in the results because participants were randomly assigned to condition.

There is still a question about generalizability, however, in that the county where the experiment was conducted (a largely white county in central

Pennsylvania) is different in several ways from the metropolitan areas where most people in the United States live.

Offenders Who Pay More Restitution, Especially Those Who Have Made More Restitution Payments, Are Significantly Less Likely to Be Arrested for a New Crime

This conclusion represents a strong example of convergent results across methodologies, samples, and statistical analytic techniques. From the several correlational studies of juvenile and adult cases by other researchers, from our three correlational studies of juvenile and adult cases, and from our follow-up of our experimental cohort (Study 15), the findings strongly suggest that paying restitution has beneficial effects and that these beneficial effects are unique to restitution. This finding suggests that judges and probation officers should be especially concerned with monitoring and collecting offenders' restitution payments.

This convergent finding has implications for decreasing offender recidivism. Moreover, this conclusion is consistent with the Model Penal Code: Sentencing's suggestion that the community needs to be involved in reintegrating the offender into society.

Specific Questions Not Addressed in the Research

Although our research touched on several important policy-related issues, there are questions that we did not investigate. One of these questions relates to the tradeoffs necessitated by imposing economic sanctions on offenders with limited incomes and assets (i.e., on most offenders).

Tradeoffs

Imposing fines and fees and costs means that restitution is less likely to be paid. Our studies in Pennsylvania, using both state-level data (Study 1) and data from four counties (Study 8), suggest that the imposition of restitution is negatively related to the imposition of fines. Similarly, in a study of economic sanctions in Philadelphia, we found that the imposition of fines was negatively related to the imposition of restitution (Study 10).

On the other hand, there could be a positive relationship between economic sanctions, a pattern suggesting that judges might believe that if offenders can pay one type of sanction, they can pay them all. In four counties in Pennsylvania, we found that the imposition of costs was positively related to the imposition of fines (Study 8). In their analysis of probation fees in Illinois, Olson and Ramker (2001) found, consistent with the negative relationship hypothesis, that probationers ordered to pay both fines and probation fees had lower average monthly fees than probationers ordered to pay only fees.

However, they also found, consistent with the positive relationship hypothesis, that probation fees were more likely to be imposed and more likely to be paid if fines were also imposed.

There is only limited research on the payment of economic sanctions, given offenders' generally inadequate ability to pay all of the sanctions imposed. However, it is obvious that there is a zero-sum issue about how offenders paying toward some sanctions likely means they are not paying toward others. Moreover, aside from this issue of tradeoffs between types of economic sanctions, there are also questions about tradeoffs between cases and between victims.

Multiple Cases and Victims

A second policy question not investigated in our research, but which became apparent in several studies, relates to the imposition and payment of restitution when an offender has multiple judicial proceedings across time, each proceeding having multiple crimes, and each crime having multiple victims. The difficult issue for a judge or for a probation officer hearing complaints from victims is to determine which proceeding, which crime, and which victim should have precedence.

For example, how should restitution payments for victims of three different crimes be prioritized? Possible options include (1) payment in terms of chronological order (i.e., the oldest first), (2) payment in reverse chronological order (i.e., the newest first, in the assumption that earlier victims have already coped with the loss), (3) the largest restitution amount first, (4) the most severely injured victim first (which will probably overlap with item 3), (5) the most proactive victim first, and (6) the victim who needs it the most first. There is no simple and no one correct answer.

Another problem arises from plea bargaining. In some states, victims can be "read-in" to a plea agreement, whereas in other states victims can be included in a restitution order only if the defendant pleads guilty to the specific offense involving those particular victims. In states with that rule, the result of the plea bargaining is that some cases (and victims) disappear when they are dropped as part of the deal, meaning that these victims will not receive restitution because there is no conviction. Although it might be beneficial to drop a charge but keep the restitution owed, in practice and probably, in law, if a charge is dropped, victims will not receive restitution.

Problem of Priorities

Economic sanctions can be difficult to apply because judges often do not have accurate information about offenders' ability to pay. Relatedly, because offenders generally cannot pay all that they owe, the imposition of economic sanctions calls for policy judgments about which type of economic sanction should be given precedence. The next section examines principles that can serve as the basis for making these policy judgments.

Prioritize the Financial Obligations

The use of multiple monetary sanctions has implications in terms of priority of payment (Olson & Ramker, 2001), both across types of economic sanctions and within any one type of sanction. With multiple types of monetary sanctions, it is unclear how monthly payments should be split among fines, fees, and restitution. Much of the objection to the current system of economic sanctions is that there are often no clear priorities for the collection of legal financial obligations (McLean & Thompson, 2007). In particular, local and state governments often get paid before others. In answer to this trend, Levingston and Turetsky (2007) suggested that child support and victim restitution should take precedence over fines, fees, and surcharges. It would also be useful to have groups that collect legal financial obligations share information, so that all of the agencies and courts to which the offender owes money are aware of the total amounts of money that are owed and the payment schedules that have been imposed (McLean & Thompson, 2007).

Guidelines might be helpful for handling such cases or the issue could be handled with a single payment plan across cases (Pennsylvania Office of the Victim Advocate, 2013). But, at the very least, a list of all of the victims and the amounts owed to them should be made known to the sentencing court.

Summary

This chapter summarized our consistent findings about restitution in Pennsylvania across studies and suggested implications for policy in Pennsylvania. The Next Chapter looks at broader implications of research on economic sanctions and makes suggestions for economic sanctions more generally.

8

Policy Implications

The first seven chapters of this book described research and policy on the imposition, payment, and effect of economic sanctions. The focus was on the research we conducted in Pennsylvania, primarily on restitution, but also on fines and fees. In this chapter I look more broadly at the benefits and costs of restitution, fines, and fees. Next, I present four policy suggestions—making restitution mandatory, imposing fines based on the offender's ability to pay, eliminating fees and costs, and societal compensation to crime victims—with some discussion about issues affecting how these ideas can be implemented. Then, because these suggestions are unlikely to be adopted, I present two ideas that have a greater chance of being adopted. Finally, I return to the question I raised in Chapter 1 about justice and economic sanctions.

A Framework for Thinking About Economic Sanctions

The use of economic sanctions should be governed by three principles: (1) concern for victims, (2) concern for offenders, and (3) concern for society. Victims are innocent sufferers who face both tangible and intangible losses. Offenders convicted of crimes face many challenges, particularly if they are incarcerated as part of their sentence. The imposition of economic sanctions can be burdensome and may make it more difficult for offenders to avoid recidivism, especially when offenders have other expenses (e.g., child support, alimony, housing, food, transportation). Society's concerns with restoring victims and punishing offenders in a fair and proportionate manner also include acknowledging governmental responsibilities. Table 8.1 summarizes the positive and negative effects of the three types of economic sanctions—restitution, fines, and costs/fees—on victims, offenders, and society. This model first appeared in my 2015 article in the *Minnesota Law Review*.

Economic Sanctions in Criminal Justice. R. Barry Ruback, Oxford University Press. © Oxford University Press 2022.
DOI: 10.1093/oso/9780190682583.003.0008

Table 8.1 Type and effects (positive and negative) of economic sanctions

	Type of economic sanction		
	Restitution	Fines	Fees/Costs
Effects of the Economic Sanction on:			
Victims			
Positive	Compensation for losses Acknowledges the harm	–	–
Negative	–	Interferes with the payment of restitution	Interferes with the payment of restitution
Offenders			
Positive	Teaches responsibility Rehabilitative Punishment Deterrence	Deterrence Punishment Can be used as an intermediate punishment	Deterrence Punishment
Negative	Perceived as (somewhat) unfair	Perceived as unfair	Perceived as unfair Perpetuates poverty
Society			
Positive	Compensates the victim Promotes restorative justice	Funds can be used for general or specific purposes	Covers some of the costs of the criminal justice system
Negative	Interferes with the payment of fines and fees/costs	Interferes with the payment of restitution and fees/costs	Interferes with the payment of restitution and fines Transfers governmental duties to offenders

Restitution

Restitution is important because it provides a formal mechanism within the criminal justice system for compensating victims for the monetary losses they suffered. Court-imposed restitution also gives victims notice that society recognizes the harm they have suffered. In addition, it promotes restorative justice, by which offenders can be reintegrated into their communities. Restitution can make offenders recognize the harm they caused, can teach offenders responsibility by making them pay for that harm, and can serve as both a punishment and deterrent (McGillis, 1986). Although offenders perceive restitution as somewhat unfair, they still perceive it as more fair than other economic sanctions. Restoring the victim is only a half promise, since restitution is not always imposed; if imposed, is unlikely to be paid at all; and, if paid at all, is unlikely to be paid in full. If we are serious about restoring victims, we cannot expect it to be accomplished completely by imposing restitution on offenders.

Fines

For victims, fines have no benefits but do have costs in that monies directed at paying fines interfere with the payment of restitution. For offenders, fines can serve goals of deterrence and punishment, and they can be used as intermediate punishments. For society, fines can be used for general governmental purposes, or they can be directed to specific purposes, such as the victim compensation fund. From the viewpoint of society, money used to pay fines may be money that is not being directed to victim restitution or to fees and costs.

Fees

Fees are used to pay some of the costs of criminal justice as well as, in many jurisdictions, the costs of maintaining the system of economic sanctions. But, as outlined later, the costs of criminal justice are governmental duties that should be assumed by government. Perhaps the most egregious fee, because it involves a constitutional right, is when poor defendants are required to pay the costs of a defense attorney (Anderson, 2009). In their study in Texas, where 30% of the probation operating budgets come from supervision fees, Ruhland, Holmes, and Petkus (2020) found that higher fees were associated with probation revocation for both a new criminal offense and a technical violation. They suggested that individuals on supervision who were delinquent in paying their fees may have been revoked as a way of saving money.

Moreover, because courts and collection agencies often have a financial stake in the payment of fees, the imposition and administration of these sanctions may conflict with justice. Courts in Nevada have increasingly had to become self-funding; in fact, judges openly worried about the operation of their courts if criminal offending decreased (Martin, 2018). In addition, the payment of fees, which collection agencies generally put first, can interfere with the payment of restitution and fines. The Department of Justice has criticized policies that target the poor in order to maximize fee collection (Apuzzo, 2016). Scholars have generally been opposed to fees (Bannon et al.,

2010; Harris et al., 2011; Reitz, 2015; Ruback, 2015), and the Model Penal Code (MPC) has called for their abolition (American Law Institute, 2020).

For victims, fees and costs have no benefits, but do have costs in that monies directed at paying fines interfere with the payment of restitution, since payment of restitution orders typically follows other financial obligations (e.g., costs, fines; Office for Victims of Crime, 1998). For offenders, fees and costs can serve goals of deterrence and punishment. However, offenders often perceive fees and costs as unfair (Study 11). Fees and costs can also greatly interfere with an offender's ability to function in society, particularly when there are surcharges (e.g., interest) on amounts that remain unpaid (Beckett & Harris, 2011). For some offenders, the amounts of these fees and costs, especially continuing ones like supervision fees, are so high that they can never be paid off, which is the situation with the private probation companies in the South.

For society, fees and costs can cover some of the costs of the criminal justice system, but they transfer governmental duties to offenders. Moreover, because these fees and costs are likely to go primarily to criminal justice administrators in local jurisdictions, they interfere with the payment of restitution (meaning victims are less likely to receive compensation) and fines (meaning that the goals of punishment and deterrence may be undermined). In addition, fees and costs are the responsibility of government, and the MPC correctly notes that fees and costs for reimbursing the criminal justice system cause a conflict of interest in the courts and agencies that impose, collect, and use these monies (Reitz, 2015). Furthermore, fees and costs are of little or no benefit to society, although private corporations seem to profit from the arrangement.

This overview of the effects of the three different types of economic sanctions leads to four conclusions: (1) restitution should be mandatory, (2) judges should be able to impose fines based on the offender's ability to pay, (3) fees and costs should not be imposed, and (4) society should compensate victims.

Restitution Should Be Mandatory

Restitution should be mandatory because it is good for victims, good for offenders, and good for society, and the fact that restitution is not mandatory may reflect subtle victim blaming (Elias, 1986). The need to focus on victims is based on the fact that victims, not governments, bear the greatest costs of crime. Although it has been argued in the United Kingdom that reducing the costs of crime to victims is not a concern of the government (Sherman & Strang, 2012), the fact that victim restitution is authorized in every state, including 20 that include it in their state constitutions, suggests that the costs victims endure are of concern to state and local governments in the United States. Most of the economic losses victims suffer are not covered by insurance or, in the United States, recompensed by government. In the United

States, victim compensation covers only a fraction of crimes because victims are often unaware of the state funding, and, even if they were aware, there are so many qualifying conditions that most victims would not be entitled to receive any state funding. In other countries, victims' losses are covered by the state, which compensates the losses because of the violation of its duty to protect citizens or because of a social welfare rationale (Elias, 1984).

Restitution is qualitatively different from other types of economic sanctions in that the funds go to the victim rather than to a state agency. The amount of restitution awarded depends on the victim impact statement that the victim files with, depending on the jurisdiction, the victim and witness agency or the prosecutor (McGillis, 1986). Amounts are for documented losses (e.g., the value of vandalized property) and out-of-pocket expenses (e.g., medical costs) directly related to the crime (Office for Victims of Crime, 1998). Restitution is arguably good for offenders because it teaches them responsibility. And restitution is good for society because of the symbolic value attached to treating victims fairly and emphasizing the importance of restoring the victim to the status quo before the crime. Restitution should take precedence over fines, as is the case in Australia (O'Malley, 2011, p. 62) and as recommended by the MPC: Sentencing (MPCS).

In most jurisdictions, victims' requests for restitution can be part of a more general process of victim allocation at sentencing, in which the victim describes the impact of the crime. The primary purposes of victim participation in sentencing are to increase victim satisfaction with sentencing and criminal justice, make the determination of crime seriousness more accurate, and make both criminal justice professionals and the offender more aware of the actual effects of the crime (Roberts, 2009). Although victim participation may accomplish these goals, it has also been criticized because it could lead to inconsistent sentencing (e.g., because of differential participation by victims or differential persuasiveness of victims), to overly harsh sentences, and to a violation of the decorum of the courtroom (Roberts, 2009, 2012).

In contrast to victim allocation in general, restitution is a relatively straightforward process that involves less discretion on the part of the judge. Providing restitution to victims could be explicitly part of a more general process of restorative justice, by which there can be reconciliation between the offender and the victim, the victim's losses are restored, and the offender is returned to the community. In this way, restitution could play a role in promoting rehabilitation.

But even if restitution is not paid, there are important symbolic aspects to the imposition of restitution. In our survey of Pennsylvania judges, one judge wrote that, "Many judges in my county feel criminals are not capable of paying restitution. My experience has been they will pay if they face jail" (Study 5; Ruback & Shaffer, 2005). Even so, it was much more common for judges to indicate that they had no real expectation that the restitution would be paid. For example, another judge said, "This court expends significant resources, including regularly scheduled collection court proceedings, to collect limited amounts of ordered restitution due to low income levels and poverty. Nevertheless, even collection of small amounts reinforces the restorative nature of the judicial system and the need to reinforce accountability to offenders" (Study 5; Ruback & Shaffer, 2005). This recognition that much of the imposed restitution will not be paid suggests that a judge's purpose in ordering it is primarily symbolic. In general, our reading of the research on the imposition of restitution suggests that, absent a mandatory rule, restitution is not frequently ordered.

The primary reason not to consider the offender's ability to pay when setting the amount of economic sanctions is that a failure to impose the economic sanction means that the system considers the offender's (and the offender's family's) needs to be greater than those of the victim or society. Specifically with reference to restitution, not to impose the payment devalues the victim and victims generally, perhaps increasing the victim's psychological distress and making the victim less likely to cooperate with the criminal justice system in the future. These harms are especially great because crime victims tend to be disproportionately poor. Second, looking at the defendant's ability to pay gives the defendant the impression that he or she can get around the system. Third, the defendant may at some point gain the money to pay the restitution (e.g., through inheritance, winning the lottery, tax refund, or recovery in a lawsuit), and, unless the sanction was imposed, recovery is essentially impossible. There are also issues of hidden income, especially illegal income.

Thus, I have argued that the defendant's ability to pay should not be considered in the imposition of restitution because the imposition of the full amount has symbolic impact: the victim was harmed by this amount. This amount is a signal to the victim, the offender, and society at large.

Against my argument, the Supreme Judicial Court of Massachusetts ruled that the trial judge must consider the defendant's ability to pay before imposing restitution (*Commonwealth v. Henry*, 55 N.E.3d 943 (Mass. 2016)). The Court in *Henry* prohibited judges from setting restitution amounts that caused a substantial financial hardship. According to the Court, conditioning probation on paying restitution that the defendant did not have the ability to pay or extending probation so that the defendant could make more restitution payments amounted to punishing defendants for their poverty and therefore violated the Massachusetts standards that the judicial process for determining restitution must be "reasonable and fair" (*Commonwealth v. Nawn*, 474 N.E.2d 545, 550 (Mass. 1985)).

In *Nawn*, the Supreme Judicial Court held that the judge's consideration of the defendant's employment history, financial prospects, and ability to pay are the central distinction between civil damages and restitution after a criminal conviction (Rodrigues, 2018). In addition, Rodrigues suggested that the defendant's ability to pay restitution was implicit in accepting a plea bargain and in the payment schedule arranged by the probation officer.

Rodrigues (2018) argued that imposing a restitution order on a defendant who is unable to pay means that the defendant likely faces additional punishments: the risk of arrest, the possibility of jail, costs for the warrant, and possible probation revocation. In addition, these sanctions are likely to waste governmental resources because the defendant is unlikely to ever pay. The Massachusetts decision goes beyond the US Supreme Court, which stated that judges can extend the length of probation so that defendants have more time to pay.

It must be noted that the victim in the *Nawn* decision was Walmart, about as nonsympathetic a victim as one could imagine, consistent with the views of the judge quoted in Chapter 4 who argued that "such losses are a part of doing business." Perhaps the only victims who might be less sympathetic are police who want restitution for "buy money" in sting operations (Duffy-Gideon, 2017). In our studies in Pennsylvania, we found that businesses, as compared to individuals, were more likely to receive a restitution award. In contrast to individuals, businesses have the resources and motivation to demand restitution, although at least one of the judges in our statewide survey said they refused to order restitution to businesses. Should *Nawn* still be the rule for more sympathetic victims, individuals who are likely to be poor and not have insurance? I believe these individuals are different from businesses.

Some states automatically convert unpaid restitution to a civil judgment. Although there are good arguments for why this might be appropriate—the defendant no longer is under criminal supervision—it also means that there is essentially no enforcement of the restitution order. Against this position is the fact that most victims will not know about an automatic civil order, and, even if they are told and understand what that means, many will be unable to afford the enforcement of the order. There is, of course, the question why the burden of the cost of an attorney and time should be on the victim to enforce the order. Another policy issue is whether interest should be allowed on restitution. With civil judgments, it would be permitted. But under Washington State law, interest would not be allowed (Vander Giessen, 2012).

One way to limit the extent to which offenders' lives are disrupted by the economic sanctions is to limit "involuntary payment to income from earnings, inheritance, lottery winnings, or gambling receipts, instead of tax rebate interception or garnishing wages earned during incarceration" (Martin & Spencer-Suarez, 2017, p. 7). Martin and Spencer-Suarez also suggested that, even though civil judgments are preferable to criminal debts, there should be a time limit on how long these criminal justice debts can affect credit reports. Martin and Spencer-Suarez (2017, p. 8) further suggested that restitution should be limited to those cases involving identifiable individual victims.

The Victims Committee of the Criminal Justice Section of the American Bar Association (American Bar Association [ABA], 2004) argued that the offender's ability to pay should not be a factor in the determination of restitution. Their report suggested that the payment of restitution could be improved if restitution were treated like child support, such that tax returns and lottery winnings could be seized. The Victims Committee also suggested that there should be a centralized system to track payments, in order to make the process more uniform and integrated.

Because crimes are committed against society, not individuals, the awarding of restitution to individual victims deviates from the general rule that victims are not parties to a criminal proceeding (Rodrigues, 2018). But restitution serves traditional goals of the criminal justice system, including rehabilitation. An important policy question is whether restitution should be imposed based on the defendant's ability to pay.

Three arguments have been made in favor of using the defendant's ability to pay in setting restitution: (1) restitution is a punishment, and the defendant cannot be punished for the nonwillful conduct of being unable to pay; (2) the "reasonable financial subsistence" standard of the MPCS requires that the defendant be able to pay reasonable living expenses and family obligations; and (3) Rodrigues (2018) suggested that collection rates might be increased if the amounts are reasonable, which would increase victim satisfaction.

In contrast, three arguments have been made against using the defendant's ability to pay in setting restitution: (1) the victim is guiltless, (2) the victim is likely to be as much in economic poverty as is the offender (as noted earlier, the impact of economic sanctions is disproportionately on minority defendants and on minority victims), and (3) if the restitution order is based on the defendant's ability to pay, then the victim is likely to receive nothing. If ability to pay is the rule, then the state should establish mandatory compensation, as I argue later.

Judges Should Have Discretion to Impose Fines Based on Ability to Pay

What does equal treatment mean in the context of money? In terms of incarceration, the time served for a specific sentence by a rich person is the same as the time served for that sentence by a poor person. But because money has different meanings for rich and poor people, a fine of $1,000 is not the same for a millionaire as for someone earning poverty-level income (currently $12,760 for a single person under the age of 65). Tonry suggested that just punishments must account for the foreseeable subjective effects on the individual offender.

Aside from trying to achieve fairness in the subjective impact of a sentence, it is important to recognize that, in actual terms, the poor may pay higher amounts of economic sanctions, particularly fees, not only relative to their income and assets, but also in absolute terms because they may face additional administrative fees if they need to pay in installments and if there are penalties for late payment or nonpayment.

Judges should have the ability to impose fines, particularly if these fines are used in lieu of incarceration. Judges should be able to impose these fines based on the defendant's ability to pay and the impact of these fines on the defendant's family and dependents. Regarding fines, the MPC (American Law Institute, 2020) suggests that, because there is little "punitive 'value'" to economic sanctions, "economic sanctions other than victim restitution may not be made formal 'conditions' of probation or post-release supervision— meaning that nonpayment cannot be a basis for sentence revocation."

With respect to fines, I think it is too early to know whether fines can be useful for deterrence and rehabilitation simply because there are few studies that have investigated the question (Gordon & Glaser, 1991, looked at a municipal court). However, given the generally successful use of fines in Europe (Hillsman, 1990) and the need for some type of inter- mediate sanction short of incarceration, judges should have the option to impose fines, particularly for offenders whose crimes are linked to eco- nomic offenses.

The key point is that fines should be imposed based on ability to pay. Fines can be useful as penalties for defendants who are wealthy (Dickman, 2009), and these sanctions may be of greater benefit to society and the crimi- nal justice system if applied to those who commit economic crimes like stock fraud and money laundering. The MPC also takes this approach, arguing that for offenders with the means to pay economic sanctions, "financial pen- alties would remain an important part of the sentencing armamentarium" (American Law Institute, 2020). But it may be useful to greatly reduce eco- nomic sanctions for the poor because they are not likely to be cost-effective (Dickman, 2009).

Most writers today advocate imposing financial obligations that are based on the offender's ability to pay. McLean and Thompson (2007) sug- gested capping amounts at 20% of an offender's income and creating real- istic payment plans. Dickman suggested removing the mandatory amounts beyond the offender's ability to pay. As Dickman (2009) noted, "the foremost reason for the nonpayment of criminal economic sanctions is the offend- er's inability to pay them" (p. 1695). Given that about half of jail inmates made less than $600 in the month prior to incarceration (Dickman, 2009), it is not surprising that many offenders cannot pay court-ordered economic sanctions.

If judges are to be able to impose fines based on defendants' ability to pay, then they need to know what that ability to pay is. Judges generally do not have much information, let alone complete information, about offenders' economic circumstances, including net employment income, other sources of income (e.g., welfare, unemployment), living expenses (e.g., rent, food, transportation), and number and costs of dependents (Hillsman & Greene, 1992). Thus, judges often must guess what amount the offender can pay. There is currently no good solution to the problem, but some jurisdictions are trying to address the issue.

Determining Ability to Pay

The primary disadvantage of economic sanctions is that their imposition is sometimes simply a fantasy in that many offenders have limited assets and incomes and may not be able to pay completely or partially the economic sanctions that are ordered (Harris et al., 2010). Ability to pay arises most often when the offender has not made adequate payment toward the economic sanctions. An affidavit of poverty, which is sufficient to establish inability to pay in the civil context (*Adkins v. E. I. DuPont de Nemours & Co.*, 335 U.S. 331 (1948)), is not sufficient in the criminal context (see Note, 2015, footnote 130).

Bearden v. Georgia (1983) speaks to penalties for nonpayment, not to the economic sanctions that are imposed (MPCS; American Law Institute, 2020, p. 189). According to *Bearden*, an offender can be incarcerated only for willfully refusing to pay, a determination that is made by the judge. Defendants are entitled to a *Bearden* hearing, at which the determination of ability to pay is made and to which defendants are entitled to counsel under the Sixth Amendment (Birckhead, 2015). However, defendants usually are not aware of this opportunity and typically defendants waive it by agreeing to a plea bargain that incorporates the requirement of paying the economic sanctions (Appleman, 2016). Based on *Bearden* and the need to treat defendants equally, one author has suggested that hearings into ability to pay could be conducted at more than one time, such as regarding the defendant's decision to pay in installments rather than at one time or before imposing any new surcharge or penalty for nonpayment (Note, 2015).

Inability to pay debt is a problem that goes beyond criminal sanctions, as there are real problems today with student debt, consumer debt (Silver-Greenberg, 2011), and child support (*Turner v. Rogers*, 2011). Nationally, medical debt lawsuits against patients have become more common, as patients with high deductibles and inadequate insurance have been unable to pay debts to doctors and hospitals. Healthcare systems often say that they are "only pursuing patients who have the means to pay but choose not to pay" (Kliff, 2019), but in general there is no requirement for these systems to screen patients for financial ability to pay. As a result, patients owing medical debt may face wage garnishment that may include, aside from the debt itself, court fees and annual interest, which can be as high as 10% (Kliff, 2019). Suggested reforms include capping interest at 3% and limiting the statute of limitations to 2 years. Given these multiple debts faced especially by offenders facing economic and other criminal justice sanctions, inaccurately finding a defendant able to pay an economic sanction includes criminal justice expenses relating to nonpayment (arrest, jail) and collateral consequences if the defendant loses a job or public benefits (O'Neil & Prescott, 2019). Moreover, criminal justice debts are not dischargeable in bankruptcy (Appleman, 2016). The existence of these multiple debts suggests there is a need to address these problems in a more integrated fashion (Bannon et al., 2010).

When setting the amount of economic sanctions, judges need to consider the offender's ability to pay, as California has required for bail-setting decisions (*In re Humphrey*, 2021). Taking ability to pay into account means that the amount set will be realistic in terms of what the offender will actually pay, and the payment schedule that is set is more likely to be adhered to. Moreover, according to Harris et al., if the offender perceives the economic sanctions as being so high that they are impossible to pay, he or she is likely to perceive the system as unfair and illegitimate and, as a result, to simply give up attempting to pay. In Study 12 and Study 14, we found that offenders said it would be very difficult for them to make payments. Similarly, Harris et al.'s (2011) interviews with offenders indicated that economic sanctions strain offenders' ability to meet other needs.

However, offenders' claims may need to be discounted somewhat. The National Center for State Courts conducted a survey of 40 courts to determine what practices might work to increase economic sanction collections (Tobin, 1996). Although many judges and court managers said they believed that offenders did not have the ability to pay fines and fees, the report also found that "experienced collectors consistently assert that all but a very few defendants have greater resources for meeting their obligations than might be immediately apparent" (Tobin, 1996, p. 55, quoting Matthias et al., 1995).

Under the framework of the MPCS, the term "reasonable financial subsistence" is used to define ability to pay in that the money available to pay economic sanctions would be whatever funds exist beyond the amount of money the offender needs to pay reasonable living expenses and meet family obligations. Colorado uses a similar standard with its prohibition of incarceration if the defendant is unable to pay without causing "undue hardship" to himself or to his dependents (O'Neil & Prescott, 2019). However, the MPCS does not provide information about the mechanics by which a court can determine reasonable financial subsistence.

Even in obvious cases where offenders are indigent, courts still impose economic sanctions. Those obvious cases of inability include homeless individuals and unemployed individuals who have no assets and are in danger of losing their possessions (e.g., car, home). Also problematic are individuals who realistically can be employed at jobs that are not much above minimum wage but would still have problems with paying expenses as well as criminal justice costs, fees, and fines. The most problematic are individuals who are not employable for a good reason, such as the mentally ill, a group that constitutes about 10–15% of individuals in the criminal justice system. The ability of offenders to pay assessed economic sanctions may also depend, beyond their own income and assets, on community characteristics that are related to offender reentry, such as social service organizations (e.g., employment assistance, drug and alcohol treatment), commercial establishments, manufacturing employment opportunities, and unemployment rates (Morenoff &

Harding, 2014). And, as noted by the Pennsylvania American Civil Liberties Union (ACLU), individuals who require a public defender or court-appointed attorney are prima facie unable to pay.

Aside from the obvious cases, ability to pay can be difficult for a court to determine for three reasons. First, it may not be possible for probation officers to reliably estimate what the offenders' ability to pay. For many offenders, work can be irregular and their monetary obligations (e.g., child support, formal or informal loans) can change, thus necessitating continual monitoring (Katzenstein & Nagrecha, 2011). A practical problem with calculating financial status arises with people who have irregular, seasonal, or temporary employment and for whom a pay stub or tax return is unlikely (Zhen, 2018). For this group of offenders, a determination of ability to pay made at the sentencing hearing is unlikely to be useful long-term.

Second, offenders may know their incomes and assets but may not be willing to make it clear to the court what those assets are. Third, some offenders might actively try to hide assets and shield income. For this reason, the Victims Committee of the American Bar Association Criminal Justice Section (ABA, 2004) suggested that courts should have a complete listing of all of the offender's assets so that the assets cannot later be hidden or given away.

For these latter two groups (i.e., those who do not disclose or actively hide their net worth), courts must develop mechanisms for assessing offenders' assets and liabilities. Accurately determining the ability to pay requires that kind of detailed information—tax records, links to the IRS and state agencies, listings of all bank accounts, and property owned by relatives to detect property that could have been transferred to avoid payment—that judges in the United States currently do not have available to them. Many courts in Europe can use actual earnings as the basis for imposing economic sanctions as day fines because governments there have access to more information about people than does the US government (e.g., income and tax records; Hillsman, 1990). In Sweden, Finland, and Norway, for example, everyone's income tax returns are published and anyone's salary can be discovered through a phone call to the tax authorities (O'Malley, 2011, p. 54; Marçal, 2017). Linking imposed economic sanctions to ability to pay will require more detailed, and expensive pre-sentence investigations and the legal authority for probation officers to discover detailed information about salaries and all assets, including assets that are jointly held.

Most courts do not have a written plan for how such a determination should be made. Maricopa County (Phoenix) had a full survey that probationers must complete (referred to in Maricopa County Adult Probation Department, nd). The Maricopa County survey is a detailed eight-page form that asks for information about 11 types of assets for the offender and the offender's spouse, 23 sources of income for the offender and the offender's spouse, and 64 different monthly expenses. There is also a self-employed income supplement. Verification is required for all of the information. In Maricopa County, offenders are required to complete the form only if they have been delinquent in payments (McLean & Thompson, 2007; see also https://www.prisonlegalnews.org/media/publications/bja_repaying_debts_guide_2006.pdf, explaining that the form must be completed when a payment is 30 days delinquent). The form (dated 2008) is available at https://www.arizonalawgroup.com/documents/AFI-Form.pdf.

Bench Cards

Another way to help judges determine a defendant's ability is to rely on "bench cards." A court settlement in Biloxi, Mississippi, between the ACLU and the court system (*Kennedy v. Biloxi*) stopped the practice whereby defendants were incarcerated if they did not pay their fines and fees in cash, in full, and immediately (Fines & Fees Justice Center, 2016). According to the settlement, defendants who do not pay their fines and fees are entitled to an ability-to-pay hearing and, if they are facing possible incarceration, to a public defender at no cost. Furthermore, according to the settlement, all municipal judges must consult a "bench card," which, in the event a defendant cannot pay mandatory state fees, advises judges to consider "(1) extending the defendant's time to pay; (2) requiring the defendant to perform community service to satisfy the state assessment fees; (3) requiring the completion of approved educational programs, job skills training, counseling and mental health services, and drug treatment programs as an alternative to, or in addition to, community service." For discretionary fines, fees, and restitution that the defendant is unable to pay, the bench card recommends that judges reduce or waive the amounts; impose community service instead of the fines, fees, or restitution; extend the time the defendant has to pay; require completion of approved educational or treatment programs; or impose some combination of these alternatives.

The Biloxi bench card also requires judges to look into and then make a determination about the defendant's ability to pay the fines, fees, or restitution. According to the bench card, if the defendant is homeless, incarcerated, resides in a mental health facility, or has an income at or below 125% of the federal poverty level, the judge must presume, subject to rebuttal evidence, that the defendant is unable to pay. The Biloxi bench card has been used as the basis for reforms across the country (Martin et al., 2018).

Ohio also has instituted reforms regarding the imposition of economic sanctions with its "ability-to-pay bench cards," which contain guidelines regarding when incarceration can be used for nonpayment of criminal justice debt. Ohio's bench cards for judges (Supreme Court of Ohio, Office of Judicial Services, 2019) help judges understand the differences between fines and costs/fees, making clear when a jail sentence can be imposed, listing factors that may be considered in the determination of ability to pay, describing the conditions when contempt of court may be imposed, and explaining when community service can be imposed as payment for court costs.

Under the Ohio system, court costs are civil, not criminal financial obligations. Not paying court costs cannot result in contempt of court or jail time, but failure to pay court costs can also mean that the defendant is ordered to perform community service, for which the defendant gets credit at no less than the federal minimum wage. Fines are a financial penalty for which the judge must consider the defendant's ability to pay. The bench card directs judges to separate costs from fines.

According to the bench card, jail time can be imposed only for unpaid fines and only if the defendant had reasonable notice, was given an evidentiary ability-to-pay hearing, had been advised of the right to counsel, and followed a specific finding that the defendant had the ability to pay the fines but willfully refused to do so. If the maximum jail sentence was imposed and served, the defendant cannot be ordered to serve additional days in jail for not paying a fine. Incarceration in jail leads to a credit of $50 per day toward the fine. A copy of the Ohio bench card is included in the Appendix (Supreme Court of Ohio, Office of Judicial Services, 2019; Collection of fines and court costs in adult trial courts, https://www.supremecourt.ohio.gov/Publications/JCS/finesCourtCosts.pdf).

Prescott (2017), who has developed an online tool that allows for the assessment of ability to pay, argues that the reforms accomplished by bench cards are minor and have relatively little impact. Web-based platforms that allow for online assessment of ability to pay are, according to Prescott, less burdensome to offenders, allow courts to save time, and provide a consistent, standardized approach that applies to everyone and that provides a written record of online statements and decisions (O'Neil & Prescott, 2019). Prescott also argues that the online tool provides for better and less biased communication.

There are several obstacles to the reform of economic sanctions in municipal and local courts (Logan, 2018). First, local governments have no incentive to change and every incentive to keep the present system because it provides a ready source of income. Second, local governments have final control over the enforcement of local codes, and local judges can be relied on to enforce these codes to generate revenue. Third, so many government units benefit from these sanctions (police, prosecutors, public defenders, jails, court clerks, and courts) that resistance is widely entrenched. Fourth, private businesses, especially probation services, often have political influence and are generally persuasive because they argue that their services cost the local governments nothing. Fifth, states benefit directly through fees that are sent directly to them and indirectly by reducing their need to subsidize local agencies.

Explicit Guidance

In addition to the survey used in Maricopa County and the bench cards used in Biloxi and Ohio, the Pennsylvania ACLU makes the following suggestion about ability to pay.

> In the absence of clear guidance, counsel should be prepared at sentencing to suggest a principled standard to the court, to determine how much the defendant should pay in fines and costs. Here are some suggestions:
> - Defendants with severe and permanent disabilities, such as individuals who receive SSI [Supplemental Security Income], should have their fines and costs substantially reduced or completely waived, since they will be unlikely to be able to afford to pay anything.
> - The defendant and the court should identify an amount that the defendant can reasonably afford to pay each month while on probation, and the fines and costs should be capped at the total the defendant would pay over the course of that supervision (e.g., $50 × 36 months of supervision).
> - The defendant should not pay fines and costs for a period of time longer than the maximum sentence. A defendant who is convicted of a crime with a possible maximum sentence of 5 years should have his payments capped at the amount he could reasonably pay over the course of that time (e.g., $50 × 60 months). If the court uses this calculation, it should subtract from that any months that the defendant will be incarcerated, as a defendant who is in jail is unlikely to have any ability to pay. (ACLU of Pennsylvania, 2020, https://aclupa.org/sites/default/files/wysiwyg/sentencing_guide_2020-03-11_1.pdf)

Civil Remedies Alone

Sobol (2016) proposed that the impact of economic sanctions on the poor can be reduced if fees intended to reimburse the state for criminal justice expenditures are restricted to civil remedies rather than arrest and incarceration. The Ohio Supreme Court's bench card for trial courts indicates that court costs are civil debts for which incarceration is not available. More generally, for costs, Sobol suggests, the state should have only those remedies that are available to private attorneys.

Sobol (2017) proposed that federal laws that govern the collection of consumer debts in the civil system can be used to reduce the abuse associated with the collection of criminal justice debt. Federal statutory remedies for civil debts prohibit abusive debt collection practices and false or misleading representations. In the criminal justice system, there is often harassment, abuse, and threats, particularly with regard to incarceration. Sobol also proposed the creation of a federal agency to combat abusive criminal justice debt collection.

The clearest way to take into account the defendant's ability to pay is to rely on *day fines*. Sobol (2016) argued that day fines have the advantage of imposing the same relative punishment on defendants (the person's daily pay) regardless of their income. Moreover, because day fines take ability to pay into account, collection should be easier. In her examination of the data from the day fine studies, Colgan (2017) concluded that payment rates increased when the level of economic sanctions decreased because, Colgan argued, paying the amount of debt owed is more possible and therefore likely to lead to greater efforts to pay.

One of the dangers of imposing economic sanctions on indigent defendants is the danger of probation revocation if the sanctions are not paid (Patel & Philip, 2012). Related to this idea is what happened in New South Wales (Australia) in the 1890s. Although fines were introduced as a way to avoid incarceration, nonpayment of fines accounted for 75% of admissions to prisons (O'Malley, 2011, p. 51). In an effort to reduce the number of prisoners, New South Wales allowed the poor to pay their fines in installments. O'Malley (2011, p. 169) argued that the failure to pay fines still accounts for a high percentage of prison admissions in Australia. He suggested that allowing offenders to pay in the form of community service would reduce the number of fiscal failures.

Fees and Costs Should Not Be Imposed

Offenders should not have to pay fees and costs. Thus, I agree with the "categorical abolitionist position" taken by the MPC. This issue is real in that convicted offenders are often called on to pay for the costs of criminal justice. The report by the Brennan Center for Justice (Bannon et al., 2010) also concluded that fees be discontinued, particularly fees that impose additional costs on the indigent, such as payment plan fees, late fees, collection fees, and interest. Most clearly, a National Public Radio report by Joseph Shapiro (2014) reported that 43 states allow a charge for a public defender, 41 states charge for jail, and 44 states charge for probation.

Marsh and Gerrick (2016) argued that the reform of criminal justice debt must go beyond greater transparency, limitations on private probation agencies, revenue caps, and requiring ability-to-pay hearings. They suggested eliminating all "poverty penalties," the extra fees that individuals face when they do not immediately pay all fines, fees, and costs. They also suggested establishing objective standards for willful nonpayment and eliminating financial eligibility barriers to alternative measures for discharging offenses, such as community service, sliding scale fines, and waivers. To truly transform criminal justice debt, Marsh and Gerrick argued for community courts that would integrate case management with social work services for alternatives such as group counseling, community restitution, and community service.

Another suggestion that has been made is that counties should not be able to keep the fees they collect since this amounts to a regressive tax and provides a perverse incentive to create even more new fees at the local level (Makowsky, interviewed in Gonzalez, 2021). What Makowsky suggests is that all of the money should be sent to the state, so that the local government gains little by establishing new fees.

A more activist approach to fees and costs would involve the willful nonpayment of economic sanctions as an example of civil disobedience. In his book *March* (Lewis et al., 2013), John Lewis described how he and his colleagues had been convicted of disorderly conduct and ordered to pay a fine of $50 each or to serve 30 days in the county workhouse. The students refused to pay, arguing that paying the fine would be supporting an unjust and immoral system. No one wants to spend time in jail but convicted offenders could greatly disrupt the criminal justice system if they all willfully refused to pay fees and costs.

Activities Covered by Costs and Fees Are Inherently Governmental Responsibilities

The argument against imposing fees and costs on convicted offenders is based on the distinction between general taxes, on the one hand, and benefit taxes and user fees on the other (Duff, 2004). General taxes are government levies on income, consumption, property, or wealth and are used to support general public services. Income taxes, corporate taxes, and sales taxes are examples of general taxes. Taxes are "what we pay for civilized society" (*Compañía General de Tabacos de Filipinas v. Collector of Internal Revenue*, 1927, Holmes dissenting, p. 100) and are "the preferred method for paying for . . . governmental functions" (US Department of Treasury, 2010).

In contrast, "benefit taxes and user fees constitute mandatory or voluntary levies imposed on persons deriving particular benefits from specific categories of publicly provided goods and services" (Duff, 2004, p. 393). Benefit taxes and user fees differ in the extent to which the benefit goes to a group or an individual. Benefit taxes are "compulsory levies applied to individuals (or institutions such as corporations) who are assumed to benefit as a group from certain government services" (Bird & Tsiopoulos, 1997, pp. 38–39). Taxes on gasoline and diesel fuel are benefit taxes because the drivers paying these taxes are members of the group of vehicle owners who benefit from the use of government-owned and -maintained roads and highways (Duff, 2004). Using fines to support government is inappropriate because payees have fewer protections, a particular concern because of the regressivity of the economic sanctions (Robinson, 2017).

User fees are amounts "levied on consumers of government goods or services in relation to their consumption" (Bird & Tsiopoulos, 1997, p. 39). With user fees, the amount of special benefits delivered to an individual can be identified along with the financing paid by the individual. To the extent that charges for water, sewage, and waste disposal are related to the consumption of the service, these charges are user fees (Duff, 2004). "The designation of user fees can also be applied to charges for the use of public transit or public recreational facilities, tuition fees for higher education, road or bridge tolls, resource royalties, and various kinds of environmental taxes" (Duff, 2004, p. 394). Under these definitions, the fees and costs imposed on convicted offenders are user fees.

Benefit taxes and user fees have both advantages and disadvantages (Duff, 2004). As an advantage, they increase economic efficiency because they cause resources to go to the most highly valued uses. They also increase the accountability of the public sector because they are more responsive to the public's demand for goods and services, and they are more fair since taxpayers pay only for those goods and services that they use. Benefit taxes and user fees are criticized, however, because they may be more burdensome on the poor than on the wealthy, they undermine the entire notion of publicly provided goods and services, and budgetary flexibility is undermined if the revenues are ear-marked for specific purposes. Duff argues that benefit taxes and user fees are appropriate for some purposes (e.g., transportation, water, sewage, waste disposal), inappropriate for others (social services, public housing), and, in between, appropriate if access is granted on the basis of right or need (e.g., healthcare, education).

According to Duff, most publicly provided goods provide both general and specific benefits. For example, a public park provides spaces for interactions for everyone and recreation for individuals. Similarly, public health interventions can reduce the impact of epidemics, benefiting both the general welfare and the health of individuals. Public and individual benefits also accompany publicly funded education, transportation, and waste disposal programs.

Although it would be possible to fund these publicly provided services through a benefits tax or user fee, there are four reasons why charging such fees is not appropriate. First, when the good or service is fundamentally public, charging fees to individual users changes the nature of the good or service. Thus, police protection, a public service, is fundamentally changed to an individual service when individuals are charged for their level of protection. Second, when benefits are distributed by right, need, or merit, benefit taxes and user fees are inappropriate. For example, if primary education is seen as a right of citizenship, then it would be wrong to charge students. Third, when the purpose of the public expenditure is to redistribute resources, as with welfare payments, it makes no sense to charge individual beneficiaries.

Finally, if the benefits tax or user fee is regressive (i.e., has a disproportionate impact on the poor), the charge is probably unfair and inappropriate unless there are some ways to offset the effect.

According to Duff's analysis, it is economically inefficient to charge the cost to the user when there are public benefits, as there are with public education. There is a continuum between pure public goods and pure private goods, which mirrors the continuum between public funding and charging specific users (Bird & Tsiopoulos, 1997). In both Canada and the United States, user fees and benefit taxes are more likely to be used at the local level rather than the state or national level (Duff, 2004), a fact that is explainable because federal level expenditures are primarily social assistance and national defense (a pure public good).

Duff argues that education (primary and secondary) and health services benefit both the general public and individuals. Moreover, because basic education is a right and healthcare is a need, he argues that a user fee approach based on ability and willingness to pay would undermine the public benefits. Duff argues that the protection of persons and property is not a proper subject for benefit taxes and user fees because of the more general public benefits.

Duff argues that even if benefit taxes and user fees are appropriately imposed, the amount of the charges must still be appropriate—"an economically sensible price" (quoting Bird & Tsiopoulos, 1997, p. 60). Duff speaks in terms of the marginal cost of production, such that rates should match the short-run marginal cost of producing the good or service, although there must also be a consideration of general benefits, uncompensated costs to third parties, and the possible need for more complicated pricing arrangements when there are declining marginal costs or substantial fixed costs. Opportunity costs must also be considered.

The government should not be contracting out inherently governmental functions. The question, though, is what makes a function fundamentally public rather than private. Minow (2003) suggests that the answer depends on traditional practices, symbolism, and political theories about the role of government. For example, because criminal prosecution has been handled primarily by the government for the past 200 years and because it has symbolism as a public action for the good of the community and private victims, it is unlikely that it would be contracted out to a private actor. The danger with private actors, especially for-profit groups, is that "the appearance of private motives in a public domain can undermine respect for government and even generate doubt whether the government is sincerely pursuing public purposes" (Minow, 2003, p. 1234).

One of the arguments for privatizing governmental functions is to reduce the size of government. Actually, of course, governmental functions have merely been outsourced, creating a government by proxy (DiIulio, 2003). Four arguments have been made in favor of privatization: (a) increasing quality and effectiveness; (b) creating competition and incentives for improvement; (c) increasing pluralism, that is, giving groups the opportunity to participate and self-govern; and (d) creating new knowledge and infra-structure (Minow, 2003).

DiIulio (2003, p. 1283) argues that efficiency is not the only criterion for "deciding who should make public policy, who should administer public policy, and who should fund public policy." According to DiIulio, it is difficult to separate making and administering public policy since so much discretion is generally involved in translating policy into action. Although DiIulio (2003, p. 1283) suggests that "[i]t is easier to separate finance from administration than it is to separate policymaking from administration," funding decisions still involve policy determinations.

If there is to be contracting out of governmental functions, the key is public accountability (Minow, 2003), which, following Hirschman (1970), means that governments "retain the option to exit relationships with private entities, the means to express disagreements with the ways in which the private entities proceed, and the capacity to remain with the private entity as a vote of confidence" (Minow, 2003, p. 1266). Government accountability comes through contracts that specify terms and enforcement, are consistent with the constitutional obligations of government, and require the reporting of information needed to assess compliance.

Governments are charging defendants with costs that are the business of government. Moreover, when states charge defendants for an attorney to defend them, these charges amount to a fee for exercising a constitutional right. Such charges are an abdication of governmental responsibility in the same way that devolving the collection and monitoring of these charges to private businesses is an improper delegation of duty. In terms of fees and costs in the criminal justice system, these costs have been imposed because there is no one to argue against them. Offenders generally do not have the right to vote, and, even if they do, they have little influence over criminal justice policy (Minow, 2003).

If Government Imposes Fees and costs, Then Government, Not Private Businesses, Should Collect and Monitor Payment of Those Charges

In recent years, private corporations have begun operating criminal justice services that had previously been performed by the government. Because they have a pecuniary interest in the behavior of the offenders they deal with, specifically wanting the offenders to continue making payments on the original owed amounts and on any additional fees, penalties, and surcharges that may have accrued (Kofman, 2019), the field has become known as "poverty capitalism" (Edsall, 2014) and an "'offender-funded' probation industry" (Human Rights Watch, 2014).

There are two reasons why local governments contract out this work to private companies (Human Rights Watch, 2014). First, these contracts reduce the costs of government and therefore the need to increase taxes to pay for the covered services. Second, because these added costs are borne by offenders, they amount to an additional punishment beyond what had traditionally been imposed on convicted offenders.

According to a Human Rights Watch report (2014, p. 3), companies that supervise offender-funded probation have an incentive for offenders not to pay off the amounts they owe: "[T]he longer it takes offenders to pay off their debts, the longer they remain on probation and the more they pay in supervision fees." That local governments need the money provided by fines and fees became apparent in response to concerns about police stops of motorists after the shooting of Michael Brown in Ferguson, Missouri in August 2014. Slightly more than 20% of the city's $12.75 million budget came from municipal court fines, and more than a third of the general revenues in one nearby town came from court fines and fees (Robertson & Goldstein, 2014).

One of the primary criticisms of private companies being involved in the criminal justice system is that they are profiting from the misfortunes of victims and offenders (DiIulio, 1988). Moreover, their focus on profit may cause them to want offenders not to succeed, so that they can make more money (Human Rights Watch, 2014). DiIulio believes that profit per se is not the factor that precludes the privatization of criminal justice functions; rather, the legally sanctioned control over crime and punishment are inherently public because criminal justice actors act on behalf of the public (DiIulio, 1988). Indeed, according to DiIulio quoting John Locke, criminal justice is one of the central functions of government (but see Logan, 1990, pp. 52–54).

Just as DiIulio believes that government can be successful at managing prisons, there is also reason to believe that probation officers can do a better job not only of supervising offenders, but also of inducing offenders to pay the economic sanctions they owe. Our evidence from Pennsylvania suggests that when specialized collections agencies are involved in the collection of fees and costs, the amount of money recovered is actually less than when probation officers are supervising the procedure (Study 4 and Study 8).

One of the real problems with private probation companies is what is called "pay only" probation, which refers to individuals who are on probation not because of a threat to public safety or need for supervision, but only because they owe fees (Human Rights Watch, 2014). Private probation agencies generally deal with offenders "whose offenses are often too minor to merit jail time" (Stillman, 2014). The Human Rights Watch report indicates that although the private probation companies account for the fees due to the court, they do not report on the amount of fees paid to the company itself.

The Human Rights Watch report (2014) argues that pay-only probation is discriminatory for three reasons: (1) offenders have to pay supervision fees only if they do not pay the total amount of their fines immediately, (2) the fees are regressive because poorer probationers pay a larger percentage of their payments in fees than do individuals who can afford to make larger payments and because poorer probationers have to stay on probation for a longer period of time because they make smaller payments, and (3) poorer individuals pay absolutely more in fees because they are on probation longer.

For the companies that Human Rights Watch observed, offenders could not pay off their debts to the court before their debt to the private probation company because the companies ensured that the two debts were paid down simultaneously. There is a hidden cost to the public for these fees in that the real threat for nonpayment is jail-time, a cost borne by the public, and one that might be greater than the amount of money owed to the court. The Human Rights Watch (p. 59) report found that courts often not only did not supervise the private probation agencies but also "delegate[d] a range of coercive powers to their probation companies."

The Human Rights Watch report concluded that courts do little to determine whether offenders are actually able to pay their fines and fees. Moreover, the private probation companies have a direct interest in making sure that courts do not decide that an offender is not able to pay the debt. The report couched the argument in terms of human rights issues.

Thus, I believe, given the public nature of the functions covered by fees and costs, they should not be imposed on offenders. Moreover, given the risks associated with privatizing their collection, if they are imposed, they should be collected by government agencies.

Stop Privatized Criminal Justice

As noted by Logan and Wright (2014), criminal justice has long been the province of private actors. This brief overview is based primarily on their article. In England until the 10th century, private prosecutions were the mechanism for handling criminal offenses. For nonhomicide cases, the offender was required to give money to the victim (a "bot") on the basis of the victim's social status. For homicide cases, the payment ("wergild") was to the victim's survivors. By the late 10th century, the government took a larger role in criminal cases, requiring local noblemen to arrest suspected criminals. At this time, payments for criminal wrongs ("amercement") were made to the king, the church, or the community, rather than to the victim. By the 1300s, the office of justice of the peace was created to handle local law enforcement. The justice of the peace office was a source of income through fees, and self-dealing was an obvious problem. By the mid-1700s, there were part-time police officers, private prosecutors, and evidence gatherers ("thief takers" who often had underworld connections), all of whom profited from rewards and government payments.

Similarly, in colonial America and in the United States until the mid-1800s, criminal justice was handled by individuals who were paid fees and received forfeiture payments, causing a focus on property crimes that yielded more financial benefit than person crimes. By the late 1800s, professional police forces were in place, although the fee and reward system was still operating. Judges received private payments for cases, and historians have characterized judges' entrepreneurial behavior as selling justice.

Criminal justice revenue also came from corrections. Dating back to colonial times, jailers charged for the costs of incarceration, even for those in Salem accused of witchcraft (Baker, 2006). Moreover, prior to the Civil War, but especially afterward in the South, states leased convicts to businesses, including mining and agriculture. This money accounted for large proportions of some state budgets (one-third of the annual budgets of Alabama and Tennessee). In 1846, Michigan enacted the first law in the country authorizing correctional fees, permitting counties to charge sentenced jail inmates for the costs of medical care (Parent, 1990).

In their review of the relevant Supreme Court cases from the 1920s, 1970s, and 1980s, Logan and Wright (2014) concluded that the imposition of economic sanctions turns on two general themes: neutrality and individualization. *Neutrality* refers to ensuring that a particular decision-maker or government agency does not benefit from a particular outcome (e.g., providing a significant percentage of a budget), although the Court has allowed surcharges and forfeitures that may undermine neutrality. *Individualization* refers to linking the economic sanction to the particular offender's crime and to the impact that payment will have on the offender.

Logan and Wright (2014) suggested that state courts and lower federal courts have added a third theme: *connectedness*. That is, courts have required that governments imposing the economic sanctions show some connection between the crime the offender committed and the way the government plans to use the money. Without such a connection, the economic sanctions, particularly fees and costs, are not reimbursement for valid expenses but mere avenues for raising revenue.

Logan and Wright (2014) indicated that economic sanctions imposed earlier in the criminal justice process (e.g., for diversion) are less likely than those imposed after adjudication to be individualized for both the offender and the offense. Not only are fees imposed early on likely to lack checks and balances against self-dealing, but there is also the danger that decisions will be based on inaccurate facts.

The more that revenue is a purpose for the economic sanctions, the greater the dangers of self-dealing and bias. Thus, Logan and Wright (2014) suggest that, to reduce these distorted incentives, all economic sanctions should be sent to the general treasury rather than to the specific agency of the decision-maker involved.

These dangers of self-dealing and bias are also often present with private companies, for whom profit is the clear incentive (Logan & Wright, 2014). Thus, private contractors are likely to impose surcharges and other costs and to advocate for outcomes beneficial to them (e.g., consecutive rather than concurrent sentences). As long as economic sanctions fund criminal justice agencies, there is likely to be continued growth in enforcement and corrections and limited debate about the future of criminal justice (Logan & Wright, 2014).

Logan and Wright (2014) suggested the creation of a state-level commission to look at the imposition and enforcement of economic sanctions to determine the impact on offenders (e.g., "piling on" the poor and disadvantaged), the fairness of collection methods (e.g., revoking drivers' licenses), and the cost-effectiveness of these sanctions (i.e., whether collections exceed costs).

Using the comparative approach of Sen (2009), Case and Deaton (2020) argued that a better world is made when injustices are removed. Their concrete examples include the widespread "agreement that making money out of human suffering is wrong, and that wealth inequality based on that suffering is unjust" (p. 245). Following their logic, I think it is fair to view private probation and poverty capitalism as unfairly making money on offenders' poverty, which is continued, reinforced, and exacerbated by unfair fees, interest, and surcharges.

The State Should Provide Compensation to Victims

There is a general concern for victims, but the fact is that even if restitution is made mandatory and even if restitution is required to be paid before other economic sanctions, most victims will still not be compensated for their losses. If crimes are reported, in most cases the offender is not caught; if caught, is often not prosecuted; and if prosecuted, lacks funds to pay restitution. Thus, the state should assume responsibility for compensating victims under one or more of three rationales: (1) a *legal tort theory*, whereby the state is seen to have failed to protect its citizens adequately; (2) a *humanitarian rationale* through which all citizens should receive assistance for their compelling needs; or (3) a *by-products theory* that recognizes victim satisfaction as a benefit to the criminal justice system.

It is important that I acknowledge my bias toward victims over offenders, although my concern is with individual, not corporate, victims. Victims who suffer because of a crime are disproportionately poor, minority, and unable to bear the loss from a criminal victimization because they often lack the resources and insurance to cover the loss. Indeed, Sullivan, Warren, and Westbrook (1999) found that criminal victimization was one of the reasons, although not one of the "big three" reasons (job loss, medical problem, divorce or separation), that the largely middle-class individuals they studied were forced into bankruptcy (Warren & Tyagi, 2003, p. 81).

Assuming there is a move toward state compensation for victims, changes must be made in the current system because it is inadequate. Federal Victims of Crime Act (VOCA) funding encourages states to implement victim compensation programs, and, after the 1988 statutory change, VOCA funding has been available for victims of domestic violence and drunk driving (Davis & Mulford, 2008). Victim compensation programs in most states are funded by fees paid by offenders (the Crime Victim Compensation [CVC] and Crime Commission Cost [CCC] funds in Pennsylvania; see Study 2). States that meet VOCA requirements can receive federal subsidies that can pay up to 40% of what is given to victims.

Even though funding is theoretically available, in practice most victims do not receive funding.

VOCA compensation funding is available in all states for medical costs, lost wages, mental health counseling, and funeral costs, but there are restrictions in terms of the type of crimes included, types of losses covered, maximum payments available, and individuals who can receive the compensation (Evans, 2014). Generally, payments take a long time. In one state, the determination of the eligibility of a claim was 8 months and the payment on a claim was 12 months (Department of Justice Office of the Inspector General, 2020). Evaluations of state victim compensation programs (Newmark et al., 2003) indicate that there are differences between states in how compensation is awarded, with some states focusing primarily on need (which means that young African American males are disproportionate recipients) whereas others focus on deservingness (which means that older white female victims are disproportionate recipients; Smith, 2006). In contrast to the generally low rate of funding, citizens seem to like compensation programs and are in favor of implementing them for property crimes (Galvin et al., 2018).

More Realistic Suggestions

My suggestions are unlikely to be implemented, particularly my suggestion of completely eliminating costs and fees. Thus, I suggest some modifications short of that dramatic change.

Reduce the Number of Fees and costs, Especially at the County Level

In our research in Pennsylvania (Study 1), we found that most of the different economic sanctions (90% of 2,629 different sanctions) relate to county-level user fees and costs. These fees are primarily aimed at generating funds for the county rather than punishing, deterring, or rehabilitating offenders. A reduction in the number of such fees would reduce the economic burden on offenders. The fact that there are more than 2,600 different economic sanctions in Pennsylvania is confusing not only to offenders, who do not know how much they owe, how much their monthly payments should be, and where the money they pay goes (Study 12; Ruback, et al., 2006), but also to judges, prosecutors, and probation officers.

Moreover, this variety of sanctions is unfair to individuals in counties that have a larger number of economic sanctions, most of which are county fees and costs. These fees and costs are imposed to shift the financial burden from the public to offenders, and counties with more of these fees and costs place more of the burden on offenders. Unfairness can occur when similar offenders in two different counties face different amounts of fees and costs solely because one county imposes a greater number of fees and costs.

One possible solution to the problem of so many different types of economic sanctions is simply to reduce the number of county fees and costs (Beckett & Harris, 2011). The large number of possible county-level economic sanctions explains most of the variation between counties, and essentially the system as it presently stands rewards counties that are more creative in creating new fees and costs. As long as the imposed fees and costs are consistent across counties, one could claim that they are uniform and therefore fair.

Although one could argue that counties should be able to impose whatever fees they wish, it would be difficult to defend these sanctions in terms of fairness to offenders. That is, it would be difficult to argue that offenders who live in certain counties should have to pay higher fees and costs merely because of where they live, not because of their actual offense.

Make Payments Easier

The National Center for State Courts (Tobin, 1996) recommended that collection of economic sanctions is likely to be improved if courts make payments more convenient, for example through credit-card payments, installment plans, incentive plans that reduce amounts for those who comply with payment plans, community service, and day fines based on income levels. The notion behind the day fine concept was that offenders should be able to afford necessities less "the amount that serves to satisfy pleasures, whatever these may be, such as wine, spirits and tobacco" (Faraldo-Cabana, 2014, p. 10; quoting Raffaele Garafalo), a concept that is also embodied in the MPCS (2020) notion of "reasonable financial subsistence": that the offender must "retain sufficient means for reasonable living expenses and family obligations after compliance with the sanction" (Section 6.06(6)).

Questions remain concerning the degree to which offenders should be allowed flexibility in payment. Events that make it difficult or impossible for the offender to pay (e.g., illness, losing a job) are probably more likely among offenders than the general public, thus suggesting that offenders should be allowed flexibility. Other questions relate to whether there should be garnishment of wages, welfare payments, and tax refunds.

The Restitution in Pennsylvania Task Force (2013) made several suggestions about how to increase the number of cases in which restitution is awarded and payments are made. To make it easier for judges to understand the law and issue restitution orders, the Task Force suggested that the state develop a toolkit for judges that clarifies and standardizes policies regarding the imposition of restitution. Other suggestions of the Task Force were more coercive: directly taking money from the offender by attaching wages or IRS refunds, limiting eligibility for public assistance, and filing contempt of court proceedings. The Task Force also recommended, based on our surveys of victims (Study 11), that victims be better informed about what restitution is and how it is imposed, collected, and distributed.

The Conference of State Court Administrators (Pepin, 2015) suggested that there needs to be a broader consideration of how economic sanctions can be met, "including community service, day fines, and non-monetary compliance such as [general education diploma] GED classes and work-skills training." The Conference also suggested that it is possible to "reduce failure to appear and improve compliance with court orders by making [legal financial obligations] LFOs easier to understand, reminding offenders about court appearances and court-ordered LFOs, and eliminating additional fees for collections-related monitoring" (Pepin, 2015).

One way that economic sanctions might be made less harsh is to make payment easier. Requiring that payments must be made in person and during business hours impacts the poor disproportionately since it is likely that they would suffer more from lost wages, childcare expenses, and transportation costs (O'Neil & Prescott, 2019).

Future Issues

There are two issues that will need to be discussed in the future. First, assuming there is variation between counties in the imposition of economic sanctions, there may be a need for economic sanction guidelines within a state. Second, there is a need for further investigations of the extent and effects of variation between states.

Should There Be State-Wide Guidelines?
A rational system would also be one that understands the cost-effectiveness of the sanctions and determines that the costs are defensible. There are administrative costs for handling economic sanctions, and it would be important to know how much it costs state courts to process a payment for state costs, including staff time for recording the amount, computer processing time (for those counties with computerized record keeping), and monitoring of paper records (for those counties without computer records of amounts owed and payments made). These costs are especially problematic because many economic sanctions involve relatively small amounts of money.

Our analyses indicated that three-quarters of all economic sanctions imposed were for less than $50 (Study 1; Ruback & Clark, 2011). Whether and how much this is a problem depends on the costs involved in imposing these sanctions, monitoring offenders to ensure that the sanctions are paid, and intervening (e.g., by issuing warnings, revoking probation) if they are not paid. Moreover, if the amounts are not paid, warnings need to be given and probation officers need to make judgments about whether probation should be revoked. For parolees who have not made payments, decisions must be made about whether parole should be revoked for a technical violation (the failure to make payments).

Three changes are needed if we are to increase the likelihood that offenders will pay the economic sanctions imposed on them. First, judges need better information about an offender's salary and assets. Now, even with pre-sentence reports, judges have little information about how much an offender would be able to pay (Hillsman, 1990). Second, the amounts imposed should be geared toward an offender's salary and net worth, as is true with the day fine concept as it is used in Europe. Third, there needs to be some system to allow people without funds to pay, either through community service for those who are on probation or though prison salary for those who are incarcerated in a state prison. The usual calculus is that 1 day in jail is equal to 1 day of fines, which is equal to 8 hours of work (Hillsman, 1990).

One option, currently embodied in the recommendations of the Pennsylvania Commission on Sentencing for drug fines, is to use community service hours as the starting point for the proposed fine (204 PA. CODE § 303.14 (2015)). These recommendations, limited to the lowest levels of offense seriousness (Level 1 and Level 2 of the sentencing guidelines), use community service hours as the starting point for the proposed fine, the rationale being that community service can be ordered without consideration of the offender's ability to pay (38 Pa. Bull 4971 (Sept. 6, 2008)). Although a system of community service would allow offenders who are without resources to pay the economic sanctions imposed on them, such a system requires that the county has the agencies and opportunities for the community service and the staff to run the programs (e.g., to supervise trash pickup). Such programs require an initial and continuing outlay of county resources.

I have argued that a structure is needed for economic sanctions in order to increase fairness through uniformity, proportionality, certainty, and clarity. One possibility for this structure is a set of guidelines for economic sanctions. Three caveats need to be raised, however. First, if a guideline system is developed for economic sanctions, alone or as a package with incarceration and other sentencing alternatives, there is the likelihood that, as with current guideline systems, prosecutors will still have most of the power and will thus be able to avoid the guidelines if they wish.

Second, if an economic sanction is not imposed, for example as part of a plea agreement, there is no one who will be able to complain. Victims, particularly of crimes that have been bargained away, may not know of the plea and thus would be unlikely to complain. If state fines were not imposed, the state would need some sort of continuing monitoring system to discover the omission. By contrast, county fees and costs, if not imposed, would be likely to elicit complaints because the county staff needed for monitoring the imposition and payment of these sanctions have both the ability and motivation to do so.

Need for Research

As indicated earlier in connection with restitution, there is variation among the states in the nature of economic sanctions. Because of this variation, more work needs to be conducted on the actual practice of how economic sanctions are imposed and monitored. For example, research conducted in Washington State may not be representative of the problem nationally because of the uniqueness of the law in Washington (e.g., the garnishment of a spouse's wages to pay legal financial obligations; Beckett & Harris, 2011). At the other extreme, Pennsylvania, the state whose economic sanctions I have investigated, may also be different from other states. In Pennsylvania, judges in some counties use a back-end adjustment to economic sanctions that are unpaid. That is, they reduce or waive the economic sanctions if the offender is complying with the conditions of supervision or "is making a good-faith effort to repay the debt" (Bannon et al., 2010, p. 40). Moreover, Pennsylvania does not charge interest on unpaid economic sanctions. Unlike some other states, Pennsylvania does not allow conversion of criminal financial obligations to civil debt. And, finally, unlike 13 of the 15 states with the largest prison populations, Pennsylvania does not have a public defender fee.

Within-state and between-state differences in economic sanctions raise questions of fairness and equal treatment that may be addressable by the law. But questions about these policies concerning economic sanctions are also in need of better information about how they actually work.

Conclusion

In this final chapter, I have argued that victim restitution should be mandatory, fines should be discretionary, fees and costs should be prohibited, and states should provide more compensation to victims. Three themes governed this argument about the imposition of economic sanctions.

First, the law and courts should be concerned about victims. They are innocent of wrongdoing but face losses that are tangible and intangible, direct and indirect. Moreover, they are especially vulnerable in that they are likely to be victimized again. Because victimization is a predictor of offending, concern about crime victims might reduce the commission of crime.

Second, the law and courts should be concerned about offenders. The criminal justice system should help offenders reintegrate into society and should not burden them by imposing extra fees or surcharges that directly support the criminal justice system, imposing fees as restitution, or imposing sanctions that are not equally imposed on all (e.g., different fees and costs in different counties). Moreover, the use of economic sanctions should be structured to help offenders learn responsibility.

Third, the law and courts should be concerned about the community. The use of economic sanctions should be cost-effective. Moreover, their use should reflect concern about future victim cooperation and reducing future victimizations. And the community should use economic sanctions to reintegrate offenders into society.

Any reforms to economic sanctions, such as guidelines, need to be understandable to four groups: decision-makers in the criminal justice system, offenders, victims, and the general public. The individuals who make decisions about economic sanctions— judges, prosecutors, probation officers, and court clerks—need to understand them and be able to explain them to others. Offenders need to understand the way economic sanctions work for purposes of rehabilitation and deterrence. They need to understand that there is a link between their criminal behavior and their economic payment. Thus, they need to know how much they owe, where the money goes (e.g., the state, the county), and for what purposes. Victims also need to understand the system so that they have a better idea about the punishment that offenders are undergoing and the likelihood that they will receive restitution. Finally, it is important that the system be understood by the general public, both to maintain some deterrent effect and to engender respect for the law. In the same way that during the COVID-19 pandemic clinical physicians focused on individual patients whereas public health experts focused on larger groups (Carroll, 2020), we need to see economic sanctions as analogous to public health—a societal problem, not a problem of individual defendants.

Economic Sanctions and Justice

In their comment on economic sanctions, Reitz and Klingele (2019), the reporters for the MPCS, characterized economic sanctions as unprincipled, unsuccessful, and unending. As has been apparent throughout the book, economic sanctions, particularly fees and fines, are *unprincipled* because defendants do not receive all of their rights, including their right to a legal hearing regarding their ability to pay, which courts interpret as having been waived by a guilty plea. Fees and fines, but especially fees, put courts and probation offices in a position of conflicting interests, as they presumably administer the law while needing the payments from defendants in order to continue operating. Because criminal justice systems need the payments from poor defendants to operate, courts and probation offices are in the position of having the irrational incentive to ensure that defendants do not pay off their economic sanctions. Last, fees and fines discriminate against the poor because they pay more relative to their financial resources than do the wealthy and, in some cases, pay more in absolute terms because of interest and surcharges.

Economic sanctions, particularly fees and fines, are *unsuccessful* because they are generally unpaid and, as presently constituted, do not meet the purposes of sentencing. Fines, if they were appropriately set and adjusted over time for inflation, might serve to punish and deter. However, because fines are generally too low for wealthy defendants, they do neither. Fees do not deter or rehabilitate, and unpaid fees and fines keep defendants under criminal justice supervision.

Fees are *unending* because local and state governments are continuing to impose economic sanctions and other legal financial obligations in order to meet budgetary needs. Incarceration and supervision costs are increasing, and taxpayers are generally unwilling to pay more for treatment and rehabilitation.

Tonry (2018) suggested that just punishment incorporates four propositions: fairness, equal treatment, proportionality, and parsimony. Fairness refers to processes that are public and applied in good faith. Equal treatment refers to the same concern and respect for all offenders. According to the principle of proportionality, the severity of punishment must be justified by the offender's blameworthiness, and it must be comparable to what other offenders receive for the same offense, less than what other offenders receive for more serious offenses, and more than what other offenders receive for less serious offenses. *Parsimony* refers to punishment not being greater than what can be justified by appropriate purposes.

Tonry was most concerned about incarceration, but his framework is also applicable to economic sanctions. A fair system would be one that is transparent and understood, imposes equal impact on offenders, is proportional to the offense, and is not exaggerated by additional penalties.

I have argued that fees and costs should never be imposed, fines should be imposed based only on ability to pay, and restitution to victims should be ordered in all cases, regardless of ability to pay. Economic penalties—surcharges, interest, penalties—are always inappropriate. I made these arguments based on the notions that fees and costs are functions of government, not user fees, and that defendants should not have to pay them. Fines can serve penological purposes, but only if they are fair for the particular defendant, with fairness depending on the impact of the economic sanction.

What is fair may depend on culture. Hillsman (1990) said that in the United States, equity is seen as consistency—that is, the same amount of money—whereas in Europe fairness demands that the impact, not the dollar amount, be the same. Structured economic sanctions (day fines) take into account both the seriousness of the crime and the offender's ability to pay (Hillsman, 1990). Thus, sentences are equally punitive for all offenders. A system of economic sanctions based on ability to pay would overcome the problem of being unfairly punitive to defendants with limited income and few assets (Colgan, 2017) and would be more likely to be paid by offenders, thereby resulting in fewer jail penalties for nonpayment.

Our research in Pennsylvania suggests that procedural justice—how fairly people feel they have been treated—is important for both victims (Study 11) and offenders (Studies 12 and 14). With regard to offenders, the criminal justice system cannot change offenders' ability to pay (the single largest predictor of payment), but it can ensure that offenders are treated fairly by the professional staff. This fair treatment, in turn, may have demonstrable positive effects on offenders' behavior, including the payment of restitution, as suggested by the positive relationship we found among offenders in Study 14.

The philosopher David Hume argued that under conditions of abundant resources, there is no need to worry about property issues or theft because everyone has enough. At the other extreme, in times of pressing emergency, people are concerned with self-preservation, not the legal system. Thus, after a shipwreck no one can be expected to act within "the strict laws of justice" (1953, p. 18). The absence of extreme scarcity is, according to Rawls, one of the objective "circumstances of justice" that make "human cooperation both possible and necessary" (1971, p. 126).

For those who do not have this circumstance of justice, the notion of economic sanctions in the form of fines, and especially fees, is unjust. Even under conditions of what Rawls would term moderate scarcity, fines and fees are not aligned with the offender's ability to pay. The current system charges offenders for procedures that are the responsibility of government, under a structure that is not coherent, and in amounts that most offenders cannot pay. This freewheeling reliance on fees and costs, and the shame of privatized criminal justice, demean us. Economic sanctions in contemporary America are not so different from those in 18th-century colonial America or 10th-century England. And, like those earlier times, many victims are not compensated for their losses.

Justice is expensive. A fair system that delivers justice by guaranteeing the rights of defendants and victims requires both trained and dedicated personnel and a sophisticated—and expensive—infrastructure within which these personnel can act. But injustice is also expensive, apparent in a society in which many do not believe that there is evenhandedness, either for offenders or victims. Economic sanctions are not the largest problem facing the justice system, but they are often unfair and would be a good starting point for reform. We can do better.

Appendix: Ohio Bench Card

THE SUPREME COURT of OHIO

OFFICE OF JUDICIAL SERVICES

COLLECTION OF COURT COSTS & FINES IN ADULT TRIAL COURTS

Court practices to enforce appropriately assessed fines, costs, and other financial sanctions are an important part of enforcing the consequences of misconduct. Courts, in general, and individual judges in particular should ensure that any fines, costs, and other financial sanctions arising out of a criminal case are reasonable and take into account a defendant's ability to pay.

Fines are a criminal sanction, while costs are a civil obligation. Although separate and distinct, the purpose of both is *not* to generate revenue for the local municipality, county, or the State of Ohio.

IMPOSING FINES, COSTS, AND OTHER FINANCIAL SANCTIONS

Court Costs	Fines

• Court costs and fees are **civil, not criminal**, obligations and may be collected only by the methods provided for the collection of civil judgments.[1]
 • Trial courts must impose court costs at time of sentencing.[2] Costs must be:
  • Stated at sentencing hearing and included in sentencing entry.[3]
  • **Segregated from fines.**[4]
 • Court costs are mandatory, but trial courts retain jurisdiction to **waive, suspend, or modify the payment of costs** at the time of sentencing or any time thereafter.[5]
 • A court **may not** order a person to appear or issue a warrant for unpaid court costs.[6]
  • The court may order the defendant to perform community service if the defendant fails to pay court costs.[7]
	• Fines are a financial sanction and criminal penalty.[8]
	 • Financial sanctions may include restitution, fines, reimbursement for assigned counsel, incarceration, and other fees.[9]
	 • Fines are a **discretionary** financial sanction, unless there is a mandatory fine attached to the offense.[10]
	 • **Ability to pay** must be considered when assessing and collecting fines.[11]
	 • A person may be jailed for a **willful refusal** to pay a fine that he or she has the ability to pay (see "Incarceration for Non-Payment of Fines," below).[12]
	 • The court may order the defendant to perform community service in lieu of fines.[13]

When both fines and court costs are owed, the court **must segregate** the amounts if jail time is imposed for nonpayment of fines.[14]

INCARCERATION FOR NON-PAYMENT OF FINES

R.C.2947.14 is the sole and exclusive method for imposing a jail sentence for willful refusal to pay a fine.[15] Incarceration for nonpayment should only be used as a last resort and after compliance with all statutory and procedural safeguards.

  Before a court may impose a jail sentence for non-payment of court fines, the court must:
- Segregate fines from court costs and other financial sanctions.[16]
- Give reasonable notice to the defendant of a hearing.[17]
- Conduct an evidentiary, economic ability-to-pay hearing.[18]
- Advise the defendant of the right to counsel.[19]
- Provide the defendant with an opportunity to be heard.[20]
- Make a specific finding that the defendant[21]
- Has the ability to pay fines; and
- Willfully refuses to pay fines.

Additional Notes About Incarceration

A person cannot be ordered to serve additional days for failure to pay a fine if the maximum jail sentence was imposed and served.[22]

  Any person jailed for failure to pay a fine shall receive credit upon the fine at the rate of $50.00 per day or per fraction of a day.[23] No commitment pursuant to this statute shall exceed six months.[24]

FACTORS COURTS MAY CONSIDER WHEN ASSESSING OFFENDERS' ABILITY-TO-PAY[25]

- Income, specifically whether annual income is at or below 125% of the Federal Poverty Guidelines.

For 2021, 125% of FPG:[26]	
$12,880 for an Individual	$26,500 for a Family of 4
$17,420 for a Family of 2	$31,040 for a Family of 5
$21,960 for a Family of 3	$35,580 for a Family of 6

- Receipt of needs-based, means-tested public assistance, such as TANF, SSI, or SSDI.
- Financial resources, assets, financial obligations, and dependents.
- Where the person resides; for example, whether the person is homeless or institutionalized.
- Basic living expenses, such as food, rent/mortgage, utilities, medical expenses, transportation, and child support.
- Offender's efforts to acquire additional resources, including any limitations to secure paid work due to disability, homelessness, institutionalization, lack of transportation, or driving privileges.

PERMITTED METHODS OF COLLECTING COURT COSTS AND FINES
(Any Method Not Permitted Is Prohibited)

Permitted Collection Methods	Costs	Fines
Voluntary Payment[27]	X	X
Payment Plan[28]	X	X
Collection Agency[29]	X	X
Community Service[30,31]	X	X
Attachment of Prisoner Accounts[32]	X	X
Execution of Civil Judgment[33]	X	X
Registration Block[34]	X	X
Imposing Jail [35,36] (see Fines *front*)		X
Driver's License Forfeiture (limited to Traffic cases only)[37,38]		X
Driver's License Warrant Block[39]		X
Extension of Probation (if within maximum allowable term of probation and if made a condition of probation)[40]		X

PERMITTED METHODS OF COLLECTING COURT COSTS AND FINES
(Any Method Not Permitted Is Prohibited)

Non-Permitted Methods of Collecting Costs, Fines, or Other Fees	Waiver/Cancellation/Discharge of Costs or Fines
<ul><li>Contempt of Court[41]</li><li>Forfeiture of Confiscated Money[42]</li><li>Refusal to Accept Filings[43]</li><li>Violation or Revocation of Probation[44]</li><li>Setting Bond based on Amount Owed[45]</li><li>Automatically applying bond to amount owed if: – Defendant is indigent or [46] – A third party posted the bond [47]</li></ul>	If at any time the court finds that an amount owed to the court is due and uncollectible, in whole or in part, the court may direct the clerk of the court to **cancel all or part of the claim**.[48] The court retains jurisdiction to waive, suspend, or modify the payment of the costs of prosecution at the time of sentencing or at any time thereafter, pursuant to R.C. 2947.23(C).[49] The court is not required, but may consider ability to pay, along with other factors.[50] If a court waives any of the court costs, it must waive all imposed costs.[51]

LIMITATIONS OF CONTEMPT FOR COLLECTION OF COSTS AND FINES

Contempt may be imposed:
- If a defendant fails to appear for a court-ordered hearing, including a hearing for non-payment of fines.
- The defendant must be served with a separate citation for contempt of court, notice, and advised of:[52]
- Right to counsel (including appointed, if applicable).
- Right to present a defense and explanation.
- Right to bond. Bond must be based on failure-to- appear and/or comply, not based on amount owed.[53]

Contempt may NOT be imposed:
- In lieu of R.C. 2947.14 to impose jail time to collect fines.[54]
- To collect costs as a civil judgment.[55]
- For failure to perform if community service is assigned in lieu of either fines or court costs.[56]
- To create a punishment based on the underlying offense or as a method to collect fines or court costs.[57]
- For failure to appear if hearing was related to the payment or non-payment of court costs.[58]

While a charge of contempt of court for non-appearance at a hearing or community-control supervision/probation violation may result in a jail sentence being issued, **neither may be used to coerce or obtain the payment of a fine, court cost, or any other financial sanction**.[59]

COMMUNITY SERVICE AS PAYMENT FOR COURT COSTS

A court may convert court costs to community service when a defendant fails to pay court costs or comply with a payment plan to pay court costs at the time of sentencing or post-judgment proceeding.[60]

- Notice should be given to the defendant and the prosecuting attorney that failure to pay court costs may result in community service.[61]
- An evidentiary hearing must be held.[62]
- Defendant is entitled to credit at no less than the federal minimum wage.[63]

COMMUNITY SERVICE SCHEDULE

Offense	Limitation	Statutory Authority
Minor Misdemeanor	Maximum 30 hours	R.C. 2929.27(B)
Second-, Third-, and Fourth-Degree Misdemeanor	Maximum 200 hours	R.C. 2929.27(A)
First-Degree Misdemeanor	Maximum 500 hours	R.C. 2929.27(A)
Unclassified Misdemeanor	Maximum 500 hours	Suspended License Offenses[64]
Felony	Maximum 500 hours	R.C. 2929.17; R.C. 2951.02
Satisfaction of Court Costs	No less than federal minimum hourly wage rate; hearing required	R.C. 2947.23; R.C. 1901.44; R.C. 1907.25
Satisfaction of Fines[65]	Not specified; hearing not required	R.C. 2929.28

The staff of the Supreme Court of Ohio would like to thank Judge **Patrick Carroll** of the Lakewood Municipal Court for his contributions to the development of this bench card.

FOR A LIST OF REFERENCES, SEE: sc.ohio.gov/Publications/JCS/finesCourtCosts_Ref.pdf

References

Abaluck, J., Kwong, L. H., Stycznski, A., Haque, A., Kabir, M. A., Bates-Jefferys, E., et al. (2021). Normalizing community mask-wearing: A cluster randomized trial in Bangladesh. National Bureau of Economic Research. Working Paper 28734. https://www.nber.org/system/files/working_papers/w28734/w28734.pdf

ACLU of Pennsylvania. (2020). An ACLU-PA guide to the imposition of fines, costs, or restitution at sentencing. https://aclupa.org/sites/default/files/wysiwyg/sentencing_guide_2020-03-11_1.pdf

Adair, D. N., Jr. (1989). Looking at the law. *Federal Probation*, 53, 85–88.

Administrative Office of Pennsylvania Courts (AOPC). (2020). 2019 caseload statistics of the Unified Judicial System of Pennsylvania. Harrisburg, PA: Supreme Court of Pennsylvania. http://www.pacourts.us/assets/files/setting-768/file-10486.pdf?cb=40b215

Albin-Lackey, C. (2014, February 5). Human Rights Watch: *Profiting from probation*. February 5, 2014. http://www.hrw.org/print/reports/2014/02/05/profiting-probation

Alexander, D., Montgomer, J., Hamilton, G., Dutton, D. W., Griswold, R. R., Russell, J. R., Salo, R. J., & Muse, M. K. (1998). Fines and restitution: Improvement needed in how offenders' payment schedules are determined. Washington, DC: U.S. General Accounting Office.

Alexander, M. (2012). *The new Jim Crow: Mass incarceration in the age of colorblindness* (rev. ed.). New York: New Press.

Allen, G. F., & Treger, H. (1994). Fines and restitution orders: Probationers' perceptions. *Federal Probation*, 58(2), 34–40.

American Bar Association Victims Committee of the Criminal Justice Section. (2004). Restitution for crime victims: A national strategy. A.B.A Section on Criminal Justice. 15.

American Civil Liberties Union. (2010). In for a penny: The rise of America's new debtors' prisons. New York: ACLU. https://www.aclu.org/sites/default/files/field_document/InForAPenny_web.pdf

American Law Institute. (2020). *Model Penal Code: Sentencing.* Philadelphia: American Law Institute.

Anderson, H. A. (2009). Penalizing poverty: Making criminal defendants pay for their court-appointed counsel through recoupment and contribution. *University of Michigan Journal of Law Reform, 42,* 323–380.

Appelbaum, B. (2019, September 1). Blame economists for the mess we're in. New York Times. https://www.nytimes.com/2019/08/24/opinion/sunday/economics-milton-friedman.html

Appleman, L. I. (2016). Nickel and dimed into incarceration: Cash register justice in the criminal system. *Boston College Law Review, 57,* 1483–1541.

Appleman, L. I. (2018). Cashing in on convicts: Privatization, punishment, and the people. *Utah Law Review, 2018,* 579–637.

Apuzzo, M. (2016, March 14). Justice Dept. condemns profit-minded court policies targeting the poor. New York Times. http://www.nytimes.com/2016/03/15/us/politics/justice-dept-condemns-profit-minded-court-policies-targeting-the-poor.html?emc=eta1

Ariel, B. (2012). Deterrence and moral persuasion effects on corporate tax compliance: Findings from a randomized controlled trial. *Criminology, 50,* 27–69.

Ariely, D. (2010). *The upside of irrationality: The unexpected benefits of defying logic at work and at home.* New York: HarperCollins.

Ariely, D., & Kreisler, J. (2017). *Dollars and sense: How we misthink money and how to spend smarter.* New York: HarperCollins.

Armony, M., Roels, G., & Song, H. (2021). Pooling queues with strategic servers: The effects of customer ownership. *Operations Research, 69,* 13–29.

Aronson, E., Ellsworth, P. C., Carlsmith, J. M., & Gonzales, M. H. (1990). *Methods of research in social psychology* (2nd ed.). New York: McGraw-Hill.

Ashford, G. (2019, September 9). The law was aimed at deadly machinery. It hit her washer. New York Times. https://www.nytimes.com/2019/09/09/nyregion/building-violations-fines-debt.html

Atuahene, B. (2020, June 11). The scandal of the predatory city. New York Times. https://www.nytimes.com/2020/06/11/opinion/coronavirus-cities-property-taxes.html

Baicker, K., & Jacobson, M. (2007). Finders keepers: Forfeiture laws, policing incentives, and local budgets. *Journal of Public Economics, 91,* 2113–2136.

Baker, K. (2006, June/July). Cruel and usual: Why prisoners shouldn't pay their way. American Heritage Magazine. https://www.americanheritage.com/cruel-and-usual2

Bannon, A., Nagrecha, & Diller, K. R. (2010). Criminal justice debt: A barrier to re-entry. New York: Brennan Center for Justice. http://www.brennancenter.org/content/resource/criminal_justice_debt_a_barrier_to_reentry/.

Bateson, M., Nettle, D., & Roberts, G. (2006). Cues of being watched enhance cooperation in a real-world setting. *Biology Letters, 22*, 412–414.

Baumer, E. P. (2008). Evaluating the balance sheet of asset forfeiture laws: Toward evidence-based policy assessments. *Criminology & Public Policy, 7*, 245–256.

Bearden v. Georgia, 461 US 660 (1983).

Becker, G. S. (1968). Crime and punishment: An economic approach. *Journal of Political Economy, 76*, 169–217.

Beckett, K., & Harris, A. (2011). On cash and conviction. *Criminology & Public Policy, 10*(3), 509–537.

Beijersbergen, K. A., Dirkzwager, A. J. E., & Nieuwbeerta, P. (2016). Reoffending after release: Does procedural justice during imprisonment matter? *Criminal Justice and Behavior, 43*, 63–82.

Bem D. J. (1972). Self-perception theory. In L. Berkowitz (Ed.), *Advances in Experimental Social Psychology* (Vol. 6, pp. 1–62). New York: Academic Press.

Benhold, K. (2013, December 7). Britain's ministry of nudges. New York Times. https://www.nytimes.com/2013/12/08/business/international/britains-ministry-of-nudges.html

Bennett, J. (2014, July 1). Kenneth Feinberg on GM Payouts: "Fast Is Possible, Fair Isn't." Wall Street Journal Law Blog (July 1, 2014, 3:47 PM). http://blogs.wsj.com/law/2014/07/01/kenneth-feinberg-on-gm-payouts-fast-is-possible-fair-isnt

Benoit, D. (2020, November 2). Ex-inmates struggle in banking system. Wall Street Journal, B9. https://prisonist.org/wall-street-journal-ex-inmates-struggle-in-a-banking-system-not-made-for-them-by-david-benoit/

Benson, B. L. (2012). Decriminalisation, restitution and privatization: The path to reduced violence and theft. *Griffith Law Review, 21*, 448–471.

Biewen, J. (2002, April 27). Weekend edition: Asset forfeiture from drug-related arrests and how some law enforcement agencies use the funds. [Radio broadcast]. Washington, DC: National Public Radio.

Birckhead, T. R. (2015). The new peonage. *Washinton & Lee Law Review, 72*, 1595–1678.

Bird, R. M., & Tsiopoulos, T. (1997). User charges for public services: Potentials and problems. *Canadian Tax Journal, 45*, 25–86.

Blumenson, E., & Nilsen, E. (1998). Policing for profit: The drug war's hidden economic agenda. *University of Chicago Law Review, 65*, 35–114.

Blumstein, A., Cohen, J., Martin, S E., & Tonry, M. H. (Eds.). (1983). *Research on Sentencing: The search for reform*. National Research Council. Panel on Sentencing, 1. Washington, DC: National Academies Press.

Board of Governors of the Federal Reserve System. (2020). Report on the economic well-being of US households in 2019, featuring supplemental data from April 2020. Washington, DC: Federal Reserve System. https://www.federalreserve.gov/publications/files/2019-report-economic-well-being-us-households-202005.pdf

Bolivar, D. (2010). Conceptualizing victims' "restoration" in restorative justice. *International Review of Victimology, 17*, 237–265.

Bonczar, T. P. (1997). *Characteristics of adults on probation, 1995*. Washington, DC: US Department of Justice.

Bonczar, T. P. (2003). Prevalence of imprisonment in the US population, 1974–2001. NCJ 197976. Washington, DC: Bureau of Justice Statistics. https://www.bjs.gov/content/pub/pdf/piusp01.pdf

Braithwaite, J. (1989). *Crime, shame and reintegration*. Cambridge: Cambridge University Press.

Braithwaite, J., Ahmed, E., & Braithwaite, V. (2006). Shame, restorative justice, and crime. In F. T. Cullen, J. P. Wright, & K. R. Blevins (Eds.), *Advances in criminological theory: Vol. 15. Taking stock: The status of criminological theory* (pp. 397–417). Piscataway, NJ: Transaction Publishers.

Brehm, J. W. (1966). *A theory of psychological reactance.* New York: Academic Press.

Brennan, P.A., & Mednick, S.A. (1994). Learning theory approach to the deterrence of criminal recidivism. *Journal of Abnormal Psychology, 103,* 430–440.

Breslow, J. (2020, May 24). Federal judge rules Florida law restricting voting rights for felons unconstitutional. National Public Radio. https://www.npr.org/2020/05/24/861776313/federal-judge-rules-florida-law-restricting-voting-rights-for-felons-unconstitut

Brett, S., Khoshkhoo, N., & Nagrecha, M. (2020). Paying on probation: How financial sanctions intersect with probation to target, trap, and punish people who cannot pay. Criminal Justice Policy Program. Cambridge, MA: Harvard Law School. https://mcusercontent.com/f65678cd73457d0cbde864d05/files/f05e951e-60a9-404e-b5cc-13c065b2a630/Paying_on_Probation_report_FINAL.pdf

Brett, S., & Nagrecha, M. (2019). Proportionate financial sanctions: Policy prescriptions for judicial reform. Criminal Justice Policy Program. Cambridge, MA: Harvard Law School. https://papers.ssrn.com/sol3/papers.cfm?abstract_id=3506268

Brickman, P. (1977). Crime and punishment in sports and society *Journal of Social Issues, 33,* 140–164.

Bureau of Justice Assistance. (1988). Restitution by juveniles: Information and operating guide for restitution programs. NCJ 115418. Washington, DC: Office of Justice Programs. https://www.ojp.gov/pdffiles1/Digitization/115418NCJRS.pdf

Burger, J. M., Bell, H., Harvey, K., Johnson, J., Stewart, C., Dorian, K., et al. (2010). Nutritious or delicious? The effect of descriptive norm information on food choice. *Journal of Social and Clinical Psychology, 29,* 228–242.

Butterfield, F. (2004, August 13). Many local officials now make inmates pay their own way. *New York Times,* https://www.nytimes.com/2004/08/13/us/many-local-officials-now-make-inmates-pay-their-own-way.html

Butts, J. A., & Snyder, H. N. (1992). Restitution and juvenile recidivism. Washington, DC: Office of Juvenile Justice and Delinquency Prevention. http://www.ncjj.org/pdf/OJJDP%20Bulletin.pdf

Cammett, A. (2012). Shadow citizens: Felony disenfranchisement and the criminalization of debt. *Penn State Law Review, 117,* 349–405.

Campos-Bui, S., Selbin, J., Jaka, H., Kline, T., Lavalais, A, Phillips, A., & Ridley-Kerr, A. (2017). Making families pay: The harmful, unlawful, and costly practice of charging juvenile administrative fees in California. Berkeley,

CA: UC Berkeley Public Law Research Paper. https://papers.ssrn.com/sol3/papers.cfm?abstract_id=2937534

Campos-Flores, A., & Kamp, J. (2020, February 8). Florida voted to give 1.4 million fellows the right to vote. It hasn't gone smoothly. Wall Street Journal. https://www.wsj.com/articles/florida-voted-to-give-1-4-million-felons-the-right-to-vote-it-hasnt-gone-smoothly-11581174000

Carlson, E. A. (2020). Prisoners in 2018. NCJ 253516. Washington, DC: Bureau of Justice Statistics. https://www.bjs.gov/content/pub/pdf/p18.pdf

Carpenter, D. M., II, Knepper, L., Erickson, A. C., & McDonald, J. (2015). *Policing for profit: The abuse of civil asset forfeiture* (2nd ed.). Washington, DC: Institute for Justice. http://ij.org/wp-content/uploads/2015/11/policing-for-profit-2nd-edition.pdf

Carroll, A. E. (2020, July 28). There are many ways we haven't tried to test for the coronavirus. New York Times. https://www.nytimes.com/2020/07/28/opinion/coronavirus-testing-antigen-pooling.html

Case, A., & Deaton, A. (2020). *Deaths of despair and the future of capitalism*. Princeton, NJ: Princeton University Press.

Charness, G., & Dufwenberg, M. (2006). Promises and partnership. *Econometrica, 74*, 1579–1601.

Cialdini, R. B. (2001). *Influence: Science and practice* (4th ed.). Boston: Allyn and Bacon.

Clerk of the Superior Court, Maricopa County, Arizona. (2020). Criminal payments. https://www.clerkofcourt.maricopa.gov/services/make-a-payment/criminal-payments

Cohen, J. (1977). *Statistical power analysis for the behavioral sciences* (rev. ed.). Hillsdale, NJ: Erlbaum.

Cohen, M. A. (2005). *The costs of crime and justice*. New York: Routledge.

Cohen, R. (1995). *Probation and parole violation in state prison, 1991*. Washington, DC: Bureau of Justice Statistics.

Cole, G. F., Mahoney, B., Thornton, M., & Hanson, R. A. (1987). *The practices and attitudes of trial court judges regarding fines as a criminal sanction*. Washington, DC: National Institute of Justice.

Colgan, B. A. (2017). Graduating economic sanctions according to ability to pay. *Iowa Law Review, 103*, 53–112.

Colquitt, J. A. (2001). On the dimensionality of organizational justice: A construct validation of a measure. *Journal of Applied Psychology, 86*, 386–400.

Commonwealth of Pennsylvania v. Kline, 695 A.2d 872 (Pa. Super. 1997).

Compañía General de Tabacos de Filipinas v. Collector of Internal Revenue, 275 US 87 (1927).

Cook, F. (2014). The burden of criminal justice debt in Alabama. Birmingham, AL: TASC Jefferson County's Community Corrections Program. http://media.al.com/opinion/other/The%20Burden%20of%20Criminal%20Justice%20Debt%20in%20Alabama-%20Full%20Report.pdf

Cunniff, M. A., & Shilton, M. K. (1991). Variations on felony probation: Persons under supervision in 32 urban and suburban counties. Washington, DC: Bureau of Justice Statistics. https://www.ncjrs.gov/pdffiles1/Digitization/131580NCJRS.pdf

Davis, R. C., & Bannister, T. (1995). Improving collection of court-ordered restitution. *Judicature, 79*, 30–33.

Davis, R. C., & Mulford, C. (2008). Victim rights and new remedies: Finally getting victims their due. *Journal of Contemporary Criminal Justice, 24*, 198–208.

Davis, R. C., Smith, B., & Hillebrand, S. (1991). Increasing offender compliance with restitution orders. *Judicature, 74*, 245–248.

Davis, R. C., Smith, B., & Hillenbrand, S. (1992). Restitution: The victim's viewpoint. *Justice System Journal, 15*, 746–758.

Department of Justice Office of the Inspector General. (2020). Audit of the Office of Justice programs victim compensation grants awarded to the Massachusetts Department of Attorney General. Audit Division 20-089. https://www.oversight.gov/sites/default/files/oig-reports/20-089.pdf

Dickman, M. (2009). Should crime pay? A critical assessment of the Mandatory Victims Restitution Act of 1996. *California Law Review, 97*, 1687–1718.

DiIulio, J. J., Jr. (1988). What's wrong with private prisons. *Public Interest, 92*, 66–83.

DiIulio, J. J., Jr. (2003). Government by proxy: A faithful overview. *Harvard Law Review, 116*, 1271–1284.

Dillman, D. A. (2007). *Mail and internet surveys: The tailored design method* (2nd ed.). Hoboken, NJ: John Wiley.

Doak, J., & O'Mahony, D. (2006). The vengeful victim? Assessing the attitudes of victims participating in restorative justice. *International Review of Victimology, 13*, 157–177.

Doyle, C. (2007). *Restitution in federal criminal cases.* Congressional Research Services. Washington, DC.

Duff, D. (2004). Benefit taxes and user fees in theory and practice. *University of Toronto Law Journal, 54*, 391–447.

Duffy-Gideon, R. (2017). Pay it backward: Buy-money repayment as a condition of supervised release. *University of Chicago Law Review, 84*, 1933–1970.

Duflo, E., & Banerjee, A. (2019, October 26). Economic incentives don't always do what we want them to. New York Times. https://www.nytimes.com/2019/10/26/opinion/sunday/duflo-banerjee-economic-incentives.html

Durose, M. (2007). State court sentencing of convicted felons. Washington, DC: Bureau of Justice Statistics. http:// www.bjs.gov/content/pub/html/scscf04/tables/scs04109tab.cfm

Dušek, L., & Traxler, C. (2020, January). Learning from law enforcement. CESifo Working Papers, 8043. Ludwigs-Maximilians University's Center for Economic Studies. Munich, Germany. https://www.cesifo.org/en/publikationen/2020/working-paper/learning-law-enforcement

Edelman, P. (2017). *Not a crime to be poor: The criminalization of poverty in America.* New York: New Press.

Edsall, T. B. (2014, August 26). The expanding world of poverty capitalism. New York Times. http://www.nytimes.com/2014/08/27/opinion/thomas-edsall-the-expanding-world-of-poverty-capitalism.html

Eisen, L-B. (2015). Curbing cash register style justice. New York: Brennan Center for Justice. https://www.brennancenter.org/our-work/analysis-opinion/curbing-cash-register-style-justice

Eisenstein, J., Flemming, R. B., & Nardullli, P. F. (1988). *The contours of justice: Communities and their courts*. Boston: Little, Brown.

Elbel, B., Kersh, R., Brescoll, V. L., & Dixon, L. B. (2009). Calorie labeling and food choices: A first look at the effects on low-income people in New York City. *Health Affairs, 28*, 1110–1121.

Elias, R. (1984). Alienating the victim: Compensation and victim attitudes. *Journal of Social Issues, 40*, 103–116.

Elias, R. (1986). *The politics of victimization: Victims, victimology, and human rights*. New York: Oxford University Press.

Ellsworth, T., & Weisheit, R. A. (1997). The supervision and treatment of offenders on probation: Understanding rural and urban differences. *The Prison Journal, 77*, 209–228.

Erez, E., & Tontodonato, P. (1990). The effect of victim participation in sentencing on sentencing outcome. *Criminology, 28*, 47–60.

Ervin, L., & Schneider, A. (1990). Explaining the effects of restitution on offenders: Results from a national experiment in juvenile courts. In B. Galaway & J. Hudson (Eds.), *Criminal justice, restitution, and reconciliation* (pp. 183–206). New York: Willow Tree Press.

Evans, D. N. (2014). Compensating victims of crime. New York: John Jay College of Criminal Justice. https://johnjayrec.nyc/wp-content/uploads/2014/06/jf_johnjay3.pdf

Faraldo-Cabana, P. (2014). Towards equalization of the impact of the penal fine: Why the wealth of the offender was taken into account. *International Journal for Crime, Justice, & Social Democracy, 3*, 3–15.

Farrington, D. P., & Welsh, B. C. (2005). Randomized experiments in criminology: What have we learned in the last two decades? *Journal of Experimental Criminology, 1*, 9–38.

Federal Bureau of Investigation. (2019). Crime in the United States, 2018. Table 6. https://ucr.fbi.gov/crime-in-the-u.s/2018/crime-in-the-u.s.-2018/topic-pages/tables/table-6

Federal Ministry of Interior and Federal Ministry of Justice. (2001). First periodical report on crime and crime control in Germany. http://www.uni-konstanz.de/rtf/ki/Download_Abridged_Version.pdf.

Feinberg, K. R. (2005). *What is life worth? The unprecedented effort to compensate the victims of 9/11*. New York: Public Affairs.

Ferguson, N. (2008). *The ascent of money: A financial history of the world*. New York: Penguin Press.

Festinger, L. (1957). *A theory of cognitive dissonance*. Stanford, CA: Stanford University Press.

Fines & Fees Justice Center. (2016). Biloxi Municipal Court procedures for legal financial obligations & community service. https://finesandfeesjusticecenter.org/articles/biloxi-bench-card-fines-fees/

Finn, P., & Parent, D. (1992). Making the offender foot the bill: A Texas program. NCT 136839. Washington, DC: National Institute of Justice. https://www.ojp.gov/pdffiles1/Digitization/136839NCJRS.pdf

Forman, J., Jr. (2017). *Locking up our own: Crime and punishment in Black America*. New York: Farrar, Straus and Giroux.

Frank, L. F. (1992). The collection of restitution: An often overlooked service to crime victims. *St. Johns Journal of Legal Commentary, 8*, 107–134.

Galaway, B., & Hudson, J. (1975). Restitution and rehabilitation: Some central issues. In J. Hudson & B. Galaway (Eds.), *Considering the victim: Readings in restitution and victim compensation* (pp. 255–264). Springfield, IL: Thomas.

Galvin, M. A., Loughran, T. A., Simpson, S. S., & Cohen, M. A. (2018). Victim compensation policy and white collar crime. *Criminology & Public Policy, 17,* 553–594.

Gillespie, R. W. (1981). Sanctioning traditional crimes with fines: A comparative analysis. *International Journal of Comparative and Applied Criminal Justice, 5,* 197–204.

Gillespie, R. W. (1988–1989). Criminal fines: Do they pay? *Justice System Journal, 13,* 365–378.

Gillibrand, K. (2020, April 26). Where's the nearest bank and ballot box? Try the Post Office. New York Times. https://www.nytimes.com/2020/04/26/opinion/kirsten-gillibrand-usps-coronavirus.html

Gilligan, C. (1982). *In a different voice: Psychological theory and women's development.* Cambridge, MA: Harvard University Press.

Gladfelter, A. S., Lantz, B., & Ruback, R. B. (2018). Beyond ability to pay: Procedural justice and offender compliance with restitution orders. *International Journal of Offender Therapy and Comparative Criminology, 62,* 4314–4331.

Gneezy, U., & Rustichini, A. (2000). A fine is a price. *Journal of Legal Studies, 29,* 1–17.

Goetzman, W. N. (2016). *Money changes everything: How finance made civilization possible.* Princeton, NJ: Princeton University Press.

Goggin, M. L., Bowman, A. O., Lester, J. P., & O'Toole, L. J., Jr. (1990). *Implementation theory and practice: Toward a third generation.* Glenview, IL: Scott, Foresman.

Goldstein, R., Sances, M. W., & You, H. Y. (2020). Exploitative revenues, law enforcement, and the quality of government service. *Urban Affairs Review, 56,* 5–31.

Gonzalez, S. (2021, February 12). Planet Money: Fines and punishment. NPR. https://www.npr.org/2021/02/12/967260423/planet-money-fine-and-punishment

Gordon, M. A., & Glaser, D. (1991). The use and effects of financial penalties in municipal courts. *Criminology, 29,* 651–676.

Greenwald, M. A., Jackson, S. L., & Baglivio, M. T. (2014). The costs of delinquency. *Criminology and Public Policy, 13,* 61–67.

Gruver v. Barton, (see *Jones v. DeSantis,* 2020).

Hallmark, S. L., Hawkins, N., & Smadi, O. (2015). Evaluation of dynamic speed feedback signs on curves: A national demonstration project. Federal Highway Administration. FHWA-HRT-14-020. McLean, VA: US Department of Administration. https://www.fhwa.dot.gov/publications/research/safety/14020/14020.pdf

Harland, A. T. (1980). *Restitution to victims of personal and household crimes.* NCJ 72770. Washington, DC: Bureau of Justice Statistics. https://www.ojp.gov/pdffiles1/Digitization/72770NCJRS.pdf

Harper, A., Ginapp, C., Bardelli, T., Grimshaw, A., Justen, M., Mohamedali, A., Thomas, I., & Puglisi, L. (2021). Debt, incarceration, and re-entry: A scoping review. *American Journal of Criminal Justice, 46,* 250–278.

Harris, A. (2016). *A pound of flesh: Monetary sanctions as punishment for the poor.* New York: Russell Sage Foundation.

Harris, A., Evans, H., & Beckett, K. (2010). Drawing blood from stones: Legal debt and social inequality in the contemporary United States. *American Journal of Sociology, 115*(6), 1753–1799.

Harris, A., Evans, H., & Beckett, K. (2011). Courtesy stigma and monetary sanctions: Toward a socio-cultural theory of punishment, *American Sociological Review, 76*, 234–264.

Harvey, T., McAnnar, J., Voss, M-J, Conn, M., Janda, S., & Keskey, S. (2014). ArchCity Defenders: Municipal courts white paper. https://www.archcitydefenders.org/wp-content/uploads/2019/03/ArchCity-Defenders-Municipal-Courts-Whitepaper.pdf

Haushofer, J., & Fehr, E. (2014). On the psychology of poverty. *Science, 344*, 862–867.

Haynes, S. H., Cares, A., & Ruback, R. B. (2014). Juvenile economic sanctions: An analysis of their imposition, payment, and effect on recidivism. *Criminology & Public Policy, 13*, 31–60.

Haynes, S. H., Cares, A., & Ruback, R. B. (2015). Reducing the harm of criminal victimization: The role of restitution. *Violence & Victims, 30*, 450–469.

Haynes, S. H., Ruback, R. B., & Cusick, G. R. (2010). Courtroom workgroups and sentencing: The effects of similarity, proximity, and stability. *Crime & Delinquency, 56*, 126–161.

Heinz, J., Galaway, B., & Hudson, J. (1976). Restitution or parole: A follow-up study of adult offenders. *Social Service Review, 50*, 148–156.

Henrichson, C., Rinaldi, J., & Delaney, R. (2015). The price of jails: Measuring the taxpayer cost of local incarceration. New York: VERA Institute of Justice. https://www.vera.org/downloads/publications/price-of-jails.pdf

Hillsman, S. (1990). Fines and day fines. In M. Tonry & N. Morris (Eds.), *Crime and justice: A review of research* (vol. 12, pp. 49–98). Chicago: University of Chicago Press.

Hillsman, S., & Greene, J. A. (1992). The use of fines an intermediate sanction. In J. M. Byrne, A. J. Lurigio, & J. Petersilia (Eds.), *Smart sentencing: The emergence of intermediate sanctions* (pp. 123–141). Newbury Park, CA: Sage.

Hillsman, S., T., & Mahoney, B. (1988). Collecting and enforcing criminal fines: A review of court processes, practices, and problems. *Justice System Journal, 13*(1), 34–35.

Hillsman, S., Mahoney, B., Cole, G., & B. Auchter. (1987). Fines as criminal sanctions. National Institute of Justice. https://www.ncjrs.gov/pdffiles1/Digitization/106773NCJRS.pdf

Hillsman, S., Sichel, J., & Mahoney, B. (1984). *Fines in sentencing: A study of the use of the fine as a criminal sanction.* Washington, DC: National Institute of Justice.

Hirschman, A. O. (1970). *Exit, voice, and loyalty: Responses to decline in firms, organizations, and states.* Cambridge, MA: Harvard University Press.

Hobbs, T. D. (2019, August 24). Parents face a growing barrage of fees as students head back to school. Wall Street Journal, p. A3. https://www.wsj.com/articles/parents-face-a-growing-barrage-of-fees-as-students-head-back-to-school-11566639001

Holcomb, J. E., Williams, M. R., Hicks, W. D., Kovandzic, T. V., & Meitl, M. B. (2018). Civil asset forfeiture laws and equitable sharing activity by the police. *Criminology & Public Policy, 17*, 101–127.

Hollin, C. R. (2002). Does punishment motivate offenders to change? In M. McMurran (Ed.), *Motivating offenders to change: A guide to enhancing engagement in therapy* (pp. 235–250). New York: Wiley.

Hudson, J., & Chesney, S. (1977). Research on restitution: A review and assessment. In B. Galaway & J. Hudson (Eds.), *Offender restitution in theory and action* (pp. 131–148). Toronto: Lexington Books.

Human Rights Watch. (2014). Profiting from probation: America's "Offender-Funded" probation industry. https://www.hrw.org/sites/default/files/reports/us0214_ForUpload_0.pdf

Hume, D. (1953/1777). *An enquiry concerning the principles of morals*. LaSalle, IL: Open Court Publishing Company.

In re Humphrey. Supreme Court of California. March 25, 2021. https://www.courts.ca.gov/opinions/documents/S247278.PDF

Institute for Justice. (2015). *Policing for profit: The abuse of civil asset forfeiture* (3rd ed.). Arlington, VA. https://ij.org/report/policing-for-profit-3/

Iratzoqui, A., & Metcalfe, C. (2017). Set up for failure? Examining the influence of monetary sanctions on probation success. *Criminal Justice Policy Review, 28*, 370–393.

Jackson, J., Bradford, B., Hough, M., Myhill, A., Quinton, P., & Tyler, T. R. (2012). Why do people comply with the law? Legitimacy and the influence of legal institutions. *British Journal of Criminology, 52*, 1051–1071.

Jacobs, S., & Moore, D. C. (1994). Successful restitution as a predictor of juvenile recidivism. *Juvenile and Family Court Journal, 45*, 3–14.

Jarvis, W. (2019, July 22). LSU just unveiled a $28-million football facility. The flood-damaged library is still "decrepit." The Chronicle of Higher Education. https://www.chronicle.com/article/LSU-Just-Unveiled-a/246750?utm_source=at&utm_medium=en&cid=at

Jones v. DeSantis, 462 F.Supp.3d 1196 (N.D. Fla. 2020).

Jones v. Governor of Florida, 975 F.3d 1016 (11th Cir. 2020).

Jones, C., & Kamp, J. (2020, September 30). In 2020 election, Florida felon voting limits could sway state outcome. Wall Street Journal. https://www.wsj.com/articles/in-2020-election-florida-felon-voting-limits-could-sway-state-outcome-11601467381

Kaeble, D., & Cowhig, M. (2018). *Correctional populations in the United States, 2016*. NCJ 251211. Washington, DC: Bureau of Justice Statistics. https://bjs.ojp.gov/content/pub/pdf/cpus16.pdf

Kaiser, K. A., & Holtfreter, K. (2016). An integrated theory of specialized court programs: Using procedural justice and therapeutic jurisprudence to promote offender compliance and rehabilitation. *Criminal Justice and Behavior, 43*, 45–62.

Katzenstein, M. F., & Nagrecha, M. (2011). A new punishment regime. *Criminology & Public Policy, 10*, 555–568.

Kelman, H. C. (1958). Compliance, identification, and internalization three processes of attitude change. *Journal of Conflict Resolution, 2*, 51–60.

Kennedy v. Biloxi, No. 1:15-cv-348-HSO-JCG (S.D. Miss) (filed Oct. 21, 2015). See https://www.courtlistener.com/docket/14433933/ kennedy-v-the-city-of-biloxi-mississippi/

Kerr, N. L., & Kaufman-Gilliland, C. M. (1994). Communication, commitment and cooperation in social dilemma. *Journal of Personality and Social Psychology, 66*, 513–529.

Kilpatrick, D. G., Beatty, D., & Howley, S. S. (1998). The rights of crime victims: Does legal protection make a difference? Washington, DC: National Institute of Justice. http://www.cvactionalliance.com/wordpress/wp-content/ uploads/2010/03/ RightsofCrimeVictimslegalprotection.pdf

Klein, A. R. (1997). *Alternative sentencing, intermediate sanctions and probation* (2nd ed.). Cincinnati, OH: Anderson Publishing.

Kliff, S. (2019, November 8). With medical bills skyrocketing, more hospitals are suing for payment. New York Times. https://www.nytimes.com/2019/11/08/ us/hospitals-lawsuits-medical-debt.html

Kofman, A. (2019, July 3). Digital jail: How electronic monitoring drives defendants into debt. New York Times Magazine. https://www.nytimes.com/ 2019/07/03/magazine/digital-jail-surveillance.html

Kohler-Hausmann, I. (2018). *Misdemeanorland: Criminal courts and social control in an age of broken windows policing.* Princeton, NJ: Princeton University Press.

Kopf, D. (2016, June 24). The fining of Black America. Priceonomics. https:// priceonomics.com/the-fining-of-black-america/

Laisne, M., Wool, J., & Henrichson, C. (2017). *Past due: Examining the costs and consequences of charging for justice in New Orleans.* New York: Vera Institute of Justice. https://storage.googleapis.com/vera-web-assets/downloads/ Publications/past-due-costs-consequences-charging-for-justice-new-orleans/ legacy_downloads/past-due-costs-consequences-charging-for-justice-new- orleans.pdf

Langan, P. (1994). Between prison and probation: Intermediate sanctions. *Science, 264*, 791–793.

Langton, L., & Truman, J. (2013). *Socio-emotional impact of violent crime.* NCJ 247076. Washington, DC: Bureau of Justice Statistics.

Levingston, K. D., & Turetsky, V. (2007). Debtors' prison: Prisoners' accumulation of debt as a barrier to reentry. *Journal of Poverty Law and Policy, 41* (July– August), 187–197.

Levitt, S. D., & Dubner, S. J. (2006). *Freakonomics: A rogue economist explores the hidden side of everything* (rev. and expanded ed.). New York: HarperCollins.

Lewis, J., Aydin, A., & Powell, N. (2013). *March: Book one.* Marietta, GA: Top Shelf Productions.

Lipsey, M. (2009). The primary factors that characterize effective interventions with juvenile offenders: A meta-analytic overview. *Victims and Offenders, 4*, 124–147.

Liu, P., Nunn, R., & Shambaugh, J. (2019, March 15). Nine facts about monetary sanctions in the criminal justice system. Washington, DC: Brookings. https://www.brookings.edu/research/ nine-facts-about-monetary-sanctions-in-the-criminal-justice-system/

Loftin, C, Heumann, M., & McDowall, D. (1983). Mandatory sentencing and firearms violence: Evaluating an alternative to gun control. *Law and Society Review, 17,* 287–318.

Logan, C. H. (1990). *Private prisons: Cons and pros.* Oxford: Oxford University Press.

Logan, W. A. (2018). What the feds can do to rein in local mercenary justice. *University of Illinois Law Review, 2018,* 1731–1759.

Logan, W. A., & Wright, R. F. (2014). Mercenary criminal justice. *University of Illinois Law Review, 2014,* 1175–1226.

Lokhorst, A. M., Werner, C., Staats, H., van Dijk, E., & Gale, J. L. (2013). Commitment and behavior change: A meta-analysis and critical review of commitment-making strategies in environmental research. *Environment and Behavior, 45,* 3–34.

Lurigio, A. (1984). *The relationship between offender characteristics and fulfillment of financial restitution.* Chicago: Cook County Adult Probation Department.

Lurigio, A. J., & Davis, R. C. (1990). Does a threatening letter increase compliance with restitution orders?: A field experiment. *Crime and Delinquency, 36,* 537–548.

Mahler, H. I. M., Kulik, J. A., Butler, H. A., Gerrard, M., & Gibbons, F. X. (2008). Social norms information enhances the efficacy of an appearance-based sun protection intervention. *Social Science & Medicine, 67,* 321–329.

Makowsky, M. D., Stratmann, T., & Tabarrok, A. (2019). To serve and collect: The fiscal and racial determinants of law enforcement. *Journal of Legal Studies, 48,* 189–216.

"Man Accused of Robbing Banks to Pay Court Ordered Restitution." (1997, June 15). *Washington Post,* p. A15.

Mani, A., Mullainathan, S., Shafir, E., & Zhao, J. (2013). Poverty impedes cognitive function. *Science, 341,* 976–980.

Marçal, K. (2017, July 27). Sweden shows that pay transparency works. Financial Times. https://www.ft.com/content/2a9274be-72aa-11e7-93ff-99f383b09ff9

Maricopa County Adult Probation Department. (no date). Payment ability evaluation. https://www.yumpu.com/en/document/read/32797253/maricopa-county-adult-probation-31012-acourt-ordered-financial

Mark, M. M., & Shotland, R. L. (1985). Toward more useful social science. In R. L. Shotland and M. M. Mark (Eds.), *Social science and social policy* (pp. 335–370). Beverly Hills, CA: Sage.

Marsh, A., & Gerrick, E. (2016). Why motive matters: Designing effective policy responses to modern debtors' prisons. *Yale Law & Policy Review, 34,* 93–129.

Martin, F. (2016, June 24). Finance is the master technology—and it's funded the world. New York Times. https://www.nytimes.com/2016/06/26/books/review/money-changes-everything-by-william-n-goetzmann.html

Martin, K., & Spencer-Suarez, K. (2017). Criminal justice debt: Costs & consequences. New York: The Fortune Society. https://issuu.com/thefortunesociety/docs/cj_report_/15

Martin, K. D. (2018). Monetary myopia: An examination of institutional response to revenue from monetary sanctins for misdemeanors. *Criminal Justice Policy Review, 29,* 630.662.

Martin, K. D., Sykes, B. L., Shannon, S., Edwards, F., & Harris, A. (2018). Monetary sanctions: Legal financial obligations in US systems of justice. *Annual Review of Criminology, 1,* 471–495.

Martindale-Hubbell. (2003). *Martindale-Hubbell law directory* (Vol. 13). New Providence, NJ: Martindale-Hubbell.

Maruschak, L. M., & Minton, T. D. (2020). Correctional populations in the United States, 2017–2018. NCJ 252157. Washington, DC: Bureau of Justice Statistics. https://www.bjs.gov/content/pub/pdf/cpus1718.pdf

Matthias, J. T., Lyford, G. H., & Gomez, P. C. (1995). *Current practices in collecting fines and fees in state courts: A handbook of collection issues and solutions.* Denver, CO: National Center for State Courts, Court Services Division.

Mazzei, P. (2020, May 24). Florida law restricting felon voting is unconstitutional, judge rules. New York Times. https://www.nytimes.com/2020/05/24/us/florida-felon-voting-court-judge-ruling.html?action=click&module=Top%20Stories&pgtype=Homepage

McGillis, D. (1986). *Crime victim restitution: An analysis of approaches.* Washington, DC: National Institute of Justice.

McLean, R., & Thompson, M. D. (2007). Repaying debts. New York: Council of State Governments Justice Center. https://nrrc.csgjusticecenter.org/wp-content/uploads/2012/12/repaying_debts_full_report-2.pdf

Mears, D. P. (2010). *American criminal justice policy: An evaluation approach to increasing accountability and effectiveness.* Cambridge: Cambridge University Press.

Meredith, M., & Morse, M. (2017). Discretionary disenfranchisement: The case of legal financial obligations. *Journal of Legal Studies, 46,* 309–338.

Miers, D. (2014). Offender and state compensation for victims of crime: Two decades of development and change. *International Review of Victimology, 20,* 145–168.

Miller, T. I. (1981). Consequences of restitution. *Law and Human Behavior, 5,* 1–17.

Ministry of Justice. (2021, February 18). Criminal justice statistics quarterly, England and Wales, October 2019 to September 2020. London: Ministry of Justice. https://assets.publishing.service.gov.uk/government/uploads/system/uploads/attachment_data/file/962357/criminal-justice-statistics-quarterly-sept-2020.pdf

Minow, M. (2003). Public and private partnerships: Accounting for the new religion. Harvard Law Review, 116, 1229–1270.

Minow, M. (2019). *When should law forgive?* New York: Norton.

Miranda v. Arizona, 384 US 436 (1966).

Moen, K. (2013). Choice in criminal law: Victims, defendants, and the option of restitution. *Cornell Journal of Law and Public Policy, 22,* 733–767.

Morenoff, J. D., & Harding, D. J. (2014). Incarceration, prisoner reentry, and communities. *Annual Review of Sociology, 40,* 411–429.

Morgan, K. (1995). A study of probation and parole supervision fee collection in Alabama. *Criminal Justice Review, 20,* 44–54.

Morris, N., & Tonry, M. (1990). *Between prison and probation: Intermediate punishments in a rational sentencing system.* New York: Oxford University Press.

Moxon, D., Sutton, M., & Hedderman, C. (1990). *Unit fines: Experiments in four courts*. London: Home Office.

Murphy, K., & Tyler, T. (2008). Procedural justice and compliance behaviour: The mediating role of emotions. *European Journal of Social Psychology, 38*, 652–668.

Nagin, D. S., & Telep, C. W. (2020). Procedural justice and legal compliance: A revisionist perspective. Criminology & Public Policy. https://onlinelibrary.wiley.com/doi/full/10.1111/1745-9133.12499?campaign=woleearlyview

Nagrecha, M. (2020). The limits of fairer fines: Lessons from Germany. Criminal Justice Policy Program, Harvard Law School. https://papers.ssrn.com/sol3/papers.cfm?abstract_id=3759196

National Center for Victims of Crime. (2004). Restitution. http://www.victimsofcrime.org/help-for-crime-victims/get-help-bulletins-for-crime-victims/restitution

National Center for Victims of Crime. (2011). *Making restitution real: Five case studies on improving restitution collection*. Washington, DC: US Department of Justice.

National Consumer Law Center. (2016). Confronting criminal justice debt: A comprehensive project for reform. https://www.nclc.org/issues/confronting-criminal-justice-debt.htmlpart1

Newmark, L., Bonderman, J., Smith, B., & Liner, B. (2003). The national evaluation of Stat Victims of Crime Act Assistance and Compensations Programs: Trends and strategies for the future. Washington, DC: Urban Institute. http://www.urban.org/sites/default/files/publication/59536/410924-The-National-Evaluation-of-State-Victims-of-Crime-Act-Assistance-and-Compensation-Programs-Trends-and-Strategies-for-the-Future-Full-Report-.PDF

Newmark, L., & Schaffer, M. (2003). *Crime victims' compensation in Maryland: Accomplishments and strategies for the future*. Washington, DC: Urban Institute.

New York Times Editorial Board. (2020, May 26). Republicans tried to suppress the vote in Florida. And failed. New York Times. https://www.nytimes.com/2020/05/26/opinion/florida-felon-voting-court.html

Nisbett, R. E., & Wilson, T. D. (1977). Telling more than we can know: Verbal reports on mental processes. *Psychological Review, 84*, 231–259.

North Carolina Sentencing and Policy Advisory Commission. (1994). *Victim restitution in North Carolina: Report to the 1994 Session of the General Assembly*. Raleigh, NC: Author.

Note. (2015). Policing and profit. *Harvard Law Review, 128*, 1723–1746. http://harvardlawreview.org/wp-content/uploads/2015/04/Policing-and-Profit.pdf

Office for Victims of Crime. (1998). New directions from the field: Victims' rights and services for the 21st century. Washington, DC: US Department of Justice. https://www.ncjrs.gov/ovc_archives/directions/pdftxt/direct.pdf

Okimoto, T. G., & Tyler, T. R. (2007). Is compensation enough? Relational concerns in responding to unintended equity. *Group Processes and Intergroup Relations, 10*(3), 399–420.

Olson, D. E., & Ramker, G. F. (2001). Crime does not pay, but criminals may: Factors influencing the imposition and collection of probation fees. *Justice System Journal, 22*, 29–46.

Olson, D. E., Weisheit, R. A., & Ellsworth, T. (2001). Getting down to business: A comparison of rural and urban probationers, probation sentences, and probation outcomes. *Journal of Contemporary Criminal Justice, 17*, 4–18.

O'Malley, P. (2009a). *The currency of justice: Fines and damages in consumer societies*. Milton Park, UK: Routledge-Cavendish.

O'Malley, P. (2009b). Theorizing fines. *Punishment and Society, 11*, 67–83.

O'Malley, P. (2011). Politicizing the case for fines. *Criminology and Public Policy, 10*, 547–553.

O'Neil, M. M., & Prescott, J. J. (2019). Targeting poverty in the courts: Improving the measurement of ability to pay. *Law and Contemporary Problems, 82*, 199–226.

Orth, U. (2003). Punishment goals of crime victims. *Law and Human Behavior, 27*, 173–186.

Oshinsky, D. M. (1996). *"Worse than slavery": Parchman Farm and the ordeal of Jim Crow justice*. New York: Free Press.

Osnos, E. (2020, August 31). Man in the middle. *The New Yorker*, 32–47.

Ottaway, A. (2018, January 24). NYC touts success of court-appearance reminder texts. Courthouse News Service. https://www.courthousenews.com/nyc-touts-success-of-court-appearance-reminder-texts/

Outlaw, M. C., & Ruback, R. B. (1999). Predictors and outcomes of victim restitution orders. *Justice Quarterly, 16*, 847–869.

Outlaw, M. C., Ruback, R. B., & Britt, C. (2002). Repeat and multiple victimizations: The role of individual and contextual factors. *Violence & Victims, 17*, 187–204.

Parent, D. (1990). Recovering correctional costs through offender fees. Washington, DC: National Institute of Justice. https://www.ncjrs.gov/pdffiles1/Digitization/125084NCJRS.pdf

Patel, R., & Philip, M. (2012). Criminal justice debt: A toolkit for action. Brennan Center for Justice. New York: New York University School of Law. https://www.brennancenter.org/sites/default/files/legacy/publications/Criminal%20Justice%20Debt%20Background%20for%20web.pdf

Pennsylvania Commission on Sentencing (PCS). (2009). A study on the use and impact of mandatory minimum sentences: Executive summary & recommendations. http://www.conversations.psu.edu/ docs/ SpecRptHR12of2007ExecSum.pdf.

Pennsylvania Commission on Sentencing (PCS). (2012). Sentencing guidelines implementation manual: 7th edition. Harrisburg, PA. https://sentencing.umn.edu/sites/sentencing.umn.edu/files/Pennsylvania%20Sentencing%20Guidelines%20Manual%207th%20Edition.pdf

Pennsylvania Commission on Sentencing (PCS). (2017). Annual Report 2016. State College, PA: Author. https://sentencing.umn.edu/sites/sentencing.umn.edu/files/pennsylvania_commission_on_sentencing_annual_report_2016.pdf

Pennsylvania District Attorneys Association. (2004). District attorneys directory. http://www.pdaa.org

Pennsylvania Office of the Victim Advocate. (2013). Restitution in Pennsylvania Task Force Final Report. http://www.center-school.org/Restitution/Restitution_Taskforce_Full_Report.pdf

Pepin, A. W. (2015). The end of debtors' prisons: Effective court policies for successful compliance with legal financial obligations. Conference of State Court Administrators. Williamsburg, VA: National Center for State Courts.

Petersilia, J. (1997). Probation in the United States. In M. Tonry (Ed.), *Crime and justice: A review of research* (vol. 22; pp. 149–200). Chicago: University of Chicago Press.

Petersilia, J., & Deschenes, E. P. (1994). Perceptions of punishment: Inmates and staff rank the severity of prison versus intermediate sanctions. *The Prison Journal, 74*, 306–328.

Petersilia, J., & Turner, S. (1993). Intensive probation and parole. In M. Tonry (Ed.), *Crime and justice: A review of research* (vol. 17, pp. 281–335). Chicago: University of Chicago Press.

Pimentel, D. (2018). Forfeiture policy in the United States: Is there hope for reform? *Criminology & Public Policy, 17*, 129–137.

Piquero, A. R., & Jennings, W. G. (2017). Research Note: Justice system-imposed financial penalties increase the likelihood of recidivism in a sample of adolescent offenders. *Youth Violence and Juvenile Justice, 15*, 325–340.

Pleggenkuhle, B. (2018). The financial cost of a criminal conviction: Context and consequences. *Criminal Justice and Behavior, 45*, 121–145.

Plunkett, L. A. (2013). Captive markets. *Hastings Law Journal, 65*, 57–111.

Porter, E. (2016, February 23). Nudges aren't enough for problems like retirement savings. New York Times. https://www.nytimes.com/2016/02/24/business/economy/nudges-arent-enough-to-solve-societys-problems.html

Posner, R. (1986). *Economic analysis of law.* Boston: Little Brown.

Prescott, J. J. (2017). Improving access to justice in state courts with platform technology. *Vanderbilt Law Review, 70*, 1993–2050.

President's Commission on Law Enforcement and Administration of Justice. (1967). The challenge of crime in a free society. Washington, DC: US Government Printing Office. https://www.ncjrs.gov/pdffiles1/nij/42.pdf

President's Task Force on Victims of Crime. (1982). Final report: Victims of Crime in America. Washington, DC: Author. http://www.ovc.gov/publications/presdntstskforcrprt/87299.pdf

Rawls, J. (1971). *A theory of justice.* Cambridge, MA: Harvard University Press.

Ray, E. T., & Kilburn, K. L. (1970). Behavior modification techniques applied to community behavior problems. *Criminology, 8*, 173–184.

Reitz, K. R. (2015). The economic rehabilitation of offenders: Recommendations of the Model Penal Code (Second). *Minnesota Law Review, 99*, 1735–1777.

Reitz, K. R., & Klingele, C. M. (2019). Model Penal Code: Sentencing—workable limits on mass punishment. In M. Tonry (Ed.), *Crime and Justice: American sentencing: What happens and why?* (vol 48; pp. 255–311). Chicago: University of Chicago Press.

Restitution in Pennsylvania Task Force Final Report. (2013). Harrisburg, PA: Office of the Victim Advocate. http://victimsofcrime.org/docs/default-source/restitution-toolkit/restitution-taskforce_final-report-2013.pdf?sfvrsn=2

Reynolds, C., & Hall, J. (2011). Courts are not revenue centers. Conference of State Court Administrators. Williamsburg, VA: National Center for State Courts. https://csgjusticecenter.org/wp-content/uploads/2013/07/2011-12-COSCA-report.pdf

Reynolds, K. (2020). Executive Order Number Seven. Governor of Iowa. https://governor.iowa.gov/sites/default/files/documents/EO7%20-%20Voting%20Restoration.pdf

Roberts, J. V. (2009). Listening to the crime victim: Evaluating victim input at sentencing and parole. In M. Tonry (Ed.), *Crime and justice: A review of research* (vol. 38, pp. 347–412). Chicago: University of Chicago Press.

Roberts, J. V. (2012). Crime victims, sentencing, and release from prison. In J. Petersilia & K. R. Reitz (Eds.), *The Oxford handbook of sentencing and corrections* (pp. 104–126). New York: Oxford University Press.

Robertson, C., & Goldstein, J. (2014, August 26). "In aftermath of Missouri protest, skepticism about the prospects for change. New York Times. https://www.nytimes.com/2014/08/27/us/in-aftermath-of-missouri-protests-skepticism-about-the-prospects-for-change.html

Robinson, M. W. (2017). Fines: The folly of conflating the power to fine with the power to tax. *Villanova Law Review, 62*, 925–951.

Rodrigues, C. (2018). The cost of justice: The importance of a criminal defendant's ability to pay in the era of *Commonwealth v. Henry*. *Northeastern University Law Review, 10*, 204–280.

Rosenmerkel, S., Durose, M., & Farole, Jr., D. (2009). Felony sentences in state courts, 2006—Statistical tables. NCJ 226846. Washington, DC: Bureau of Justice Statistics. http://www.bjs.gov/content/pub/pdf/fssc06st.pdf

Rothfeld, M., & Reagan, B. (2014, September 17). Prosecutors are still chasing billions in uncollected debts. *Wall Street Journal*, https://www.wsj.com/articles/prosecutors-are-still-chasing-97-billion-in-uncollected-debts-1410984264

Rowley, M. (1990). Comparison of recidivism rates for delinquents processed in a restitution-diversion program to a matched sample processed in court. In B. Galaway & J. Hudson (Eds.), *Criminal justice, restitution, and reconciliation* (pp. 217–226). Monsey, NY: Willow Tree Press.

Roy, S. (1995). Juvenile restitution and recidivism in a midwestern county. *Federal Probation, 59*, 55–62.

Ruback, R. B. (2002, May). Restitution in Pennsylvania: A multimethod investigation. Final Grant Report for NIJ Grant No. 97-CE-UX-0001, Submitted to the National Institute of Justice. Unpublished manuscript, Pennsylvania State University.

Ruback, R. B. (2004, June). The imposition of economic sanctions in Philadelphia. *Federal Probation*, 21–26.

Ruback, R. B. (2011). The abolition of fines and fees: Not proven and not compelling. *Criminology & Public Policy, 10*, 569–581.

Ruback, R. B. (2015). The benefits and costs of economic sanctions: Considering the victim, the offender, and society. *Minnesota Law Review, 99*, 1779–1836.

Ruback, R. B., & Bergstrom, M. H. (2006). Economic sanctions in criminal justice: Purposes, effects, and implications. *Criminal Justice and Behavior, 33*, 242–273.

Ruback, R. B., Cares, A. C., & Hoskins, S. N. (2006, April). Evaluation of best practices in restitution and victim compensation orders and payments. Final report to the Pennsylvania Commission on Crime and Delinquency. http://www.portal.state.pa.us/portal/server.pt/community/victims_services/7633/restitution/517810.

Ruback, R. B., Cares, A. C., & Hoskins, S. N. (2008). Crime victims' perceptions of restitution: The importance of payment and understanding. *Violence and Victims, 23*, 697–710.

Ruback, R. B., & Clark, V. A. (2009). Eliminate disparity in economic sanctions. In N. A. Frost, J. D. Freilich, & T. R. Clear (Eds.), *Contemporary issues in criminal justice policy: Policy proposals from the American Society of Criminology Conference* (pp. 75–82). Belmont, CA: Cengage/Wadsworth.

Ruback, R. B., & Clark, V. A. (2011). Economic sanctions in Pennsylvania: Complex and inconsistent. *Duquesne Law Review, 49,* 751–772.

Ruback, R. B., Clark, V. A., & Warner, C. (2014). Why are crime victims at risk of being victimized again? Substance use, depression, and offending as mediators of the victimization-revictimization link. *Journal of Interpersonal Violence, 29*, 157–185.

Ruback, R. B., Gladfelter, A. S., & Lantz, B. (2014). Paying restitution: An experimental analysis of the effects of information and rationale. *Criminology & Public Policy, 13*, 405–436.

Ruback, R. B., Hoskins, S. N., Cares, A. C., & Feldmeyer, B. (2006). Perception and payment of economic sanctions: A survey of offenders. *Federal Probation, 73*(3), 26–31.

Ruback, R. B., & Innes, C. A. (1988). The relevance and irrelevance of psychological research: The example of prison crowding. *American Psychologist, 43*, 683–693.

Ruback, R. B., Knoth, L. K., Gladfelter, A. S., & Lantz, B. (2018). Restitution payment and recidivism: An experimental analysis. *Criminology & Public Policy, 17*, 789–813.

Ruback, R. B., Ruth, G. R., & Shaffer, J. N. (2005). Assessing the impact of statutory change: A statewide multilevel analysis of restitution orders in Pennsylvania. *Crime & Delinquency, 51*, 318–342.

Ruback, R. B., & Shaffer, J. N. (2005). The role of victim-related factors in victim restitution: A multi-method analysis of restitution in Pennsylvania. *Law and Human Behavior, 29*, 657–681.

Ruback, R. B., Shaffer, J. N., & Logue, M. A. (2004). The imposition and effects of restitution in four Pennsylvania counties: Effects of size of county and specialized collection units. *Crime & Delinquency, 50*, 168–188.

Rubin, H. T. (1988). Fulfilling juvenile restitution requirements in community correctional programs. *Federal Probation, 52*, 32–42.

Ruhland, E., Holmes, B., & Petkus, A. (2020). The role of fines and fees on probation outcomes. *Criminal Justice and Behavior, 47*, 1244–1263.

Sally, D. (1995). Conversation and cooperation in social dilemmas: A meta-analysis of experiments from 1958 to 1992. *Rationality and Society, 7*, 58–92.

Sampson, R. J. (2010). Gold standard myths: Observations on the experimental turn in quantitative criminology. *Journal of Quantitative Criminology, 26,* 489–500.

Sampson, R. J., & Lauritsen, J. L. (1990). Deviant lifestyles, proximity to crime, and the offender-victim link in personal violence. *Journal of Research in Crime and Delinquency, 27,* 110–139.

Sampson, R. J., Raudenbush, S. W., & Earls, F. (1997). Neighborhoods and violent crime: A multilevel study of collective efficacy. *Science, 277,* 918–924.

San Antonio School District v. Rodriguez, 411 US 1 (1973).

Sances, M. W., & You, H. Y. (2017). Who pays for government? Descriptive representation and exploitative revenue sources. *Journal of Politics, 79,* 1090–1094.Schneider, A. L. (1986). Restitution and recidivism rates of juvenile offenders: Results from four experimental studies. *Criminology, 24,* 533–552.

Schneider, A. L. (1990). *Deterrence and juvenile crime: Results from a national policy experiment.* New York: Springer-Verlag.

Schneider, P. R., Griffith, W. R., & Schneider, A. L. (1982). Juvenile restitution as a sole sanction or condition of probation: An empirical account. *Journal of Research in Crime and Delinquency, 19,* 47–65.

Schnittker, J., & John, A. (2007). Enduring stigma: The long-term effects of incarceration on health. *Journal of Health and Social Behavior, 48,* 15–130.

Scott, W. R. (1992). *Organizations: Rational, natural, and open systems* (3rd ed.). Englewood Cliffs, NJ: Prentice Hall.

Scott-Hayward, C. S. (2009). The fiscal crisis in corrections: Rethinking policies and practices. VERA Institute of Justice, Center on Sentencing and Corrections, New York. http://www.vera.org/files/The-fiscal-crisis-in-corrections_July-2009.pdf.

Sen, A. K. (2009). *The idea of justice.* Cambridge, MA: Harvard University Press.

Shadish, W. R., Cook, T. D., & Campbell, D. T. (2002). *Experimental and quasi-experimental designs for generalized causal inference.* Boston, MA: Houghton Mifflin.

Shaffer, J. N., & Ruback, R. B. (2002). Violent victimization as a risk factor for violent offending among juveniles. Washington, DC: Office of Juvenile Justice and Delinquency Prevention. https://www.ncjrs.gov/pdffiles1/ojjdp/195737.pdf

Shapiro, D. L., Buttner, E. H., & Barry, B. (1994). Explanations: What factors enhance their perceived adequacy? *Organizational Behavior and Human Decision Processes, 58,* 346–368.

Shapiro, J. (2014, May 19). As court fees rise, the poor are paying the price. National Public Radio. https://www.npr.org/2014/05/19/312158516/increasing-court-fees-punish-the-poor

Sharpe, C., Christy, & Ward, J. T. (2019). Imposition and collection of fines in Pennsylvania criminal cases: Preliminary results from an analysis of 10 years of court data. ACLU of Pennsylvania. https://www.aclupa.org/sites/default/files/field_documents/imposition_and_assessment_of_fines_in_pennsylvania_criminal_cases_final_0.pdf

Sharpe, C., Dilks, J., & Christy, A. (2018). Imposition and collection of court costs in Pennsylvania criminal cases: Preliminary results from an analysis of 10 years of court data. ACLU of Pennsylvania. https://www.aclupa.org/sites/

default/files/field_documents/imposition_and_assessment_of_court_costs_
in_pennsylvania_criminal_cases_final_revised.pdf

Sherman, L. (1993). *Policing domestic violence: Experiments and dilemmas.*
New York: Free Press.

Sherman, L. W., & Strang, H. (2012). Restorative justice as evidence-based
sentencing. In J. Petersilia & K. R. Reitz (Eds.), *The Oxford handbook
of sentencing and corrections* (pp. 215–244). New York: Oxford
University Press.

Shichor, D., & Binder, A. (1982). Community restitution for juveniles: An
approach and preliminary evaluation. *Criminal Justice Review, 7,* 46–50.

Silver-Greenberg, J. (2011, March 17). Welcome to debtors' prison,
2011 edition. Wall Street Journal. https://www.wsj.com/articles/
SB10001424052748704396504576204553811636610

Sims, B. (2000). Victim restitution: A review of the literature. *Justice Professional,
13,* 247–269.

Singla, A., Kirschner, C., & Stone, S. B. (2019). Race, representation, and
revenue: Reliance on fines and forfeitures in city governments. *Urban Affairs
Review, 56 ,* 1132–1167.

Skolnick, J. H. (2008). Policing should not be for profit. *Criminology & Public
Policy, 7,* 257–262.

Slocum, L. A., Wiley, S. A., & Esbensen, F. (2016). The importance of being
satisfied: A longitudinal exploration of police contact, procedural injustice,
and subsequent delinquency. *Criminal Justice and Behavior, 43,* 7–26.

Smith, B., Davis, R., & Hillenbrand, S. (1989). *Improving enforcement of court-
ordered restitution.* Chicago: American Bar Association.

Smith, D. A. (2019). Expert report of Daniel A. Smith, Ph.D. US District Court
for the Northern District of Florida. https://www.aclu.org/sites/default/files/
field_document/gruver_v_barton_-_expert_report_of_daniel_a._smith_
ph.d.pdf

Smith, H. P. (2006). Violent crime and victim compensation: Implications for
social justice. *Violence and Victims, 21,* 307–322.

Sobol, N. L. (2016). Charging the poor: Criminal justice debt & modern-day
debtors' prisons. *Maryland Law Review, 75,* 486–540.

Sobol, N. L. (2017). Fighting fines & fees: Borrowing from the consumer law to
combat criminal justice debt abuses. *University of Colorado Law Review, 88,*
841–912.

Sparks, R., Bottoms, A.E., & Hay, W. (1996). *Prisons and the problem of order.*
Oxford: Clarendon Press.

Spaulding, K. R. (1989). "Hit them where it hurts": RICO criminal forfeitures and
white-collar crime. *Journal of Criminal Law and Criminology, 80,* 197–292.

Stecklow, S. (2001, January 2). Finnish drivers don't mind sliding scale,
but instant calculation gets low marks. Wall Street Journal. https://
www.wsj.com/articles/SB978398058976592586

Steffensmeier, D., & Allan, E. (1996). Gender and crime: Toward a gendered
theory of female offending. *Annual Review of Sociology, 22,* 459–487.

Stillman, S. (2014, June 23). Get Out of Jail, Inc: Does the alternatives-
to-incarceration industry profit from injustice? New Yorker. https://
www.newyorker.com/magazine/2014/06/23/get-out-of-jail-inc

Stripling, J. (2017, October 15). The lure of the lazy river. The Chronicle of Higher Education. https://www.chronicle.com/article/The-Lure-of-the-Lazy-River/241434?utm_source=at&utm_medium=en&cid=at

Sullivan, T. A., Warren, E., & Westbrook, J. L. (1999). *As we forgive our debtors: Bankruptcy and consumer credit in America*. Washington, DC: Beard Books.

Supreme Court of Ohio, Office of Judicial Services. (2019). Collection of fines and court costs in adult trial courts. https://www.supremecourt.ohio.gov/Publications/JCS/finesCourtCosts.pdf

Thaler, R. (1985). Mental accounting and consumer choice. *Marketing Science, 4,* 199–214.

Thaler, R. H., & Sunstein, C. (2008). *Nudge: Improving decisions about health, wealth, and happiness*. New Have, CT: Yale University Press.

Timbs v. Indiana, 586 US _____ , 139 S.Ct. 682 (2019). https://www.supremecourt.gov/opinions/18pdf/17-1091_5536.pdf

Tobin, R. W. (1996). Funding the state courts: Issues and approaches. Williamsburg, VA: National Center for State Courts. http://cdm16501.contentdm.oclc.org/cdm/ref/collection/financial/id/5

Tobolowsky, P. M., Gaboury, M. T., Jackson, A. L., & Blackburn, A. G. (2010). *Crime victim rights and remedies* (2nd ed.). Durham, NC: Carolina Academic Press.

Tobolowsky, P. M., Beloof, Gaboury, M. T., Jackson, A. L., & Blackburn, A. G. (2016). *Crime victim rights and remedies* (3rd ed.). Durham, NC: Carolina Academic Press.

Tonry, M. (1992). Mandatory penalties. In M. Tonry (Ed.), *Crime and justice: A review of research* (vol. 16, pp. 243–273). Chicago: University of Chicago Press.

Tonry, M. (2018). Punishment and human dignity: Sentencing principles for twenty-first-century America. In M. Tonry (Ed.), *Crime and justice: A review of research* (vol. 47; 119–157). Chicago: University of Chicago Press.

Tonry, M., & Lynch, M. (1996). Intermediate sanctions. In M. Tonry (Ed.), *Crime and justice: A review of research* (vol. 20, pp. 99–144). Chicago: University of Chicago Press.

Tumey v. Ohio, 273 US 510 (1927).

Turner v. Rogers, 131 S.Ct. 2507 (2011).

Tyler, T. R. (2006). *Why people obey the law*. Princeton, NJ: Princeton University Press.

Tyler, T. R. (2011). *Why people cooperate: The role of social motivations*. Princeton, NJ: Princeton University Press.

Tyler, T. R., & Huo, Y. J. (2002). *Trust in the law: Encouraging public cooperation with the police and courts*. New York: Russell Sage Foundation.

Tyler, T. R., & Lind, E. A. (1992). A relational model of authority in groups. In M.P. Zanna (Ed.), *Advances in experimental social psychology* (vol. 25, pp. 115–191). San Diego, CA: Academic Press.

United States v. Bajakajian, 524 US 321 (1998).

United States v. Ursery, 518 US 267 (1996).

University of Pennsylvania Law Review. (1953). Fines and fining: An evaluation. *University of Pennsylvania Law Review, 101,* 1013–1030.

https://scholarship.law.upenn.edu/cgi/viewcontent.cgi?referer=https://
www.google.com/&httpsredir=1&article=7955&context=penn_law_review

US Bureau of the Census. (2006). Government finance and employment classification manual. https://www2.census.gov/govs/pubs/classification/2006_classification_manual.pdf

US Bureau of the Census. (2010). 2005–2009 American Community Survey 5-year estimates. http://factfinder.census.gov/servlet/DatasetMainPageServlet?_program=ACS&_submenuId=downloadcenter_0&_lang=en&_ts=

US Commission on Civil Rights. (2017). Targeted fines and fees against communities of color: Civil rights & Constitutional implications. Washington, DC: Author. https://www.usccr.gov/pubs/2017/Statutory_Enforcement_Report2017.pdf

US Department of Justice. (2015). Investigation of the Ferguson Police Department. US. Department of Justice Civil Rights Division. https://www.justice.gov/sites/default/files/opa/press-releases/attachments/2015/03/04/ferguson_police_department_report.pdf

US Department of Justice. (2019). United States Attorneys' Annual Statistical Report: Fiscal Year 2017. https://www.justice.gov/usao/page/file/1199336/download

US Department of Treasury. (2010). Taxes and society. https://www.treasury.gov/resource-center/faqs/taxes/pages/taxes-society.aspx

US Government Accountability Office. (2017). Federal criminal restitution: Factors to consider for a potential expansion of federal courts' authority to order restitution. GAO-18-115. https://www.gao.gov/assets/gao-18-115.pdf

Vander Giessen, M. L. (2012). Legislative reforms for Washington State's criminal monetary penalties. *Gonzaga Law Review, 47*, 547–585.

Van Ness, D. (1990). Restorative justice. In B. Galaway & J. Hudson (Eds.), *Criminal justice, restitution, and reconciliation* (pp. 7–14). New York: Willow Tree Press.

Van Voorhis, P. (1985). Restitution outcome and probationers' assessments of restitution: The effects of moral development. *Criminal Justice and Behavior, 12*, 259–287.

Walsh, A. (1986). Placebo justice: Victim recommendations and offender sentences in sexual assault cases. *Journal of Criminal Law & Criminology, 77*, 1126–1141.

Walsh, T. (2014). Juvenile economic sanctions: A logical alternative? *Criminology and Public Policy, 13*, 69–77.

Warren, E., & Tyagi, A. W. (2003). *The two-income trap: Why middle-class mothers and fathers are going broke.* New York: Basic Books.

Washington State Institute for Public Policy. (2017, May). Benefit-cost technical documentation. Olympia, WA: Author http://www.wsipp.wa.gov/TechnicalDocumentation/WsippBenefitCostTechnicalDocumentation.pdf

Weber, M. (1947). *The theory of social and economic organization.* (A. M. Henderson & T. Parsons, Trans.). Glencoe, IL: Free Press.

Weisburd, D., Einat, T., & Kowalski, M. (2008). The miracle of the cells: An experimental study of interventions to increase payment of court-ordered financial obligations. *Criminology & Public Policy, 7*, 9–36.

Weisheit, R. A., Wells, L. E., & Falcone, D. N. (1995). *Crime and policing in rural small-town America: An overview of the issues*. Washington, DC: Bureau of Justice Statistics.

Wenzel, M. (2002). Principles of procedural fairness in reminder letters: A field experiment (Centre for Tax System Integrity Working Paper No. 42). Canberra: The Australian National University. https://pdfs.semanticscholar.org/9fd6/278f2ca51e6f84dd425ffd906bedff716e5c.pdf

Western, B. (2002). The impact of incarceration on wage mobility and inequality. *American Sociological Review, 67*, 526–546.

Western, B. (2006). *Punishment and inequality in America*. New York: Russell Sage Foundation.

Wheeler, G. R., Hissong, R. V., Slusher, M. P., & Macan, T. M. (1990). Economic sanctions in criminal justice: Dilemma for human service? *Justice System Journal, 14*, 63–77.

Wheeler, G. R. Macan, T. M., Hissong, R. V., & Slusher, M. P. (1989). The effects of probation service fees on case management strategy and sanctions. *Journal of Criminal Justice, 17*, 15–24.

Williams, M. R. (2002). Civil asset forfeiture: Where does the money go? *Criminal Justice Review, 27*, 321–329.

Wilson, J. Q. (1989). *Bureaucracy: What government agencies do and why they do it*. New York: Basic Books.

Wilson, W. J. (2008). The economic plight of inner-city black males. In E. Anderson (Ed.), *Against the wall: Poor, young, black, and male* (pp. 55–70). Philadelphia: University of Pennsylvania Press.

Worrall, J. L., & Kovandzic, T. V. (2008). Is policing for profit? Answers from asset forfeiture. *Criminology & Public Policy, 7*, 219–244.

Zelinsky, E. A. (2007). *The origins of the ownership society: How the defined contribution paradigm changed America*. New York: Oxford University Press.

Zhen, T. (2018). (Color)blind reform: How ability-to-pay determinations are inadequate to transform a racialized system of penal debt. *N.Y.U. Review of Law & Social Change, 43*, 175–222.

Zvonkovich, J., & Ruback, R. B. (2017, November). State laws on economic sanctions. Paper presented at the annual meeting of the American Society of Criminology, Philadelphia, PA.

Name Index

For the benefit of digital users, indexed terms that span two pages (e.g., 52–53) may, on occasion, appear on only one of those pages.

Subject Index